A
REMEMBERED
FUTURE

Harold Fisch

A REMEMBERED FUTURE

A Study in Literary Mythology

*INDIANA
UNIVERSITY
PRESS*

Bloomington

Manufactured in the United States of America

Library of Congress Cataloging in Publication Data

Fisch, Harold.
  A remembered future.

  Includes bibliographical references and index.
  1. Mythology in literature.   I. Title.
PN56.M95F5   1984   809'.9337   83-48899
ISBN 0-253-35003-4
1   2   3   4   5   88   87   86   85   84

For Menachem, David, Yossi, Shiffy, Eli,
and Those Who Share the
Future with Them

CONTENTS

Acknowledgments

Grateful acknowledgment is made to the publishers for permission to reprint passages from the following works:

"Ash-Wednesday" in *Collected Poems 1909–1962* by T. S. Eliot, copyright 1936 by Harcourt Brace Jovanovich, Inc., copyright © 1963, 1964 by T. S. Eliot. Reprinted by permission of Harcourt Brace Jovanovich, Inc., and Faber and Faber Ltd.

"Burnt Norton" in *Four Quartets* by T. S. Eliot, copyright 1943 by T. S. Eliot; renewed 1971 by Esme Valerie Eliot. Reprinted by permission of Harcourt Brace Jovanovich, Inc., and Faber and Faber Ltd.

A Canopy in the Desert, by Abba Kovner, translated by Shirley Kaufman. © 1973 by Shirley Kaufman. Reprinted by permission of University of Pittsburgh Press.

"The Dead of the Desert," by C. N. Bialik, from *Selected Poems*, translated by Ruth Nevo, copyright © 1981 by Dvir Publishing House Ltd.

"The Dialogue of Zion and God," by Eleazar ben Kallir, from *The Penguin Book of Hebrew Verse*, edited and translated by T. Carmi (Allen Lane 1981), pp. 223–24. Copyright © T. Carmi, 1981. Reprinted by permission of Penguin Books Ltd.

"Jezreel," by Abraham Shlonsky, from *Modern Hebrew Poetry: A Bilingual Anthology*, translated by Ruth Finer Mintz (Berkeley and Los Angeles: University of California Press, 1966). Reprinted by permission of publisher.

"Massadah," by Yitzhak Lamdan, from *Modern Hebrew Poetry: A Bilingual Anthology*, translated by Ruth Finer Mintz (Berkeley and Los Angeles: University of California Press, 1966). Reprinted by permission of publisher.

"A Note on War Poetry" in *Collected Poems 1909–1962* by T. S. Eliot, copyright 1936 by Harcourt Brace Jovanovich, Inc., copyright © 1963, 1964 by T. S. Eliot. Reprinted by permission of Harcourt Brace Jovanovich, Inc. and Faber and Faber Ltd.

"War (1911)," by Georg Heym, from *The Penguin Book of German Verse*, translated by Leonard Forster (Penguin Poets, Revised edition 1959), pp. 435, 437. Copyright © Leonard Forster, 1957, 1959. Reprinted by permission of Penguin Books Ltd.

"The Waste Land" in *Collected Poems 1909–1962* by T. S. Eliot, copyright 1936 by Harcourt Brace Jovanovich, Inc., copyright © 1963, 1964 by T. S. Eliot. Reprinted by permission of Harcourt Brace Jovanovich, Inc., and Faber and Faber Ltd.

I would like to express thanks to many colleagues, students and friends—too many to list individually—who have shared their thoughts with me on this or that detail of this study. Warm thanks are due also to the staff of the Indiana University Press for their unfailing helpfulness. Finally, it is a pleasant duty to acknowledge the assistance of the Research Authority of Bar-Ilan University, Israel, in defraying the incidental costs of preparing the manuscript of the work here offered to the public.

A
REMEMBERED
FUTURE

1

Historical Archetypes

To SPEAK OF "historical archetypes" would be, it seems, to speak in riddles, for archetypes are, almost by definition, timeless. Leslie Fiedler declares that "the archetypal critic is delivered from the bondage of time."[1] C. G. Jung's patients, we are told, were able to reconstruct Greek myths in their dreams without knowing anything of ancient Greece, for the archetypes live within us in a timeless continuum that knows not before or after. Maud Bodkin, in an early work on archetypal patterns, quotes some lines from the last section of T. S. Eliot's *The Waste Land*, remarking that they "create for us the bare form of an emotional situation realizable in any period of history, or pre-history, and multiplied, beyond actual occasions, infinitely, in dreams and delirium."[2] In *The Waste Land*, Bodkin finds evocations of an eternal initiation or rebirth pattern as well as of the myth of Isis and Osiris. Dream, legend, and sophisticated modern poem testify to the same bundle of psychic contents. For Lévi-Strauss, later on, the "savage mind" is, of course, also the modern mind; we are at one with the tree- and cave-dwellers in the way in which we seek to resolve the binary oppositions (incest versus exogamy; the raw versus the cooked) by which our minds are structured. Northrop Frye, who has given impressive currency to the notion of archetypes as the basic myths of all literature (the Myths of Autumn, Winter, Spring, and Summer), speaks of "the obliterating of boundaries separating legend, historical reminiscence and actual history."[3] A corresponding stance is required of the critic: "When a critic deals with a work of literature, the most natural thing for him to do is to freeze it, *to ignore its movement in time* and look at it as a completed pattern of words, with all its parts existing simultaneously."[4]

It is this insistence that literary structure is spatial rather than temporal that has provoked the most serious criticism of Frye and the structuralists. Geoffrey Hartman remarks that Frye "fails to bring together the form of art and the form of its historical consciousness."[5] For narrative is surely an unfolding of events in time. Drama too seizes events at a critical turning-point. The time consciousness of the reader/spectator is always involved. More than that, it may be claimed that poems have reference to other poems that have gone before; footfalls constantly echo in the memory. T. S. Eliot's *The Waste Land*, for example, recalls for us phrases from Dante, Webster, Shakespeare, Spenser, and others. It is true that these other poems are felt to exist simultaneously in a sort of timeless present, yet there is also a lengthening perspective, a sense of an irrecoverable past to be both fused and contrasted with the present.

"Sweet Thames run softly till I end my song." The image of the river in this line of Spenser is, of course, a primordial image for time itself, indeed an archetypal image. In the context of Eliot's poem, the line is a way of wishing that Spenser's world might continue into the future, that the "sweet Thames" might continue to flow. The elegiac, plangent tone of the verse, however, is a reminder that such continuities are no longer achievable. But it is not true to say of this poem that time is "obliterated." On the contrary, the sense of rupture so central to the poem is closely bound up with the awareness of time, of history and its inexorabilities. In short, we have here an archetypal language, or rather, metalanguage, which suggests quite the opposite of a "completed pattern of words, with all its parts existing simultaneously."

There evidently are "archetypes"—patterns that recur in a vast number of texts enabling us to claim for them a kind of universality.[6] This study will be concerned with a number of such patterns. But they are evidently not all as "synchronic" or ahistorical as the formalists have maintained. Seen properly, they often reveal

and seek to define the tensions of historical time itself. The myth of
the wanderer, for instance, is as universal a myth as anyone could
find. Odysseus, Moses Herzog, the Ancient Mariner are all wanderers and they all obey the law of the eternal return; the circle
must be closed. To that extent their myth is ahistorical. But the
myth expresses something more than the rounded shape of the
journey and the inevitable return to the point of departure. There
is also the wandering itself, the sense of distances traversed, the
weary movement through time and space, which echo the very nature of our own existence. In that existence, the point of departure
is hardly remembered, the destination is scarcely known. Odysseus
is not merely a wanderer: we should remember that he is also a
survivor. And each one of us responding to his story responds in his
own character as survivor. We hold on precariously, never quite
sure where the next stage of the journey will take us and whether
we shall reach the goal or not. The very openness of time, the non-
recurring quality of the events that befall the wanderer on his way
are themselves, one may suggest, structural features of the myth.

At one point in his *Anatomy of Criticism*, Northrop Frye suggests that we may think of the different *mythoi* of literature as ultimately part of one unified myth, that of the quest.[7] The hero's
struggle, his disappointments, his death, and his final success or
recovery at the end of the cycle are all comprised in this archetype
of archetypes. It reflects the "law of the eternal return." But might
one not suggest that, infolded with this and at the same time dia-
lectically opposed to it, is another supreme myth, which we may
term, the Test? Joseph K. in Kafka's *The Trial* or Job in the Old Testament can certainly be spoken of as quest-heroes, the former de-
feated, the latter, seeming to triumph. But fundamental to both
these stories is the sense of a trial or test. Nor is this a ritual test of
identity or endurance as in so much folk and romance literature,[8]
or a suitor-test as in Shakespeare's *The Merchant of Venice*. It is our
fundamental moral nature that is tested; life as a whole indeed becomes a test—we are constantly challenged and a response is demanded of us. Whether we have correctly understood the challenge
and whether our response is in any way relevant to the challenge
remains doubtful, but the sense of our being tested or tried is a universal way we have of arranging our experiences. Nor does it apply
only to those who, so to speak, stand before God. Lord Jim is not a
Christian hero of the faith; nevertheless, he is a man who is re-

morselessly and continuously tested. Camus in *The Myth of Sisyphus* dismisses all religious assurances and calls upon us to accept the ultimate absurdity of existence. But for him there is a test nonetheless: the test is to remain alive, to learn to live without hope. The trial is as agonizing as that of Bunyan's hero in *The Pilgrim's Progress* even though it takes place in a metaphysical vacuum. In other words, we are talking about an archetype that asserts itself in texts of all kinds as an almost inevitable way of giving order to the randomness of things. Prince Hal is tested by royalty; Falstaff is tested by rejection. The evaluation of the test (the grade, so to speak, to be given to the examinee) remains debatable, but of the test itself as a dynamic principle in literature and life there can be no doubt.

As against the cyclical shape of the quest, the test is open-ended. We never know quite how it will end. "Then I saw," says Bunyan's hero at the end of his pilgrimage, "that there was a way to hell even from the gates of Heaven." The conditions of the test are what keep the options open. We may make a further distinction here. The rounded form of the quest narrative yields such a genre as the epic (Aeneas is first and foremost a quest-hero); the open-ended character of the test yields a different form, which we might term the pilgrimage. The pilgrimage is thus an alternative to the epic. Lord Jim's career, like that of many other heroes of Conrad, is a pilgrimage. There is an uncertain but nevertheless persistent movement forward along a narrow path; ascent and descent are not arranged in regular sequence, and there is the ever-present possibility of error. Here is a fundamental literary genre and one that can surely be categorized as archetypal.

But we are not talking about a law of nature. If myths and archetypes belong to man-in-general, nature-in-general, and literature-in-general, then the test is not a myth in that sense. It does not reflect the cycle of the seasons so much as the special conditions of human existence, the time of human life. And, we may add, not human existence necessarily at all times and places. There are times when the test is more real than at others; it is evidently more prominent in Shakespeare than in the Greeks. Is Oedipus tested? Or is he not rather trapped? There is a difference. Angelo in *Measure for Measure*, on the other hand, is elaborately tested ("Let there be some more test made of my mettle"), and it is not by chance that the play is full of trials, of legal processes. The comic character, Pompey, is tried, but so is Claudio, so is Isabella, and so is Angelo. One of the fundamental questions of the play is: who is fit to judge and how are we ultimately to be judged? This is, of course, a comedy (the Myth of Spring?), and we know that things will work out for the best. To that extent the trials are rigged, but there is suspense nevertheless, the suspense of real historical existence with its "trials" and tribulations.

Archetypes are therefore not as simple and harmonious as has been supposed. Mixed up with the nonhistorical or ahistorical kind are others that may properly be termed "historical archetypes." Shakespeare's plays give us marvelous examples of such opposing or mingled structures. The plot of *Hamlet* is clearly mythical in the sense of reflecting the fatal cyclical movement of tragedy, and as such it has appealed to the "Myth and Ritual" school of criticism. In fact, it was the subject of an early essay by Gilbert Murray entitled "Hamlet and Orestes" (1914), in which he sees the play as based on a nature myth and manifesting primitive man's sense of the cyclical movement of the seasons.[9] Old Hamlet had been a winter god: he "smote the sledded Polacks on the ice" (I.i.63). Claudius is a summer god, the usurper who comes along in high summer when his victim is sleeping in the orchard in the afternoon. When the play opens some months later, it is again winter; in the first scene and again in the fourth, we are informed of how bitter cold it is. Young Hamlet dressed in black is the winter god over again; he will kill Claudius but he will be unseated by another spring god (Fortinbras?) who comes at the turn of the year. It will be seen that the wheel comes full circle: this is an essential part of the play's "Senecan" structure, with its circular pattern of action and reaction, murder, retaliation, and more murder.

But the Myth and Ritual school show themselves unaware of another decidedly noncircular movement opposed to this pattern, though subtly interwoven with it. If the Ghost urges Hamlet to act in the name of nature ("If thou hast Nature in thee, bear it not"), he also presents the need to kill Claudius as a high moral duty, a test. He must kill but he must not taint his mind; he must cleanse the realm, eradicate its evil, but he must take care to spare the innocent—a novelty in the revenge tradition. More than he is a winter god, therefore, Hamlet is a man burdened with a task, one almost too heavy to bear. It is a task of self-discovery and self-determination. Here is an invitation to the wayfaring hero to discover some kind of destiny not comprised in the term "nature" at the same time as he performs the ritual gestures associated with a myth of nature. There is a structural irony in the play on which we would do well to ponder. Instead of the simple formula proposed by Gilbert Murray, we are presented with a duality in the very management of the plot. Coinciding with, and yet contradicting the circular advance of the Senecan plot, there is a hesitant and persistent search for meaning. There is no clear progress upon a well-defined path of practical endeavor, but rather an ever-defeated and ever-renewed pilgrimage. *Hamlet* is the prototype of all heroes who are tested, on whom responsibility is placed, a responsibility almost too heavy to be borne: "The time is out of joint. O cursed spite, / That ever I was born to set it right" (I.v. 188–89). Hamlet is the man with a burden on his back. He must carry it to the end of the road, but there is no knowing how or when or where that road will end.

II

We have here a problem of definitions. Criticism has not shown itself much aware of "historical archetypes," and we lack terms and methods for dealing with them. An earlier philosopher-critic who came near to defining this category was Ernst Cassirer. In his doctrine of "Symbolic Forms" he distinguished between myth consciousness and the consciousness of history as such. The former, based on "biological time," can yield a rounded, harmonious pattern, a myth of origins or of grand, universal world-cycles. But it is essentially spatial and is grounded in nature. It can at best rise to the apprehension of a cosmic order, the order of destiny. But it cannot apprehend the unrepeated quality, the portentousness of historical time.[10] By contrast, true time-consciousness, for which, according to Cassirer, the Hebrew prophets provide the classic example, reaches into the past through memory and gains a perception of the future (what Leibniz called *percepturitio*) as something hidden and yet unfolding out of the past. There is here no unchanging pattern as in the biological time of nature. Thus "Nature can offer no support to the prophetic consciousness."[11] Nature is given, objective, history is open, its events, irreversible. In particular, the openness to the future, the quality of expectation, provide a human dimension specific to prophecy. This orientation, he claims, is essentially different from the Greek *gnosis*. Symbolic Forms, that is to say, the mental structures by which we apprehend the world, embody such time awareness. Elsewhere, Cassirer goes further and points out that this awareness is the very ground of our humanity: "The ego finds and knows itself only in the threefold form of the temporal consciousness."[12] And this "threefold form" consists of "a unity of present intuition, memory and expectation." Cassirer goes on (very pertinently for our present purpose) to make the following observation: "For the meaning of historical time is built not solely from recollection of the past, but no less from anticipation of the future. It depends as much on the striving as on the act, as much on the tendency toward the future as on the contemplation and actualization of the past."[13]

Cassirer did not, it seems, develop a literary or linguistic model for applying this intuition of the centrality of historical time to particular texts. And if we look to the structuralists of France or of the Prague school, we shall find little assistance either. True, they are much exercised with the structure of our thinking (what Cassirer had termed "Symbolic Forms") and the way that structure is revealed in culture, in language, in texts of all kinds. But they have chiefly given preference to synchrony, to "deep structure," with its unchanging order, as of pure intelligible form. And here there is little room for the unpredictable quality of human existence, the onward striving, the sense we have of the uniqueness of events. Dazzled by the mathematical clarity and simplicity of Propp's analysis of folktales or of Lévi-Strauss's treatment of the Oedipus myth, we are less likely to attend to the qualities that characterize individual works of literature as singular utterances of the human voice speaking to us in our singularity. From the point of view of the structuralists, we are confronted in literature as in language not with process or development but primarily with system, not with diachrony but synchrony.

From within the French intellectual community, however, there have been reservations and criticisms. Paul Ricoeur, for instance, has mounted a formidable critique of some of these positions. The common division between synchrony and diachrony and the subordination of the latter to the former, he maintains, contradict the historical condition of our existence to the point where change becomes unintelligible. More than that, they contradict the essential nature of language. Language as described by Saussure and some of the semiologists is a closed system, closed within itself and "separated from all references to a world." But this is not how, as human beings, we use language. We speak of something to someone.[14] Every such utterance is a saying, an event in time. "It is necessary then to balance the axiom of the closure of the universe of signs by attention to the primary function of language, which is to *say*. In contrast to the closure of the universe of signs, this function constitutes its openness or its opening."[15]

It is no accident that Ricoeur's criticism stems largely from his interest in hermeneutics, and specifically the interpretation of Scripture. For, as he tells us, the biblical word not only refers to itself and to the Word within us; it also *says* something, claiming a connection with reality, historical and physical.[16] After all, the first saying in the Bible is creative: "And God said Let there be light."[17] We may add that the giving of names in Genesis 2 is the establishment not of an autonomous system of signs but of a meaningful relation between Man and that which is outside of Man. After Adam names the creatures, they become part of a comprehensible universe. Or, as Walter Benjamin has put it, "God's creation is completed when things receive their names from man."[18] Through language we make a gesture of communication, reaching out to that which is not ourselves. We also attach ourselves to the past, making it real again for us in the present (cf. Exod. 13. 8). In the biblical understanding, poetry is primarily an act of remembering: "And when many evils and troubles have come upon them, this poem shall confront them as a witness, for it will live unforgotten in the mouths of their descendants" (Deut. 31. 21). Ancestral memories are linked with messianic promises and the linking is made possible by the texts to which we give our assent.

But how are we to conceive of a structure that binds beginnings to endings in this way and yet leaves us in the openness of real historical time? If, with Ricoeur, we deny the axiom of closure, will not all patterns inevitably begin to dissolve, including what we have here chosen to call "historical archetypes"? Here is the capital difficulty that besets us. Another contemporary French structuralist, A. J. Greimas, while he has done little to resolve the difficulty, has usefully pinpointed it. In an essay on "Structure and History," he speaks of "the specific character of diachronic transformations" and of the problem they pose for the analyst. This has to do, he says, with "the irreversible character of their application,"[19] which cannot easily be handled by systematic criticism. A number of paradigms distributed along a time axis may seem to be transformations one of another, but they are not quite interchangeable. Or rather, they are only interchangeable in one direction. To illustrate Greimas's observation, we may take the case of *Hamlet* once again. In Gilbert Murray's reading of the play, Claudius's killing of Old Hamlet and Hamlet's own killing of Claudius are related to one another as a pattern of repetition. They are both part of the circular revenge-plot: that which was is that which will be. And yet when viewed as events in an unfolding history—and that is also how they demand to be viewed—only one of them echoes the other, i.e., Hamlet's killing of his uncle echoes the uncle's killing of his father. But Hamlet's act does not, in its turn, call for a further act of bloodletting of the same kind. It belongs to what has gone before but also veers away from it. It marks the beginning of a new order. The world at the end of the play is not quite the same as it was at the beginning. The difference between history and myth is that history has within it a potentiality for change.

What kind of pattern is it that can embody changes of this kind? We may consider a formula of Frank Kermode's. He finds in many fictions a "structure of adventures," in which the beginning implies the end. The shape of novels (and to some extent dramas also) is determined by what he calls "the sense of an ending."[20] As in the biblical mode of Apocalypse, by which our literary tradition has been largely conditioned, "past, present and future are related inextricably"[21] by the felt need for a foreordained conclusion, an *eschaton*, whether of disaster or blessing. Time is in this way given form, significance. It is not mere duration, the time of the clock, but rather the "time of men in certain postures of attentiveness."[22] This is well said and it catches the sense of expectancy with which we read novels, relating them to our own mode of existence. We desire to impose a pattern on the flux of time, to see it teleologically poised and directed. We also obscurely seek such a *telos* in our own lives. We live for the sake of what is to come and in some sense that promise is already beheld as present, like the biblical *eschaton*, in every moment. But if the notion of apocalypse can be seen to shed meaning and value on our quotidian existence, does it not also in a manner tend to abolish the felt contingency of such existence, its human density and unpredictability?

True, we do not live without pattern, but it would seem that we should be looking for a pattern—if that is the right word—which does not have quite the degree of closure assumed by Kermode. His temporal order has something of the symmetry and balance of arrangements in space. His notion of an end present in every moment is a little too tidy for life or for literature either. It is also a little too tidy to do justice to the Bible itself. The truth is that the Bible does not (except in the final book of the New Testament and in a few verses of Daniel and the later Prophets) talk too much about the end of days. But it does talk about tasks imposed in the historical present, about accidental judgments and purposes mistook. If we read Samuel and Kings, we find that history works much more by trial and error than by the sense of an ending. There is, of course, movement and direction, but such terms as trial, pilgrimage, promise, and warning are more to the point than apocalypse. And this applies not only to the Bible. How does *Hamlet* end? A simple but not entirely inaccurate way of putting it would be to say that it does not end at all. Horatio is commanded to live on and tell the story of Hamlet to the unsatisfied, and, as the play closes, we see him beginning to do just that. As with the Ancient Mariner, it is almost true to say that the ongoing purpose is in the telling itself. Biblical consummations are similar. The Exodus from Egypt, the seeming ending of a story of trial and sacrifice, is really a beginning. In particular it is the beginning of a story that has to continue to be told into the future. The future witness is of its essence (cf. Exod. 10.2). Ruth is a good example of a biblical story with a seemingly well-defined beginning, middle, and end. The end comes with the birth of Obed and the cry "A son is born to Naomi." If, in line with Christian typology, we change the lowercase "son" to "Son," then we get the suggestion of the final consummations of apocalypse. But typology is not history: if we attend to the dynamics of the story itself, we shall see that it resonates into the distant past and into the far future. But it denies closure. The birth of Obed is not the end but the beginning of a history that will continue to David and beyond. The verses of genealogy at the end pick up the thread of genealogy from the beginning. Here is a tale that is part of an ongoing history of promise and struggle, of suffering and redemption.

A better term than apocalypse or *aevum* (also proposed by Kermode) is covenant.[23] Biblical history in Ruth and elsewhere is covenant history. This is a dynamic, not a static form, not a pattern given but a pattern unfolded through trial and error. The human partners have a share in its unfolding. The essence of the covenant is dramatic, the memory of an encounter in which responsibilities are undertaken and promises exchanged by both parties. These responsibilities and promises remain with us through the time of our lives and beyond. We may seek to escape the former, and the latter may be hidden (as at the beginning of the story of Ruth), but they are potentially present and will one day reassert themselves. There will be unexpected obstacles but also unexpected opportunities. The course ahead is never clearly marked out, because while we are coerced by the terms of the covenant, we are also free agents. We may choose, and this choice gives to every moment a quality of peril and uncertainty. The American founding fathers felt themselves to be involved in just such a covenant enterprise as they sailed the seas to make a new beginning in a New World. John Winthrop aptly quoted to them the covenant formula from Deuteronomy 30: "I have set before you this day life and death, blessing and cursing: therefore choose life." They had the sense of momentous possibilities for good or ill on every side as they stepped forward into an unknown land. "The world was all before them where to choose," one may say. That line from Milton reminds us also that, in spite of the typological scheme that governs the "plot" of *Paradise Lost*, there is along with this an implicit denial of closure, an openness asserted at the end of the poem, suggesting the openness of real time and real history as men endure them. For Milton too had a strong sense of the covenant principle in literature and in life.

The covenant is a condition of our existence in time, rather than an end foreseen. We cooperate with its purposes never quite knowing where it will take us, for "the readiness is all." The phrase is Hamlet's, and *Hamlet* is much more a covenant drama than is generally recognized. The protagonist is existentially in the situation of a covenant hero (or victim). In Act I there is a transforming encounter as a secret is revealed and a task imposed. We see in Hamlet a task-burdened figure, not obeying a pattern like Oedipus, but rather seeking it. It will only be finally discovered in the randomness of circumstances as he confronts time and its challenges—the time not of nature but of men. There is a long backward perspective, a long and profound expectancy as he strives imperfectly to shape his life in accordance with the task he has received. There is memory but there is also forgetfulness, coherence but also a lack of coherence, as befits human situations in history, the history of trial and self-discovery. If we use the term "historical archetype" for such a dramatic structure, it is because we lack a better term. For the covenant is not so much an archetype, a controlling metaphor, as the ground of many metaphors, a dynamic of relationships whereby many archetypes are shaped and to which they deeply have reference.

III

This book seeks to sketch and understand a number of myths or archetypes that seem to start at the beginning of the modern period (in the sixteenth or seventeenth century), have their apogee in the nineteenth century, and continue down to our own times. Their dynamic phase begins roughly with the Romantic Age, which Leslie Fiedler has aptly termed the "primal garden of the unfallen archetypes."[24] There are many reasons for the interest the romantic poets showed in mythology (ancient and new), but the impulse that most concerns us here is the impulse to come to terms with history. The "Burden of the Past"[25] lies heavily on the poets of the new age. Even as they seek to break free, they are enthralled by the past. "The days gone by," writes Wordsworth,

> Return upon me almost from the dawn
> Of life: the hiding places of man's power
> Open. . . .
>
> (*Prelude* XII, 278–80)

From Goethe on, the men of the nineteenth century are obsessed with development and organism. Wordsworth's poem from which the above lines are quoted has as its subtitle: "Growth of a Poet's Mind." Continuities and origins are important, the more perhaps because of the deep fear of discontinuity. But the metaphor of organism, so dear to Wordsworth and his friend Coleridge, was not the only "Symbolic Form" found helpful in coming to terms with time and its mutability. In this study we shall be concerned with several other myths and metaphors no less pervasive in the period.

At this point we should perhaps make a distinction between the mythologizing of history and the historicizing of myth. Of the former a good deal has been written. It is a major preoccupation of

Herder and Coleridge and the men of their generation. It leads to schemes of universal history based on what was felt to be the vitality of primitive myth.[26] Such visionary history has had many practitioners, from Blake to Thomas Mann. Blake gives us in his prophetic books and in such a poem as "The Mental Traveller" the outline of what has come to be known as the Orc-cycle. Orc (or Luvah), beginning as a god of revolution, seems to develop into a nature god, his ritual birth, copulation, and death suggesting the monotony of a world order that knows neither salvation nor change but only the sameness of eternal forms. Blake had an intuition of other possibilities also, such as those associated with Los, who is much more a god of historical time as such. Mythologized history is everywhere in the period of Hegel and Comte: it is an ingredient in classical Marxism, with its vision of the vicious circle of revolution and counterrevolution, just as it is an ingredient in the thinking of Nietzsche, with his romantic glorification of Aryan origins and his feeling for the Dionysiac in art and literature. There is a profound attraction for the men of the nineteenth century in such images. Perhaps we have here (following Cassirer's formulation) a projection of the inner biological need to root human contingencies in some more timeless pattern of repetition. Mann later was fascinated by life as "sacred repetition"—Cleopatra, for instance, in her mythic role as Isis or Venus.[27] Shakespeare had a keen intuition of this also, but he also saw Cleopatra in a perspective of irony as an erring female—"no more but e'en a woman" (*Antony and Cleopatra*, IV.xiii). Along with the mythic apotheosis of the hero and heroine, a morally bracing wind of realism blows through Shakespeare's play. This is not always to be found in the mythologized history of the nineteenth century or beyond that—in the enchanted historiosophies of Yeats, Spengler, and Berdayev.

But alongside and sometimes subtly combined with this felt need to relate time and its mutabilities to timeless schemes drawn from the region of myth and nature, we may note in the nineteenth century a time consciousness of a different kind. It has to do with the awareness of living in an age of change and crisis, of living precisely in a period for which there were no set schemes, no adequate historical prototypes, and where events revealed themselves as irreversible, even our own actions being in a deep sense unpredictable, and nonrepetitive. Such is the consciousness of Dostoyevsky's Underground-man or of the speaker in Matthew Arnold's "Dover

Beach." History has become a "darkling plain" where "ignorant armies clash by night." In trying to grapple with their existential crisis, with the awareness of historical rupture, so characteristic of this time, writers often seized upon myths or legends of a non-historical kind and gave them a new historical urgency. This is what I have termed the historicizing of myth. Thus the Faust myth becomes in America and elsewhere a major archetype of the nineteenth century, as we shall see. It lurks behind *The Scarlet Letter*, *Wuthering Heights*, *Le père Goriot* and many other texts. It comes to express the terrors of modern man as he endures the crisis of his own insurrection against traditional bonds. The archetype now acquires an intensity that is *sui generis*, belonging to a particular time, that of a world in travail. This is what is meant by speaking of the literary expression of the Faust myth as an "historical archetype." It has a sixteenth-century genesis (and, we may add, a twentieth-century dénouement) and is to that extent to be differentiated from anything more generalized and universal.

It is hardly new to say that even the theories of the unconscious that make their appearance at the end of the nineteenth century are historically conditioned. Freud's system, which parades itself as a "biological" investigation of the permanent laws of human nature, nevertheless starts from an intuition of the constraining power of our personal past. The Oedipus phase is presented as a permanent aspect of human maturation, but surely the notion of the Father who will destroy us if we do not destroy him is part of a specifically nineteenth-century myth to which hundreds of texts bear witness. Nor is Freud's own rebellion against his Jewish father (a special case of nineteenth-century historical crisis) entirely irrelevant in this context.[28]

But it is not only that a new intensity, a new quality of historical urgency is given to imaginative contents that might seem to be timeless and universal. There is also in many cases a modification of the contents themselves. Under the stress of historical crisis, archetypes undergo structural modification. There is new interest in the figure of the wanderer in the nineteenth century.[29] Students would normally wish to consider the wanderers of all ages (Odysseus, Perseus, Wotan, etc.) and the wanderers of the nineteenth century—Arnold's Scholar Gipsy for example, and the Wandering Jew of so many nineteenth-century fables—synchronically, i.e., as transformations of a single archetype. But I will suggest that it is more important to observe the mutations in the synchrony itself. The new wanderers are functionally different, expressing a new need to dramatize the pressures of historical change. Arnold's wanderer

> Still nursing the unconquerable hope,
> Still clutching the inviolable shade,
> With a free onward impulse brushing through,
> By night, the silver'd branches of the glade—

represents the need to affirm a standard of permanency and sanity in the face of the intolerable spiritual prostration of his own time:

> For what wears out the life of mortal men?
> 'Tis that from change to change their being rolls:
> 'Tis that repeated shocks again, again,
> Exhaust the energy of strongest souls
>   And numb the elastic powers.

The Scholar Gipsy, "born in days when wits were fresh and clear," mediates for us the two contradictory emotional directions of the poem: on the one hand he serves to articulate the sense of irretrievable loss; on the other, he becomes the sign of a still conceivable and tangible past. This is a far cry from the wanderer's classic function as a sign of circularity. Arnold's wanderer serves as a modality of communication in the face of historic rupture. Of course, the communication is only possible by means of texts. The Scholar Gipsy, we are told, is "Living as thou liv'st on Glanvil's page." "Glanvil's page" (and by metonymy Arnold's own poem) is in fact all that we have by way of an image of the past. The revenant of which the poem speaks is the text itself. The wanderer is the poem. The poem does not so much recall the past as it personifies through the figure of the wanderer the action of memory itself, its comforts and frustrations.

We shall often find ourselves in this region of metapoetics. The new transformations of myth often seem to parade and question their own mythic nature. Sometimes—and these are among the most interesting examples of our subject—the timeless world of myth turns out on scrutiny to have a traitor in the house. Keats's *Ode to a Grecian Urn* will do as an example of this: On the face of it, the poem is a celebration of the perfection of the changeless world of myth—symbolized by a transcendent chord of music, a transcendent moment of love, a transcendent moment of devotion. But in the inevitable counterpoint, the world of suffering and change is by no means abolished. The "cold pastoral" (how revealing that adjective is!) is set off against "breathing human passion" and the unassuaged woe of a world in travail:

> When old age shall this generation waste,
> Thou shalt remain in midst of other woe
> Than ours, a friend to man.

The poet seems to say how much better off we would be if we could inhabit the aesthetic paradise of the Urn, but it is not the satisfaction of such achieved myth-consciousness that the poem communicates. It dramatizes much rather the "mad pursuit," the "struggle to escape," and the "wild ecstasy." These suggest a violence of movement at odds with the stillness of the Urn. At the same time, paradoxically, these gestures seem to point to a poetics of *escape* from history and *pursuit* of myth, but in this they betray their own hopelessness. There can be no successful escape or pursuit, and the gestures remain frozen in the stillness of death that is the Urn. Ultimately, the poem in its pathos and beauty betrays itself as a criticism of its own myth of sublimation. It conjures up for us an aesthetic paradise that has become barren and lifeless.

Another romantic poem of attempted escape, written more than eighty years later by the Hebrew poet C. N. Bialik, shows an even more decided counterpoint. The archetypal motif embodied in "The Pool" (1905) is that of Narcissus gazing at his image reflected in the water—a motif mediated through the *Roman de la Rose* and the tradition of romantic allegory. The Pool here is the mirror that so regularly comes to represent romantic self-consciousness. As in many poems of Wordsworth or Hölderlin, the poet seeks to cultivate a tranquil mood of meditation. But for the Jewish poet such a mood of stillness is even more problematical than it had been for Keats or Wordsworth or Hölderlin. For Bialik, like so many Jewish writers of the past hundred years, had to endure the traumas of modern history in their most acute form. The Pool is riven by storm. There are "six hundred thousand gusts of wind" (the number of the Israelites passing through the wilderness after the Exodus from Egypt), and later on, the narrator, now seen

as a child gazing into the dreaming depths of the Pool, is violently
disturbed by the commanding voice of the "hidden God" (of Isaiah
45.15):

> And suddenly shattering the silence
> Echoes the voice of "the hidden God":
> "Where art thou?"
> And the woods gaze astonished
> And great cypress-trees, green denizens of the forest,
> Look on me amazed, in majesty
> And silence asking: "What does this one in our midst?" [30]

The meaning of "the voice of the 'hidden God'" has been much discussed by Bialik's critics. It signifies guilt, alienation ("What does
this one in our midst?"), but above all it surely represents the call
of unrevoked responsibility. It addresses to us the question heard
by Adam in the Garden, *Ayĕka*, "Where art thou?" It announces an
urgent historical purpose. That is why it is also linked in the system of the poet's imagery to the Judge Samson. The narrator's relation to the Pool is that of Samson in the arms of Delilah (line 12).
Even as he seeks to cultivate the tranquility of a green thought in a
green shade, he is forced to recognize his continuing allegiance to
the absent God. The covenantal imperatives are too strong for him.
Poetry is not enough.

Structurally, Bialik's poem resembles the longer lyrics of the romantic poets of the early nineteenth century.[31] An outdoor scene of
nature is interiorized by the meditating consciousness. As in Wordsworth's "Lines Composed a Few Miles Above Tintern Abbey," an
earlier memory is superimposed upon a later memory of the same
scene, and what results is a mood of tranquil restoration to be laid
up for future use. As with Coleridge's "Dejection: An Ode," the poem
of Bialik proceeds by means of long irregular stanzas, commotion
giving way to joy and repose in slow undulations. Above all we
have with Bialik, as with his romantic precursors in this genre of
the memory poem, a revelational tone and a posture of prayer. But
the difference again should be noted. For them the revelation essentially is from within the meditating consciousness itself—"I
may not hope from outward forms to win / The passion and the life,
whose fountains are within"—says Coleridge. This will not quite
do for Bialik. The Pool epitomizes tranquility, the hidden treasure
of a world of dreams. But the dream will be disrupted by another

kind of revelation, one that explodes on us from outside the magic circle of the mind, from that region of historical crisis which Wordsworth had sought to banish from his poetry, terming it "the fretful stir / Unprofitable, and the fever of the world." Bialik cannot escape this fever. The sudden *Ayĕka* breaks the mood of tranquil self-absorption, and likewise, standing alone as it does, it sharply arrests the flow of the slow pentameters by which that mood had been communicated.

We could say that the movement in Bialik's poem is the reverse of what had happened earlier on to Wordsworth. Wordsworth tells us in *The Prelude* how, from being an "active partisan" much involved in the stirring events in France in the years immediately following the Revolution, he had undergone a kind of recoil from history and "yielded up moral questions in despair" (XI.305). It was then, around the year 1796, that, guided by his sister Dorothy, he retired into the countryside to cultivate his vocation as a poet of the inner weather:

> She, in the midst of all, preserved me still
> A Poet, made me seek beneath that name,
> And that alone, my office upon earth.
> (Ibid., 346–48)

The phrase "and that alone" is noticeably strident. There is, of course, no such thing as taking on oneself the name of poet "alone," but that is nevertheless what Wordsworth claims to be doing, revealing at the same time what a lonely business it will be and ultimately how unattainable. But the direction is what counts: it is from a greater to a lesser consciousness of the world of change and trial.

If Bialik's direction is different from Wordsworth's, this will be found very often to be the case with the Jewish writers we shall discuss from time to time in this book. Having inherited the meditative posture of Wordsworth and other romantic poets, Bialik in the end finds himself rudely interrupted in his attempt to devote himself to a poetics of emotion recollected in tranquility. History may not be mocked. Because of their extraordinary exposure to historical pressures—pressures that reached a dreadful climax in the mid-twentieth century—and because of their peculiar sensitivity also to the language of the Bible, where many of our historical archetypes have their origin, much space will be devoted in these pages to the evidence of Hebrew writers. The present work turns out to be in fact, from time to time, something of a comparative study of American and European writings on the one hand and Hebrew (or, more generally, Jewish) writings on the other. For Hebrew authors, while they tried very hard, from the period of the Enlightenment on, to write like everyone else, often found themselves—almost against their will—doing something different. Bialik's Pool signifies a world of natural forms and the biological time-consciousness that responds to such forms. Read as metalanguage, it also signifies a poetics of timeless archetypes that Bialik seeks to make his own. But he cannot in the end achieve such identification. The voice of history invades the Garden of the unfallen archetypes. He finds he cannot take his ease in that Garden, for he is enthralled by memory, the unappeased memory of a future still to be fulfilled.

2

The Pact with the Devil

"To ANY TRUE GREEK," said Nietzsche in *The Birth of Tragedy*, "*Faust*
would have seemed quite unintelligible." In contrast to the serenity
of Alexandrian culture, to the Socratic confidence in the powers of
human knowledge, and in contrast to the myth world of the an-
cients, we have that symbol of modern restlessness, the man "who
storms unsatisfied through all the provinces of knowledge and is
driven to make a bargain with the powers of darkness."[1] Nietzsche
did not pursue the thought. It was left to his disciple, Oswald Spengler, to see in the Faustian idea the fundamental determinant of modern culture, the key to a new "dynamic lay-out of the universe."[2]

Moreover, it is essentially a Western, *Christian* phenomenon; we
get a hint of it in the later Middle Ages with Leonardo da Vinci but
it really begins with the Reformation. The sense implicit in Christianity of the importance of the individual soul and the infinite powers it possesses will eventually bring the new man into existence.
The new man, says Spengler, is Martin Luther. "He completely liberated the Faustian personality. The intermediate person of the
priest, which had formerly stood between it and the Infinite, was
removed. And now it was wholly alone, self-oriented, its own priest
and its own judge."[3] For Luther the devil is a real presence, within
and without. The world as we know it cannot be understood with-

out him, nor without him can we understand our own drives, our own violent and uncurbed desires. Life is a desperate battle against the devil.

What we are here concerned with is, in the most essential meaning of that term, an historical archetype. The first full account of the legend is presented as a history, the *Historia von D. Johann Fausten* (1587) based on the life of an actual necromancer—an exact contemporary, by the way, of Luther, at the beginning of the sixteenth century. Time, its purpose and meaning belong to the very essence of the pact between Faustus and Mephistophilis. Christopher Marlowe's Doctor Faustus bargains away his soul for "four and twenty years," which he will pass "in all voluptuousness." The most intense evocation of the onward movement of time is achieved in Marlowe's incomparable closing scene, where his hero has "but one bare hour to live"—an hour marked out for us by the striking of the clock:

> The stars move still, time runs, the clock will strike,
> The devil will come, and Faustus must be damned.

The play brings together the poles of time as human beings experience it: the long scale of years, with its vista of limitless opportunity, and the short scale of minutes, which leaves us no breathing space or possibility of achievement or rest. Corresponding with this there are two kinds of rhythm in the play: there is the swelling, lyrical blank verse of the early scenes expressive of his "four and twenty years of liberty," and there is the urgent, short-breathed rhythm expressive of intolerable suspense, as in the lines just quoted.

In all the multiple transformations of the Faust myth, the exigency of passing time (felt either as opportunity or as dread) remains its core, its fundamental "deep structure." Macbeth, who yields his "eternal jewel to the common enemy of man"—a Faust figure if ever there was one—decides to "jump the life to come" seeking his be-all and end-all here "upon this bank and shoal of time." Lady Macbeth imagines their time to come will be gloriously fulfilled, a succession of nights and days intensely lived:

> you shall put
> This night's great business into my dispatch;
> Which shall to all our nights and days to come
> Give solely sovereign sway and masterdom.

Goethe's *Faust*, so different in moral pattern and aim from Marlowe's play or Shakespeare's, nevertheless preserves this essence:

> Stürzen wir uns in das Rauschen der Zeit,
> In's Rollen der Begebenheit.
> (Let's hurl ourselves in time's on-rushing tide,
> Occurrence's on-rolling stride)

declares Goethe's hero. Man's life is defined by his ceaseless activity:

> Nur rastlos bethätigt sich der Mann.
> (Man's active only when he's never at ease.)[4]

He will lose his wager at the moment when he pauses and seeks to arrest the flow in order to take pleasure in the immobile beauty of some scene or occasion:

> Werd' ich zum Augenblicke sagen:
> Verweile doch! du bist so schön!—
> Dann magst due mich in Fesseln schlagen. . . .
> Die Uhr mag stehn, der Zeiger fallen,
> Es sei die Zeit für mich vorbei!
> (If the swift moment I entreat:
> Tarry a while! you are so fair!
> Then forge the shackles to my feet. . . .
> The clock may stop, its hands fall still,
> And time be over then for me.)[5]

At the metapoetic level, we may say that we have in these words an affirmation of pure diachrony; any notion of the reality and value of aesthetic space, of timelessness—what Blake called "the moony habitations of Beulah"—is declared to be the antithesis of the Faustian experience. That is why it is here represented as a violation of the pact. When he entreats time to stop he will have failed.

It is not that the Faustian pact is simply a modality whereby time is shaped, a drama performed in a given medium that we call historical time; it is much rather that by which time itself is constituted, the myth determining what history is to be. Faustus is granted his time span of twenty-four years under the terms of the contract. It does not exist in any other form. Central to the myth is the awareness of the time of this world as a commodity purveyed by the devil. Here we have the precise antithesis of the account of the Creation in the first thirty-four verses of Genesis. There time is sanctified; each day, as it is brought into existence, is declared to be good, and, when the work of the six days is accomplished, they are gathered up under the covenantal sign of the Sabbath, to be shared in by God and Man.[6] Lurking behind this notion of the Sabbath of created time is the longer time-scheme of history itself, which also has its "Sabbath" or "end of days," signifying not only a terminus but the consummation of a purpose, a *telos*.[7] The parallel end-moment in the Faustian covenant is, of course, the dark and terrible end of the hero: "The devil will come, and Faustus must be damned." The awareness of the end point, "the sense of an ending," is again not an incidental aspect of the Faustian pact. Time is given meaning and direction by the catastrophe that awaits us. Time is not neutral: it is diabolically shaped. And lurking behind the personal doom of the Faustian hero is the doom of the world, the coming of the dark millennium. The "decline of the West" of which Spengler writes is already implicit in the earliest formulations of the myth. Marlowe's hero is aware that he will pay a dreadful price for the marvels he enjoys. We receive our powers under terms that include our ultimate overthrow. The blessings of our culture have within themselves the seeds of the destruction of that culture. It is a seeming absurdity. Nevertheless, it follows logically from the basic apprehension of the world and time as gifts of the Devil rather than as blessings of God. Once that is established, it follows that knowledge will bring its own nemesis; that the power we have will prove satanic; that we will become slaves of our machines, victims of our own economic inventions. This is the essence of Spengler's vision.

Sadly, all this has tended to be a self-fulfilling prophecy. And that is the nature of "historical archetypes." The myths of which we are speaking not only reflect historical situations; they also tend to shape and condition the historical process. Men act out the Faustian dream or nightmare in real life. Space flight is an example of this. Going back to Leonardo, it receives insistent expression in the romantic period (Byron's Faustian hero Cain is taken on a flight into space—his guide is Lucifer) and throughout the nineteenth century, to be translated into technology in our time. Art anticipates scientific invention.

Jules Verne seized hold of the Faustian myth as dream, Spengler seized it as nightmare. And his pessimism too was to be vividly reinforced by what was happening to Europe just as his life came to an end in 1936. Ten years later his own countryman Thomas Mann, reflecting deeply on Germany's part in all this, was to write the Faust novel to end all Faust novels. In Adrian Leverkühn's terrible end we have an intimation of the abyss into which Germany has descended. He takes with him apparently all that is best in the culture of the West, of which he is the supreme symbol. He stands for its music, its art, its highest reaches of soul. But he has sold his soul irredeemably and the demons wait for him on the other side. It is more than a literary archetype: it seems to be Europe's central myth in the modern era. During the composition of *Doktor Faustus*, Mann tells us that he had read much of Nietzsche, that he had thought a great deal about Luther, who is actually introduced as a central figure in the book (Mann's friend Erich Kahler drew a direct line from Luther to Hitler), and also that he had read practically the whole of Conrad in large doses each night before going to sleep.[8]

Conrad, as a matter of fact, had the whole thing worked out almost half a century earlier. In *Heart of Darkness* (1902) we have surely the essential kernel of *Doktor Faustus*. Mr. Kurtz is the noblest European of them all. "All Europe," we are told, "contributed to the making of Kurtz." He was a writer, a poet, an artist in words and in paint, but he had sold himself into savagery, and the end is darkness, madness, and death.

It is clear and often noted that all the major expressions of the Faustian myth have reference to art itself. Mikhail Bulgakov gives us a fantasy version of this in *The Master and Margarita* (1928?), where one of Mephisto-Woland's main achievements is to save the writer's masterpiece and restore it to him. The hero of the myth who sells his soul to the devil is in an important sense the demonic artist and poet for whom beauty is an irresistible fascination. More than she is the symbol of the desires of the flesh, Helen of Troy in Marlowe's play is the goddess who makes the poet immortal with a kiss. What Mephisto offers to Goethe's Faust is not mere time, mere duration but the intensity of an hour of pure artistic creation: "ein ganzes Stundglass voll genialer Teufelzeit." Here is the ultimate ecstasy, the intoxication that Faustian man will achieve. He will descend like Orpheus into the depths and win from the dark gods the gift of poetry. It is clear that the Faustian myth represents, from this point of view, a modern historicized version of the myth of Orpheus. Margarita in Bulgakov's novel is an Orpheus figure. Conrad's Marlow going up-river in search of Kurtz, whom he will try to bring back from the heart of darkness, is Orpheus all over again, descending into the underworld in search of Eurydice. Thomas Mann has the clearest possession of this dimension of the myth.[9] His hero is, above all, the artist seized by romantic nihilism. From his pact with the devil a terrible beauty is born. Descending into the depths, he will pluck for us the flowers of evil in all their fragile, trembling beauty. A musical composition as perfect as Leverkühn's final work will never be achieved again. For, like its composer, it too is doomed, lost—a memory of all that was fair beyond words in European art and civilization. But this has turned out to be a dream, "the latest dream I ever dream'd on the cold hill side." We awake bereft.

Orpheus has thus become for Mann a figure in an historical drama: he appears with the beginning of the Renaissance, enchanting stones and trees with his music; in the period of romantic subjectivity he descends into the depths of his own consciousness and discovers its disintegrating fascination, and in our twentieth century he is torn to pieces by the Thracian women.[10] That would seem to be one important way of defining the Faustian archetype. A timeless myth is transformed into a dynamic historical pattern structured by the dialectic of renaissance and decline. And it is the decline that we chiefly sense in Mann and Spengler. In the strict terms of the myth, hope will not be recovered. This is the difference again between the myths of nature and the myths of history. With Orpheus and Eurydice, as with Proserpine—in their original characters—we may comfort ourselves with the thought that with the return of the spring, the cycle will be repeated. The Faustian myth does not harbor such consolations. Built into it is the irreversibility of historical time. Thomas Mann's novel, in consequence, does not have the cathartic ending of a Greek tragedy. There will never be another Leverkühn, just as there will never be another "Lamentation for Doctor Faustus." We must accept the finalities of history.

Nevertheless, there is in many of the texts we are considering an overtone of salvation. Conrad's *Heart of Darkness* suggests at first sight the absoluteness of a dark apocalypse. Behind the façade of civilization is the primeval forest. Africa is the symbol of what lurks within us all—"The Horror." The darkness of the Thames and the Congo is the same, and what awaits us at the end of the river is the hole into which Kurtz's body is finally consigned. The corpse casually thrown to the side of the road over which Marlow stumbles, the dead and dying lying unregarded "in every pose of contorted collapse," are the first amazing prevision in literature of the imagery of Belsen and Auschwitz. But this is not quite the final meaning of the book. There is a continuing character, Marlow, who symbolically retraces Kurtz's journey but nevertheless stands for endurance and recovery. It seemed to him at the end "that the house would collapse before I could escape, that the heavens would fall upon my head." But this does not occur: unlike Orpheus, he is not torn to pieces by the Maenads. He survives, and draws his breath with pain to tell the story. The fact is that the literary evidence, if properly sifted, confirms the doubts of many of Spengler's critics. The Faustian myth is undoubtedly central to the European experience from Shakespeare and Marlowe on, but it is all far more complex and the "decline" far less inevitable than Spengler held. It is worth remembering that Goethe's *Faust* ends with the rose petals with which Gretchen welcomes the immortal part of Faust in heaven. Nor is this just an afterthought. The prologue in heaven is based on Job: Faust is going to be tried and tested. And if that is so, maybe he will, like Job, pass the test. This is not a sentimental nineteenth-century importation. Heine, who wrote a ballet version of *Faust*, reminds us that at the very beginning of the legend, we have the story of Theophilus of Adana, a hero who is in the end saved from Hell by the grace of Mary.

II

In the modern history of the diabolical compact, the American experience is crucial. Covenant and bond have, from the time of the Mayflower compact, been the normal form of response to the challenges and opportunities presented by the new continent. But the bond has always been deeply ambiguous. Even as the new men pledge their loyalty to God and to one another, the devil creeps in and takes a hand. As remarked earlier, John Winthrop, setting sail for America with the men of the Massachusetts Bay Colony, summoned them into a covenant based on the speech of Moses to the Israelites in Deuteronomy 30. Like the Israelites, they were about to cross their Jordan to enter their Promised Land: when they arrived they were to observe the commandments and thereby "choose life." But, as Robert N. Bellah points out, "the covenant was broken almost as soon as it was made."[11] As they achieved power and possessions, the dark covenant of rapacity and demonism came as a substitute for, almost a parody of, the moral covenant that commands virtue. The dream and the nightmare lived side by side. Hobbes's State of Nature, in which every man is at war with every man, alternated with the biblical garden of Eden.

Shakespeare anticipates the dilemma in one of his many Faustian characters, Angelo, in *Measure for Measure*. He is a good Christian, indeed a Puritan, up to the moment when he is given absolute power over the state: "Mortality and mercy in Vienna / Live in thy heart and tongue. . . ." The temptations that come with power are too strong for him, and the devil ("the cunning enemy") steps in. This, of course, is a comedy, and so in the end the Duke intervenes to save him from the full consequences of his diabolism. Unfortunately, there was no such kindly *deus ex machina* available to the new settlers in America. Too often they muttered to themselves, "blood thou art blood," and proceeded reluctantly to sign themselves over to the common enemy of man. The black covenant came to stay.

Puritanism had itself in a manner prepared the way for this development. Luther and Calvin had seized on the doctrine of election—the dynamic of the Old Testament—but they had abandoned the practical morality of Works that informed it and laid their emphasis instead on the evangelical principle of Grace. "And if by Grace, then it is no more of Works," said the apostle Paul (Rom. 11.6). The effect of this "Covenant of Grace," as Tawney and others have shown, is that spirituality is concentrated in the inner life, while the newfound powers exercise themselves in a world from which God is absent. The practical result is that the devil takes over.

The early Puritans were dimly conscious of this danger. William Perkins in 1591 spoke of the possibility of a diabolical covenant, a dark replica of the covenant with God,[12] and later described the experience of "satanical molestation" in terms that very closely resemble the plight of Angelo in Shakespeare's play. *Pecca fortiter*, Luther had said, "Sin strongly." There will be no half-measures now that we know for sure that the devil is in charge. Angelo is the same. Once he feels the drive of his instinct, he abandons himself to it. "I have begun, / And now I give my sensual race the rein." This is what happens, Angelo concludes sadly, "when once our grace we have forgot."

The demonic covenant may thus be viewed as a direct outgrowth of the Puritan doctrine of Grace. Puritanism, in its evangelical character, had sought to deny the world. My kingdom, it declared, is not of this world. But the world will not be denied. Wars matter, the acts of men matter, in politics and economics. In a word, history matters. This was part of the "new dynamic lay-out of the universe," as *homo americanus* experienced it. The reaction to the Covenant of Grace thus takes the form of violently reinstating the covenant idea *in the world*. Owing to the effect of the Covenant of Grace, the world will not be sanctified by the commandments given at Sinai, and yet it is in the world, in the realm of history, *as with the Hebrew prophets*, that salvation will be sought. The pact with the devil thus represents the dynamics of the biblical, Old Testament covenant without its ethical content. Consciously or unconsciously, the new Faustian man attaches himself to the biblical model, draws strength from it. He acts out a kind of sinister parody of the Old Testament covenant. For the Hebrew Bible taught that men are justified by work in the world. To be sure, that work was the work of righteousness, but it was work nevertheless. If the new men were activists ("Up and be doing, for the Lord is with thee," declared John Eliot), upheld by a sense of mission that enabled them to do amazing things, it was because that was what the newly discovered Bible of the Reformation taught them to be. In short we have here the eruption into modernity of a kind of bastard Hebraism.

This will perhaps explain why the devil is so often represented as a Jew! Joshua Trachtenberg has shown that the Devil-Jew-Judas triangle is a medieval commonplace,[13] but it achieves new force at the beginning of the modern period. If one struggles in vain against one's own aggressions called into play by the new extraordinary opportunities, then who but the Jew is responsible? For it is he who tells us, in direct contrast to the Evangelist, that his Kingdom *is* of this world. ("It is not in heaven that thou shouldst say, who shall go up to heaven and bring it to us, and make us hear it that we may do it" [Deut. 30.12].) As a result, the dynamic possibilities offered by the new politics and the new economics are often traced to the devil, who is also a Jew. The first Machiavelli on the English stage is Marlowe's Jew of Malta, Barabas. Sixteenth-century man could not escape the evil attracton of Machiavelli, who had given a license for the exercise of this-worldly ambition. This is part of the revolutionary tide of modernity, and so it is given vivid dramatic form by means of the mythic triangle of Jew-Machiavelli-Devil. We have a similar phenomenon in Shakespeare's *The Merchant of Venice*. Nine times in the course of that play, Shylock is linked with the devil. At the beginning of the play, Antonio enters into a compact, a *bond*, with Shylock. The word "bond" is repeated obsessively throughout. It is evidently the basis of a new reality. It is the "bond" that holds Antonio in its diabolical grip, but it also enables Antonio and his friend, Bassanio, to pursue their commercial ambitions, for, absurdly, the "Jew" holds the key to the new economic power and opportunity. The fact that the new usurers were Christians rather than Jews is ignored.[14] What we have here is a kind of guilt substitution. In the figure of the Jew-devil, the Puritan seeks to hide himself from his own self-reflection as he pursues his ambitions in a world stripped of the restraints of righteousness. There is a dark anticipation here of the Nazi mythology, which idealized the Faustian superman as the essence of the German spirit, while it illogically cast the Jew as the devil in the Faust story.[15]

III

Nineteenth-century America turns out to have the richest array of examples of the archetype we are discussing,[16] in keeping perhaps with the truly Faustian progress of the New World itself. Moreover, this literary testimony is of special interest because we can see how, in spite of the fierce attractions of the diabolical compact, the biblical salvation-myth remains in some sense a viable alternative, a muted countertheme. Melville's *Moby-Dick*, as Leslie Fiedler has noted, is a major Faust story. In a central chapter, Ahab is seen making his crew "parties to the indissoluble league" (chap. 35). Later on, at the forge (chap. 112), he tempers the barb intended for Moby-Dick in the blood of his three pagan companions, at the same time uttering a formula of baptism "*in nomine diaboli.*"

Melville is clearly reacting here to the monstrous presumption of man in seeking control over the world, even over the source of life itself (for that is what the sperm whale surely stands for). This presumption invites a biblical judgment. "Canst thou draw out Leviathan with a fish-hook?" The clear answer implied by the book of Job had been no. But Ahab had tried to answer yes. Melville's Ahab is something like the "mortal God" of Hobbes's *Leviathan* (a book that, as Bellah has shown, lurks behind the self-awareness of the new American).[17] He is the absolute monarch into whose hands the members of the crew have all, by compact, surrendered their individual ambitions. Will that hold? Or shall we have a better covenant—that suggested by Father Mapple's sermon on the book of Jonah, or by the Epilogue, where the narrator Ishmael survives to bear witness to a happier vision of man's future? "The unharming sharks, they glided by as if with padlocks on their mouths; the savage sea-hawks with sheathed beak." It is a redemptive moment, marked with an appropriate motto from Job: "And I only am escaped alone to tell thee."

On the whole, nineteenth-century American fiction tries to suggest redemption, even for the Faust figures themselves. Dimmesdale and Hester are both saved in their different ways at the end of *The Scarlet Letter*, while Roger Chillingworth, the devil figure who has all but mastered the souls of both of them, is thwarted and diminished like Mephistopheles at the end of Goethe's *Faust*. "Thou hast escaped me," Chillingworth mutters to Dimmesdale. And, "since there was no more devil's work on earth for him to do," we are told, "all his strength and energy seemed at once to desert him." That is what Hawthorne very much wants to believe. Above all, he wants to believe in a happier future for America, to be achieved with the release from sexual taboos. The scarlet letter, we are told, will cease to be a stigma, and the women who come to the aging Hester's cottage for counsel will be told that "at some brighter period, when the world should have grown ripe for it, in Heaven's own time, a new truth would be revealed, in order to establish the whole relation between man and woman on a surer ground of mutual happiness." In short, a better time is coming. Maybe Hawthorne would have thought differently today. In his time, it was still possible to be hopeful. The pact would fade away and something fairer and more sunlit would take its place. In a similar fashion, the devil is hoodwinked at the end of "Young Goodman Brown," as Hawthorne tries to persuade himself that the witches' sabbath in which all New England seems to have participated was perhaps no more than a very bad dream.

Writers of more realistic fiction from the beginning of our century seem to be equally obsessed with the Faust theme, but there is perhaps less confidence in the happy ending. In *The Titan* (1914), Dreiser sums up the career of his Faustian hero, Cowperwood, the creator of the railroads, whereby the great wilderness would be conquered: "Rushing like a great comet to the zenith, his path a blazing trail, Cowperwood did for the hour illuminate the terrors and wonders of individuality." Where does the energy come from? he asks: "The soul within? And whence comes it? Of God?" Evidently not, for he continues, "What thought engendered the spirit of Circe, or gave to Helen the lust of tragedy? By what demon was the fate of Hamlet prepared? And why did the weird sisters plan to ruin the murderous Scot?" The references to *Hamlet* and *Macbeth* are apt. Hamlet commits his body and soul to the service of a Ghost without knowing for certain whether it was "a spirit of health or goblin damned." The swearing ceremony in Act I, at which the Ghost in the cellarage provides an infernal commentary, is very Faustian. Macbeth is a more obviously Faustian character. True, he is haunted by images of salvation, of "heaven's cherubins hors'd upon the sightless couriers of the air," but he has clearly sold his soul to the devil ("and mine eternal jewel / Given to the common enemy of man"), and he will be damned for it.

Faulkner deserves separate treatment. He abounds with dark strangers who gain possession of the lives of others. The whole history of the South before and after the Civil War seems to be one great example of the theme we are discussing. But Faulkner is also derivative: Varner's contract with Ab Snopes in *The Hamlet* (1940), the act from which the whole family history takes its rise, reads like a "low-mimetic" version of Ahab's bond with his crew in *Moby-Dick*. Later on we have a burlesque interlude in which the Prince of Darkness argues with Flem Snopes about the latter's soul. But he turns out to have none. Evil is left supreme, but in the decay of the South the spiritual energy—the soul—which once informed it is somehow absent. The Faust figure continues to perform his gestures, but with a certain hopelessness. If there are no souls to be damned, there is also no great prize to be won. We are too deeply conscious of anticlimax and absurdity to believe in such mighty consummations. Paul Valéry at about the same time (*Mon Faust*, 1941) strikes a similar note of anticlimax. With the death of the soul, says Faust to Mephisto, "the whole system of which you were a linchpin is falling to pieces." Absurdly, only Mephistophilis is left to nurse the old-fashioned belief in good and evil.

In Faulkner's *Absalom, Absalom!* (1936), the survivor is the idiot negro, Jim Bond. The demonic Thomas Sutpen and his son Henry have gone and so have their victims. We are left with a land exhausted and hopeless. The story resembles *Wuthering Heights*, from which Faulkner seems to have drawn some features. Like Heathcliff, the first Sutpen is a "demon . . . who came out of nowhere and without warning upon the land" and then proceeded to plant himself in the lives of the indigenous inhabitants and finally to destroy them. But in Emily Brontë's novel we will emerge into the light of a better world. With Cathy and Hareton occupying the center of the stage at the end of the book, there is the intimation that the demons have been thoroughly exorcised: "They are afraid of nothing," we are told in the closing paragraphs. "Together they would brave Satan and all his legions." Such assurance is no longer possible in Faulkner's world.

The last great Faust novel is, as we have remarked, that of Thomas Mann, *Doktor Faustus* (1947). It is the last because, more than it is a demonstration of the force of the Mephistophilian pact, it is a lament for the tragedy of Europe, and of America too, for that matter. Mann himself, writing it in America, felt he was writing a novel to end novels—like Joyce's *Ulysses*. He was deeply touched, he tells us, by a remark of Harry Levin's to the effect that "the best writing of our contemporaries is not an act of creation, but an act of evocation."[18] He will describe not the fascinations of power but its ironies and deceptions, not the grandeur of Faustian man, but the pathos of a lost world, the music of a lost civilization. We are haunted by the music of Faust and of Germany. There is, of course, a survivor, an Ishmael figure. But Serenus Zeitblom, Ph.D., has too small a mind to offer any real hope for the future. He is also too servile for the role. In fact, what horrifies the reader most on reflection is not the list of enormities proclaimed in Leverkühn's final speech, but an early remark by the mild schoolmaster: "I have never, precisely on the Jewish problem, and the way it has been dealt with, been able to agree fully with our Führer and his paladins." The word "fully" opens abysses.

IV

Many of the great nineteenth-century myths have disappeared from serious literature in our own time for the simple reason that we have witnessed their literal translation into fact. Space travel, now that it has been achieved, will be the subject of ironic speculation (as in Bellow's *Mr. Sammler's Planet*) rather than of unconscious desires. In like fashion, the Faust theme proper, except for an occasional echo, seems to come to an end in literature at the moment when history shows us the final horrible results in life. In the Nazi period the word was made flesh. The Heart of Darkness became fact, and with that dreadful incarnation there was seemingly no further need for literary treatments. Having seen where it all ends, we stand appalled and helpless at the results.

It would appear indeed that historical archetypes not only have historical beginnings, but they may have historical terminations also. This would again make them significantly different from the timeless myths of the anthropologists, which are alleged to have not only universality but also permanency. Faust ends when its meaning is fulfilled; at that point it ceases to function as myth. One can go further than that: its end in historical time is implicit in the structure itself.

> Cut is the branch that might have grown full straight,
> And burned is Apollo's laurel bough,
> That sometime grew within this learned man . . .

says the Chorus at the end of Marlowe's play. The pathos of discontinuance is the very matter of the story. And the discontinuance is poetic discontinuance. What is implied is not only the inevitable, violent end of Faustian man from Macbeth to Adrian Leverkühn, but the inevitable end of the marvelous poetry of Faustian man, its pride and power. "Apollo's laurel bough" refers as much and perhaps more to the language of the myth as to Faust himself. It is that which is due to be lost with the ending of the structure that supports it. There is an indescribable pathos in the thought of the loss of so much beauty. There is, however, some comfort in this very interpretation, for it now appears that what is at issue in our time is not the end of the world, as Spengler thought, but the end of the myth.

It is true, of course, that man does not live by bread alone: he needs myths for survival. So that if the myth of inevitable disaster has exhausted itself—exhausted itself largely by coming true—it may be that what we need are myths of continuance to replace it. Melville had an intuition of this when, as noted earlier, he brought his fable to an end not with the overthrow of the *Pequod* and its crew but with the deliverance from death of the continuing character, Ishmael. Ishmael too, like Ahab, had been a Faust figure.[19] He had gone to sea in search of that boundless solitude, which, according to Spengler, was "the homeland of the Faustian soul." But we see in him at the end the symbol of the survivor who has abandoned all Faustian ambitions. He has become the witness, the teller of the tale, the mediator of a saving text.

A word about the Jewish literary evidence would be in place here. The Jew seems to have played a major part as presumptive villain in the Faust myth, and he has also emerged paradoxically as principal victim in its final, diabolical phase. What do Jews themselves say about it? In what form do they experience it? There are, of course, many Jewish stories about demons and their deluded victims, from the legends associated with Rabbi Joseph della Reina in the fifteenth century to the actual history of Shabbetai Zewi in the seventeenth century. And in our time we have a seemingly inexhaustible variety of such tales in the writings of Isaac Bashevis Singer. The demons and Satan, he said, symbolized the world for him.[20] But we miss the true Faustian note struck by Marlowe:

> Oh, what a world of profit and delight,
> Of power, of honour, of omnipotence
> Is promised to the studious artisan!
> All things that move between the quiet poles
> Shall be at my command. . . .

Such Promethean confidence in the possibilities provided by the powers of evil is somehow missing in the Jewish tradition. Demonic bargains there may be, but the sense of the power and opportunity that go with them is lacking. All the real power seems to be on the other side, on the side of the God of Abraham. He has seized us inexorably in the bondage of the covenant. Singer's ultimate hero is not a defiant rebel but Jacob, in *The Slave*, a tormented figure, who cannot escape his Jewish destiny. A parallel example is provided by the play *God, Man, and the Devil* (1900), by the popular Yiddish dramatist, Yakov Gordin—a play that evidently helped to shape Kafka's "The Judgment."[21] Satan tempts the hero, Herschele, by having him win a lottery. As a result his moral character is subverted. From being humble and saintly he becomes overbearing and heartless to those around him, his father and wife in particular. It is with them that we sympathize. The focus is on Herschele's moral corruption rather than his Promethean daring. The Prologue in Heaven at the beginning is Job mediated through Goethe's *Faust*, and Herschele himself, suffering at the end the retribution due to his folly and evil deeds, becomes a kind of Job figure. His suicide will mark the atonement for his sins. In a decisive rejection of the Faustian model, Herschele declares to the devil character, Mazik: "No Jew it was who said that he wants to take everything possible in life and still desire more."[22] Gordin is here echoing and rejecting Goethe's *Faust* and the boundless appetite for experience of Goethe's hero. He seems to be saying that this is something the Jew cannot embrace.

There are seeming exceptions. Abraham Cahan's *The Rise of David Levinsky* (1917), a novel of Jewish immigrants in New York at the beginning of the century, exhibits a fictional shape very similar to that of Dreiser's Cowperwood trilogy. The hero succumbs to the same sexual temptations, and the same attractions of power and wealth urge him forward. Levinsky too blazes cometlike (though he is a somewhat pale comet compared with Cowperwood) to his zenith and wonders regretfully whether he was aided in getting there by some wicked demon. The wicked demon for him, of course, is America itself. "Beware of Satan, Davie. When he assails you, just say no"—his teacher had warned him back in Antomir. But unfortunately David on arrival said yes. The American experience comes to represent that fatal deviation from the sacred covenants to which Levinsky's life as a child had been devoted. To step ashore in New York is to accept a darker dream, a different hope. But *The Rise of David Levinsky* is not in this respect a *Jewish* novel. As Isaac Rosenfeld has said, it is "an exemplary treatment of one of the dominant myths of American capitalism."[23] While the vocabulary is Jewish, the syntax is pure American.

What one would like to say is that Faust is not a Jewish myth at all. It is not without significance that Meir Letteris in his Hebrew rendering of Goethe's play in 1865 renamed its hero Elisha Ben Avuya. Ben Avuya was a notorious second-century heretic whose impieties were regarded with such horror that the Talmud refers to him simply as *aher*, "the Other." Rebel he certainly was, and one who had thrown in his lot with the powers of darkness. True also that he represented the fascination of forbidden knowledge—a factor that made him attractive to the writers of the modern Hebrew renaissance who were able to translate that knowledge into their own terms, i.e., the forbidden knowledge of the *haskala*, the European enlightenment. But he did not whisper in their ear that the world was theirs to conquer if they would only sign. He was not a Faustian figure in the Spenglerian sense of giving the signal for a new "dynamic lay-out of the universe."

There are many modern treatments of the Ben Avuya theme (for instance, Milton Steinberg's novel *As a Driven Leaf*, 1939); the one I should like to point to especially is a verse play by the Hebrew poet Shin Shalom written in the climacteric year 1945 under the title *Shabbat HaOlam*, "The Sabbath of the World." Precisely contemporary with Thomas Mann's *Doktor Faustus*, it may stand as the parallel Hebrew response to the same world-situation. Elisha is fundamentally a lost soul—that is the main thrust of the play—because he has rebelled against the Jewish covenant symbolized by the Sabbath. As a child of modernity, he turns his face away from the tradition and proclaims a new dispensation of freedom and light. But for Shin Shalom writing in the year 1945, such freedom and light are seen as existing in a spiritual vacuum. Inexorable though the need for them may be, they carry no sense of promise. Their reward is only endless loss. Basically, Ben Avuya is a Job figure, not a Faust figure: he is reacting to disaster, to "the ruin of the world." And he takes the road counseled by Job's wife: he is moved to "curse God and die." But he does not have the last word. That belongs to his pious disciple, Meir, and his wife, Bruria, who hold on to their faith, absurdly, it would seem, in spite of holocaust and exile, in spite of the ruin of the world.

For the Jew, evidently, there is no total abrogation of the sacred covenant. It is the ground of his eternal discontent: it holds him even when he seeks to escape into "forbidden paths." It drags him back to Nineveh to bear witness. In S. Y. Agnon's hauntingly beautiful novella, "The Betrothed" (1943),[24] a man and a woman are bound to one another by a promise made long ago, but they drift apart. Jacob Rechnitz seeks to deny his "bond" with Shoshana (the "lily of the valleys" of the Song of Songs), the oath first uttered by them in her father's garden in Vienna when they were children. But in the ancient sea-town of Jaffa, where Jacob now lives, it will be ratified anew. In a dreamlike episode, Shoshana runs a race on the seashore with six other maidens of Jaffa. Winning it, she also wins Rechnitz for herself and brings about the fulfillment of their age-old vows. The symbolism is patent. Behind the story lies the shape of the biblical covenant between God and Israel.

In other works, however, Agnon faces up more directly to the fierce and demonic antitheses to the biblical covenant. *Shira* (a posthumous work published in 1971), deals with the fascination of the unhallowed. The bond between the woman Shira and the hero is a kind of witchcraft. It is brought about by "that one who was created for our harassment"—i.e., the devil, and accordingly it lacks the grace and beauty of the sacred covenant celebrated in "The Betrothed." And perhaps for that reason too this was the one novel that Agnon was unable to finish though he made several tries. Agnon knew all about the bargain with the devil (perhaps from Chamisso's *Peter Schlemiel*) and used it as a motif in several early stories. But his final, summarizing statement, like those of Shin Shalom and Thomas Mann, came out of the spiritual prostration and horror of the Second World War. In *The Day Before Yesterday*, published in that same year, 1945, we are presented with a nightmare world lacking traditional signposts. Its hero, Yitzhak Kummer, has abandoned the pieties of tradition. Driven to the holy land by forces that he scarcely understands, he finds himself moving about in it as a stranger, a frustrated wanderer, alienated from those around him and ultimately alienated from himself. Finally, he moves into the shadow of insanity, and, bitten by the mad dog Balak, who symbolizes the darkness within him, as well as the diabolical forces in the world around him, he dies in agony.

But this is not quite the conclusion of the novel. True to his biblical models, Agnon delivers his world from death, burning, and madness. After Yitzhak's death there is a symbolic downpour of rain. The problems are not solved, but the parched earth is revived. Man returns to his labor under the sun. After flood and holocaust, we witness the return of fertility as the land yields its blessing and becomes in very truth, as the narrator terms it, "the Garden of the Lord." Total nihilism and total discontinuance are, it seems, impossible.

3

Doubles and Dybbuks

ON THE DAY BEFORE the trial of his brother Dmitri for the murder of his father, Ivan Karamazov is visited by the devil. It is Faust and Mephistophilis all over again, as his visitor reminds him, also the temptation of Job, but the aspect clearly emphasized is that the visitor is, at bottom, no other than a projection of a fragment of Ivan's own disturbed psyche. It is not by chance that Ivan's nightmare comes on the eve of his final mental derangement. Ivan's distinction is that he clearly recognizes what is happening to him; in this he becomes the representative of the romantic hyperconsciousness of the nineteenth century. In his agony, he identifies his visitor as a mental hallucination: "You are my hallucination. You are the incarnation of myself, but only of one side of me . . . of my thoughts and feelings, but only the nastiest and stupidest of them." And later Ivan, telling Alyosha of his visitor, remarks that "He is myself . . . all that's base in me, all that's mean and contemptible" (chap. x). We are thus in the realm of mental pathology. Dostoyevsky here anticipates Freud and modern depth-psychology generally; the Faust myth reveals itself as an aspect of a simpler and more general structure, that of the "Double." Faustian man is man divided against himself, threatened by his own shadow as man always has been.

Can it be that the Faust myth then resolves itself into a matter of neurosis rather than historical crisis? If so, we would have to reconsider the conclusions already reached and perhaps revise them according to a model based on universal-psychological postulates. Clearly, there is substance in such an argument. The good angel and the bad angel, who pull Dr. Faustus in opposite ways in Marlowe's play, providing thereby the very key to the play's dramatic symmetry, are in a real sense projections of Faustian man's divided psyche, the devil being no more than his own darker self. Adrian Leverkühn in *Doktor Faustus* and Jasper in Dickens's strange work, *The Mystery of Edwin Drood*, are Jekyll and Hyde characters, doppelgängers; so is Harry in Hermann Hesse's *Steppenwolf*. Here in Hesse is the modern distillation of the genre, the tragic vision of Dostoyevsky transformed into a vision of the absurd. But *Faust* lingers in the background of the story. "Two souls, alas, dwell in my breast." Goethe's hero had said. On this saying Harry, in *Steppenwolf*, meditates long and deeply. From this point of view, both the Faustian myth and that of the double resolve themselves into a literary-psychological structure easily amenable to Freudian description. The shadow self, normally suppressed, leaps out and threatens the stability of the acknowledged and more respectable self. Or else we have the double as immortal self, a vessel for preserving our identity, a kind of ideal or narcissistic image of ourselves, whereby we somehow face and overcome death.[1]

But we must beware of deceptions, more especially of the self-deceptions to which students of literary mythology are prone in their implicit claim that there is nothing new under the sun. True, the legend of Narcissus goes far back into antiquity, as do the darker forms of the double, but the real question is, what makes these images so peculiarly relevant at a particular historical moment? Why should the nineteenth century be so full of doubles? New elements have clearly been introduced that transform the pattern, giving it an altogether new urgency. The double as a static notion may be discerned in Homer[2] and in Shakespeare's *Two Gentlemen of Verona* or in *The Comedy of Errors*, where the image of the soul seeking its partner provides a pleasing network of symmetries to delight the audience. But what we find in the nineteenth century and later is a dynamic version of the double—one that prompts us to a violent response. The demon must be exorcised or he will destroy us. Fable has become nightmare. *The Picture of Dorian Gray* is Narcissus or Pygmalion with a difference: the difference is what counts. Man, we may say, has always had his shadow-self; but now that shadow, dangerously detached, has become—to use one of Henry James's very relevant titles—a "Beast in the Jungle." The Faust myth as it unfolds in the new era is a drama both new and terrifying. A psychological description provides us with little more than a list of the *dramatis personae* and their functions. It will not tell us why the signing of the pact should be so fraught with consequences. What is interesting about Ivan Karamazov is not the nature of his malady but its *portentousness*, its profound relevance to the whole situation that the plot unfolds, a situation very carefully located in time. We shall come across other examples of ancient, indeed "universal," archetypes being summoned at a particular moment into a special vivid existence. The "Wasteland" imagery that T. S. Eliot uses in his poem seems to be almost as old as human memory, and Eliot is at pains to emphasize its universal character. Nevertheless, as we shall see later, the special resonance of the poem is due to its capturing the essence of a new and unprecedented historical reality. Images of the wasteland in earlier writing turn out to be in a deep sense anticipations. The same applies to earlier manifestations of the double. They merely light up for us the new and disturbing reality of the nineteenth century.

In the case of Dostoyevsky, a closer examination of the episode of Ivan's nightmare reveals its emphatically diachronic character; it has a clear historical reference. The devil introduces himself to Ivan as the representative of the new man "lifted up with a spirit of divine Titanic pride . . . from hour to hour extending his conquest of nature infinitely by his will and his science." The "new man," he tells him, "may well become the man-god, even if he is the only one in the whole world and, promoted to his new position, he may lightheartedly overstep all the barriers of the old morality of the old slave-man, if necessary" (Book XI, chap. ix). Here is a fragment of Ivan's psyche that has crazily detached itself from the rest; for he himself had held to the motto that "all things are lawful." But his horror is not so much at seeing part of himself hypostatized before his eyes as at witnessing that hypostasis projected threateningly onto the screen of the future. If the moral restraints of the past are unbearable, then the moral anarchy of the future is equally unbearable. It is a measure of the complex crisis symbolized by Ivan's malady that in an earlier chapter the same devil is seen to lurk behind the Grand Inquisitor as the representative of evil and inexorable authority, that of our inherited institutions. The ambiguities are thus manifold and leave us without a way of resolving the fearful tensions endured by the "new man" on whose soul the burden of past and future equally rest.

In *Notes from Underground* (1864), another account of the darker self, there is an even greater degree of history consciousness. The contradictions in the soul of the Underground-man are those of the age he lives in, an age of moral scrupulousness that is nevertheless more systematically barbarous than that of Cleopatra, who enjoyed sticking gold pins into the breasts of her slave-girls. The new man is more ingeniously bloodthirsty because he also looks upon himself as a moral and civilized person for whom bloodshed is abominable. Here is the fearful contradiction for which the Underground-man's condition becomes a paradigm:

> Have you noticed that it is the most civilized gentlemen who have been the subtlest slaughterers, to whom the Attilas and Stenka Razins could not hold a candle, and if they are not so conspicuous as the Attilas and Stenka Razins it is simply because they are so often met with, are so ordinary and have become so familiar to us.[3]

The hidden life of the Underground-man, his compulsive desire to abase himself and others, links itself to the ancient Huns at one end of the scale, and, at the other end, to the respectable middle-class citizen who joins the S.S. and becomes a mass-murderer. *Notes from Underground* reveals the hollowness of nineteenth-century optimism and its belief in progress, but it is metonymic not of an age but of a process, a process that will be fulfilled when the "banality of evil" reaches its acme in our own time.

To set Dostoyevsky's fiction against the reality of twentieth-century consummations is thus not to introduce an outside point of reference. The text itself explores the paradoxicality of these directions. The Crystal Palace (built in 1854 and destined to last until 1936) is his symbol of the future: it becomes the image of a positive sunlit direction; it is expressive of the belief in progress toward an end. But viewed from Underground, that end becomes a chimera; the Crystal Palace reveals itself as a glittering but empty fantasy, the intensity of all our striving, as meaningless: "Man is a frivolous and incongruous creature, and perhaps like a chess player, loves the process of the game, not the end of it."[4] Such awareness is dramatized in the second half of the work when the Underground-man strives to join in the "real life" activities of his drinking companions and their highly successful leader, Zverkov, only to be spurned and insulted. The passionate striving toward a meaningless object is here given tragicomic shape. He is left at the end shrinking into himself and desiring to remain alone in his underground-world, a figure of alienation. From Dostoyevsky a straight line takes us to Kafka's Gregor Samsa in *Metamorphosis*. The Underground-man had said that he felt like an insect settling down into his corner: Gregor actually becomes one. The "normal" self is eclipsed.

Dostoyevsky was drawn frequently to the theme of the double. In his work of that title (*The Double*, 1846), his hero Mr. Golyadkin ends up in the hands of an alienist; in fact it is the precise literary metaphor for alienation. Presumably cases of mental disorder involving "split-personality" had a special interest for Dostoyevsky, but in the period we are considering they have become a fundamental image, a means of articulating a crisis that involves us all. Nor is Dostoyevsky the only writer who tends to see the dark or shadow-self as the "new man" who terrifies us by threatening our moral integrity, by disrupting the order of the past. In Yakov Gordin's play, *God, Man and Devil*, referred to earlier, Mazik, the Mephisto figure, is significantly dressed "in the new European style." He is meant to represent the threat to a world still hospitable to family loyalty and the pieties of tradition. Often among Jewish writers we have the contrast of old and new interiorized in the same person. In Abraham Cahan's *The Rise of David Levinsky*, mentioned earlier, the hero has a double identity: one is that of the new American man-of-business, the other, which he never loses, is that of the Talmud student in old Antomir. As he looks back at the end of his life, it seems to him that the latter was his true identity. However, what stands out for the reader is David's essential duality. In England too, Israel Zangwill had written a series of novels and stories at the turn of the century to illustrate the crisis of what he called "double-living." His characters are all ambiguous figures harboring within themselves loyalty to a tradition as well as the need to abandon its particularity. There is for Zangwill no solution to the crisis of dual identity, for it is his problem as a writer. A child of the ghetto himelf, his imagination is nourished by its imagery and forms, and yet he feels the centrifugal pull of a wider world of inventions that he can never make his own. The most real thing in his writing is the duality itself. Yet clearly the pathos of the figures in these fictions is not owing to psychic duality as such, nor is that the issue; it is a matter of psychic duality realigned as historic rupture. We are liberated from the past, and yet the past, whether conceived as our own personal prehistory or as the collective vessel of tradition, lives within us.

Even the patterns of duality that Nietzsche proposes at this period—Apollonian versus Dionysiac and (more particularly) Socratic versus Dionysiac—are ways of talking about historical crisis. "Socratic man has run his course," he tells us, and he calls upon his readers to welcome the new ecstasies wrought by the wand of Dionysus.[5] A Dionysiac future beckons us with its joy, its power, and its loosening of the bonds of individuation. This Dostoyevsky too senses in the chapter describing Ivan's nightmare, but unlike Nietzsche he recoils from it in horror.

The most frequent formulation of the myth of the double is that which visualizes the shadow-self as a symbol of the past.[6] This is so pervasive in the nineteenth century as to be something of an archetypal pattern all by itself. Oswald in Ibsen's *Ghosts* is haunted by the evil done in the past (it is Ibsen's dominant theme); like Golyadkin he ends in madness. His overt self strives to escape from darkness into light, toward the sun of a Dionysiac future that he glimpses as joyous consummation, but the past will overpower him and thrust him down. Sometimes there will be a happier outcome as the ghosts are laid and the hero is enabled to reach a healthy maturity: this is the fundamental shape of Samuel Butler's *The Way of All Flesh*. Of this type too is Conrad's "The Secret Sharer," where the Captain gains the true mastery of himself and his new command when he has faced his alter ego and released himself from the disabling bondage to a darker and earlier self. In Henry James's short story "The Jolly Corner" there is a similar release for Spencer Brydon from his might-have-been-self, that other identity belonging to his American past, which must be faced and overcome before he can know love and happiness. To arbitrate between the conflicting claims of past and present is a major theme for James, a necessary stage in the search for one's true identity. But it is worth noting that the roles are reversible. In the story just mentioned, the house in New York comes to represent the past; the "old silver-plated knobs of the mahogany doors . . . suggested the pressure of the palms of the dead." Emerging from it into the street, he says, is like emerging from an Egyptian tomb.[7] Brydon's new self is what he has acquired in Europe: he will become whole when he has freed himself from the ghost of his American past or somehow come to terms with him. Elsewhere in James's fiction, as for instance in *The American*, it is the other way around. The old world with its ghosts is identified with the European experience, while America is very literally the New World. Personae change in the surface structure, but the fundamental pattern remains; it is a triangle of forces involving Self, Past, and Future in dialectical relation to one another. Walter de la Mare's little-read novel *The Return* (1910) is a story of reincarnation where the hero's personality is invaded by a Cain figure, a Huguenot outlaw who had died a hundred and fifty years earlier. Arthur Lawford too will emerge (like the Captain in "The Secret Sharer") into the daylight, improved by his experience. Such stories are essentially tales of maturing and growth, a variety of *Bildungsroman*.

II

As in the last example, ghosts are often literal ghosts, wraithlike presences who threaten one or invade one's person in the form of demoniacal possession. This notion became prevalent in England and elsewhere in the romantic period as part of the machinery of the Gothic novel, and perhaps for that reason stories of this kind have not been given the serious attention they sometimes deserve. In a time of radical novelty, of emancipation from tradition in all its forms, the past is seen nevertheless to lay its palsied hands on the present. The figure of the revenant stalks through romantic literature in many forms, sometimes highly melodramatic:

> Raymond, Raymond, thou art mine!
> Raymond, Raymond, I am thine.
> In thy veins while blood shall roll,
>   I am thine!
>   Thou art mine.
> Mine thy body, mine thy soul!

These doggerel verses are spoken by the Bleeding Nun, a figure from the past who threatens to blight the life and loves of the young hero in M. G. Lewis's Gothic novel *The Monk* (1796). She is got rid of eventually, her bones being decently reinterred and laid to rest. And, paradoxically enough, her removal is accomplished with the help of Ahasuerus, the Wandering Jew. It is he who releases Raymond from the spell of the revenant, and thus enables him to go forward into the light, liberated from inherited guilt. Raymond might very well have remarked, in the words of Joyce's Stephen Dedalus, that history was a nightmare from which he was trying to awake. It was the Jew who helped him to wake up by releasing him from the bondage of the past.

But the Wandering Jew is himself a revenant, a compulsive visitor who comes to remind us of such past events and responsibilities as we would rather forget, and as such he is a great favorite among the romantic poets. Thinly disguised as the Ancient Mariner in Coleridge's ballad, he lays his skinny hand on the Wedding Guest and forces him to hear his tale of woe and deliverance, of old unhappy far-off things. And yet the same Wandering Jew is for Coleridge a persona of the poet himself, a rebel and iconoclast, that is to say, a man of the new order. It is Ahasuerus who, in Shelley's early poem *Queen Mab* (1813), announces that a new era is beginning, and that Reason and Freedom are "now establishing the imperishable throne of truth" and thus frustrating the curse of ancient religious tyranny.[8]

The romantic writer's relation to the past is thus nothing if not ambiguous. Romantic literature, says W. J. Bate, is "crazily split down the middle by two opposing demands."[9] He notes that there is both a nostalgia for the past and a sense of the inexorable need to be liberated from its oppressive burden. This is the problem that underlies, for instance, many of Edgar Allan Poe's short stories. In "A Tale of the Ragged Mountains," the hero is possessed by a past incarnation, a double from the India of Warren Hastings. The experience is represented as a form of mesmerism (another psychic phenomenon popular in the period) and it leads to his death. He tries to show the dead burying their dead in "The Fall of the House of Usher." But it is the ancient house itself, fatally flawed though its fabric is, that holds our attention. Until we have come to terms with it, we can hardly come to terms with ourselves. It oppresses the imagination, and when it falls (as it does at the end of the story), it leaves us shocked and horrified. "There was a long tumultuous shouting sound like the voice of a thousand waters." Chaos is, so to say, come again.

The most insistent of all the revenants for the romantic poets is probably John Milton. Keats was obsessed with the Miltonic model, and Wordsworth declared in a famous sonnet: "Milton, thou shouldst be living at this hour!" Some would say he was, because Wordsworth himself bore a remarkable facial, as well as stylistic,

resemblance to the dead poet. But it is Blake more than anyone
else who brings Milton back from the dead. He celebrates Milton's
return in full and meticulous detail. Arriving in the poet's garden
at Felpham in the year 1803, Milton enters Blake's body through
his foot. It is a moment of incomparable revelation, and also one of
disaster. Following "the vast breach of Milton's descent," Blake
tells us that

> . . . all this Vegetable World appeard on my left Foot,
> As a bright sandal formd immortal of precious stones & gold:
> I stooped down & bound it on to walk forward thro' Eternity.
> (*Milton* 21.12 – 14)[10]

The significance of this event is that Blake may now draw directly
on the biblical inspiration of the seventeenth century, an age of
faith and vision. It is an age in which Ololon (the "Emanation" of
Milton) can be pictured as a "sweet river of milk and liquid pearl"
flowing through Eden. And fortified with this vision, Blake, now
the reincarnation of Milton, can become the true poet of Revolution. The present has become suffused with the glory of the past.

And yet, viewed from another angle, this long "prophetic" poem
of Blake's is one long fierce contention with Milton and all that
Milton had stood for. Blake rejects the older poet's Puritan world
view, the "thunders loud and terrible" that his presence conjures
up. His body, he says, "was the rock Sinai"—which for him represents all that is negative in institutional religion. And, as a result,
when Blake gazes at his left foot in another passage, he sees "a
black cloud redounding spread over Europe." All that is bad in the
Europe of Pitt and George III, its blindness, its institutionalized
forms, its social tyrannies, may be traced back to the evil authority
of the past, with Milton as the dark Urizenic figure looming up out
of the center of that past!

Blake's way of dealing with this "crazy split" in his own relation
to the inheritance is to insist that the past has to change. In the
course of the poem Milton is cured of his Puritan proclivities. We
see him at the end casting off and annihilating his selfhood. He
"bathe[s] in the Waters of Life, to wash off the Not Human" (Plate
41). Thus the irreversibilities of history are abolished, and the poet
can come to terms with a past that has become plastic and malleable. Blake's world, like that of the space traveler, is one in which
the law of gravity no longer operates. Time itself is abolished, so
that in the infinite space of metahistory he may build the great city

of Golgonooza, where mankind is delivered and all contraries are made one.

Blake thus seems to find an easy way to bring together the obligations of the past and the promise of the future. He simply ignores what is normally regarded as the chief difference between them, namely, the freedom we have with regard to the future and our lack of freedom in relation to the past. It may change us, but we cannot change it—or so it would generally seem. Milton in his time had certainly felt these inexorabilities: Adam after the Fall will never be quite the same as Adam before the Fall; never more will he behold the face of God or Angel. But unlike Milton, Blake takes the privilege of the romantic poet to affirm the abolition of our time-bound existence:

> nor time nor space was
> To the perception of the Virgin Ololon, but as the
> Flash of lightning . . .
> (Milton 36.17–19)

In this and other similar passages, the poet seems to suggest that we can find a way of transcending time, of being liberated from our bondage to the clock and the historical process. The moment is eternal and this "vegetable" earth of time and space is but the shadow of eternity.[11] In the light of the poet's vision it can melt away. When time becomes awkward we just, so to say, walk out of it, abandon it, rather like the Marx Brothers, who, faced with a vertical barrier, simply treat it as horizontal.

This, however, is not quite the whole story. Blake's awareness of time is more involved than this. We may understand him better if we consider the function of Los in the poem. After the union with Milton celebrated in Plate 21, occurs a moment scarcely less dramatic, in which Los, the god of time and history, but also of the poetic imagination, descends toward the poet, stands behind him in fire and terror, until he too becomes united with the poet! (Plate 22.5f.)

> & he also stoop'd down
> And bound my sandals on in Udan-Adan . . .
> And I became One Man with him arising in my strength.
> (Milton 22.8–12)

By situating the union with Milton in the perspective of a further union with Los, or rather by making it a threefold union of Blake-

Los-Milton, Blake is indicating that the encounter with Milton is a poetic encounter, the fusion of two poetic natures. The poet does not celebrate the arrival of a ghost from the past—the figure of a poet brought to life—but rather the re-possession of a poetic text. Not Milton but Milton's poetry is the theme of the drama; and in relation to the poetry of the past we may truly speak of the past changing, becoming malleable. In relation to recovered voices, texts, we are not bound by inexorabilities; we are not fixed in the resin of history. There is a sense in which texts handed down are, by interpretation, fused with present insights and needs. This is the work of hermeneutics; it creates simultaneity in spite of change.

What I am suggesting is that Blake's *Milton* in its deeper sense portrays the drama of the hermeneutic process. Every text from the past is a kind of revenant and every revenant is a kind of text. And this is true in other works. Ivan's nocturnal visitor is really a bundle of literary associations: he is Goethe's Faust, he is the Satan of Job, he is perhaps Vautrin in Balzac's *Le père Goriot*. He is, in short, a way of reading the literary inheritance of the past, and every such reading involves a change in the pattern so delivered. Not only does the image inevitably accommodate itself to our present needs and occasions; it also demands to be related to our sense of the future. Once Milton enters Blake's foot "in the nether Regions of the Imagination," Blake is furnished for a voyage; he becomes like Hermes, a traveler, a messenger—hence the golden sandals.[12] He bears a word, a dream that will continue to have meaning for the future, a word that will be subject to constant reinterpretation. That is why, once he has stooped down and bound on his bright sandal, he is fitted for a journey. He will "walk forward thro' Eternity." Blake could hardly have found a clearer image for the ongoing interpretation of poetic texts. It is in that region that we retain our liberty from the bondage of time, but without ever losing our consciousness of history as process, and of tradition as tradition.

Borges's story "The Other Death" (1949) would serve to confirm and summarize what has just been said. This is the tale of a revenant who turns out to be a literary echo, or rather the effect of a group of literary echoes. More than that, it reviews the process of its own composition and thus reflects metacritically on the very phenomenon we are here discussing. It begins with a seemingly straightforward account of the death of one Pedro Damian, who had fought with the Argentinian rebels in a skirmish against Uruguay at Masoller in 1904 and had finally died of a fever in 1946 while reliving the battle in his delirium. Then a number of different and contradictory reports superimpose themselves one upon the other. First there is the doubt as to whether Damian distinguished himself in the battle or whether he revealed abject cowardice that he spent the rest of his life making good. This would make him into a repeat version of Lord Jim, whose tale is here recalled. Then comes a different story attested by reliable witnesses, which seems to take the place of the first. According to this, Damian died bravely in 1904 while leading the attack. The narrator now concludes that the Peter Damian whose death was reported to him in 1946 was either another person of the same name or else was the ghost of the first, who, by the grace of God, was permitted to return to his native place and live on for forty years after his life had been so cruelly cut short. But how can these various "historical" accounts exist side by side? Does the past exist at all or are there perhaps two (or more) different histories suitable to two (or more) different generations of readers? "In the first, let us say, Pedro Damian died in Entre Rios in 1946; in the second, at Masoller in 1904. It is the second history that we are living now."[13] What emerges at the end is the essential textuality of the events themselves. For first and foremost Damian is a figure in a story—the very story that Borges is writing. But even the outlines of that story fade as we become aware of the various literary sources by which it has been shaped. Borges in his reflexive virtuosity reveals an astonishing network of intertextual relationships. His own story becomes a trace produced by the action on one another of a memory of a poem by Emerson, "The Past," which speaks of the absolute fixedness of past events ("None can reenter there. . . . Alter or mend eternal Fact"); of Conrad's *Lord Jim*, in which the past is nevertheless redeemed; of the twenty-first canto of Dante's *Paradiso*, where in a vexed passage the poet seems to recall two different persons once living, both named Peter Damiani, the one a saint, the other a sinner. And finally there are the words of Pier Damiani himself (the saint of Dante's poem), an eleventh-century cardinal, who had asserted in a treatise that "it is within God's power to make what once was into something that has never been."

Borges is not indulging in fantasy; he is sharing with us his perceptions of the plasticity of recalled events. He is telling a tale that dramatizes the hermeneutic process itself. At the end we realize that when all the onion layers of history have been peeled away we have something resembling the contents of Damian's final delirium. For what happens in the past to ourselves and to others is but "the shadow of a dream." Moreover, the dream does not stop with the story itself. Our own reading of these texts represents a continuation of the hermeneutic process. The narrator in Borges's story becomes the reader's own double as he tries to make sense of the story. The narrator also expresses the reader's own skepticism ("it is my suspicion that Pedro Damian—if he ever existed . . ."). As we become *possessed by* the story it becomes for us too a revenant. The same applies to Blake's poem. Blake-Milton-Los combines itself with the present reader so that we have Blake-Milton-Los-X, where the coordinate X, like the narrator in Borges's story, strives to make sense of the poem and to resolve its major contradictions. We too are invited to put on the golden sandals and carry our reading of these literary images forward into the future.

III

At this point I would like to introduce a parallel Jewish myth, that of the "Dybbuk." Though the legendary materials on which the dybbuk stories are based are premodern, the term only achieves currency in the seventeenth and eighteenth centuries with the rise of Hassidism. And it becomes a major folk theme only in modern times.[14] In essence, the spirit of a dead person enters and *cleaves* to the living. The term "dybbuk" means "a fast-cleaving." A "denuded soul" (usually one that has sinned) has to cleave to another person. The victim too is not entirely innocent, hence his vulnerability to invasion. Stories of dybbuks in action in various parts of the world, especially in Eastern Europe, are common right down to the twentieth century. A knowledge of the past and a power of prophesying the future are not unusual in dybbuk stories—an aspect of demoniacal possession already mentioned in the Talmud.[15] But the Talmudic, Kabbalistic (and possibly, Pythagorean) sources of the dybbuk do not concern us here, nor do its implications for parapsychology, the study of mental illness and the like. What concerns us is its power as myth and as literary structure.

In brief, the dybbuk archetype conceives the relation between the past and the present under the image of possession. It is not merely a case of a revenant, but of a revenant who enters and controls the personality of the living. What had been for "Monk" Lewis a bit of Gothic fustian, now becomes the main theme of the literary work, and a serious theme at that. "I am thine! / Thou art mine. / Mine thy body, mine thy soul!" said the Bleeding Nun. This, in effect, is what the dybbuk says to the person whom he invades.

We begin with the work that made the term "dybbuk" famous in many parts of the world; it is, of course, S. Ansky's play, *The Dybbuk*, the extraordinary popularity of which on the Hebrew stage from 1922 onwards[16] suggests that here we have a collective myth of great power. Its portrayal under the direction of the great Eugene Vakhtangov had, like the classic dramas of ancient Greece, the effect of a ritual. In this case it was a ritual designed to assuage the anxieties created by the impact of the past upon the present, as indicated by its subtitle: "The Two Worlds." The date of the original composition of this "Gothic" masterpiece, 1916, need not surprise us, because for Jews the crisis of emancipation reached its acute phase in the early twentieth century, in the writings of Brenner, Tchernichowsky, and Bialik—the latter two, incidentally, are among the chief Hebrew translators of the English and German romantic poets of the early nineteenth century. Bialik also translated Ansky's play (which had originally been written in Russian and then in Yiddish), and it was in Bialik's translation that it finally reached its true audience, namely, the new *Yishuv* in Palestine, where the new Jew found himself at the crossroads of history. He had cast off one world and had eagerly turned to another, but his soul was not at rest. The Burden of the Past was upon him. And it was a schizophrenic burden: he could live neither with it nor without it.

In Ansky's play, the heroine, Leah, is in the grip of the spirit of her dead lover, Hanan. She had been promised to him by her father before her birth, but her father, Sender, had failed to honor the terms of the pact. Central to the whole drama is the ambiguity in the personalities of the two chief characters and also the ambiguity in the experience of possession itself. Hanan is an intensely devout student of Kabbalah: we see him in a central scene gazing in rapture at the Scrolls of the Law in the Holy Ark: "The scrolls of the law . . . there they stand like comrades, shoulder to shoulder, so calm, so silent. All secrets and symbols hidden in them. And all miracles from the six days of creation, unto the end of all the generations of men."[17] Here we have again the hermeneutic posture that we noted in Blake's poem and in Borges's tale. We have here too the sense of the visionary span of history from the Creation on, but also the sense of the primacy of the Word, through which history can be understood. Hanan is here a witness to antiquity, but more than that he witnesses to the still-compelling force of an ancient literary inspiration. There is something "hidden," closed-up in the ancient texts that he must release and deliver to the future "generations of men." His restlessness, his unappeased search for fulfillment (which is the theme of the play) are bound up with the frustrations of the student of ancient words who is not content with mere antiquity. "I am one of those," he declares, "who sought new paths." He is a witness to the new restlessness. In the climax of the play, speaking through the mouth of Leah, he confronts the rabbis who have come to expel him and fiercely claims his right to love and freedom. The symbolism is utterly clear: he is the new emancipated man, a rebel in league with the devil, like Cain in Byron's play.[18] Leah, too, is attached with the utmost devotion to the memory of her deceased mother. This is the hinge of her personality, and yet she is also (through a Kabbalistic wordplay on the letters of her name) literally "the godless one"—her love for Hanan symbolizing her rejection of her father's authority and of the traditional society to which he belongs.

The same "crazy split" is to be noted in the nature of the union between the dybbuk and his victim. Hanan's lodgement in the heart and body of Leah is a source of ecstasy, a traumatic release from an environment dominated by bourgeois narrowness and rabbinical obscurantism. But it is also a state of subjection: the dead lover, whose power over her stems from ancient solemn obligations and ancient solemn words, relentlessly invades her personality. She struggles to be free from the grip of Hanan. This she finally achieves when the dybbuk is expelled with bell, book, and candle. But she does not survive the expulsion. As in the fall of house of Usher, the collapse of the fabric of antiquity and, with it, the breaking of the spell, are themselves disastrous. Leah dies. As for the basic problem of the "two Worlds," Ansky offers no solution except perhaps a sentimental one. The two lovers will be united beyond the grave in an afterlife where the pressures of history no longer operate.

We may say that the hermeneutic task is harder for Ansky, the Jew, than it is for Blake. It is not by chance that Ansky presents the burden of the past under the sign of a prenatal contract. Ancient texts not only inspire: they also constrain; they have authority. A way must be found to make their revolutionary message available for the future, but their commands may not be violated. This dilemma does not affect Blake. Blake, in his gnostic fashion, feels he can strip off that part of the Miltonic inheritance which is comprised under the term "the Rock Sinai." Milton had stood for a combination of Law and Liberty. Blake will have none of this; Blake-Los can preempt the biblical inspiration of Milton while proclaiming a total freedom from the Law, that Urizenic, repressive side of Milton's Puritan personality. There is, in short, no "precontract." Ansky cannot deceive himself about this. Ancient texts are not that malleable. History can be reenacted, reinterpreted, but it cannot be subverted. This is the ground of the essential pathos of Ansky's play. We are bound by the terms of the precontract, the inexorabilities of the historical forms we have inherited; but he can and does console himself and his audience with the dream of the lovers going hand in hand in some paradisal world to come. In other words, there is no solution, and the audience, whose basic spiritual problem the play has ritually enacted, go home, wiping their tears away, comforted only by the thought that in death all contraries are made one.

In S. Y. Agnon's remarkable short story "Edo and Enam" (1950),[19] the heroine, Gemulah, has two "lovers." There is her husband, Gamzu, a one-eyed antiquarian bookseller who is clearly a man of the tradition with a warm attachment to the synagogue and the house of study. And there is also Dr. Ginat, a man likewise engaged in the study of ancient things, but in a modern spirit, his approach being objective and scientific. Her psyche is torn between the two. Once a month, when the moon is full, Gemulah loses her normal personality and is possessed by what one can only describe as the Spirit of the Past. She leaves her bed in a trancelike state, and, walking in her sleep toward the lodgings of Ginat, she sings the strange hymns of her ancestors in the lost language of Edo. These are the Enamite hymns to the study of which the philologist Ginat has devoted his life. And something of his passionate involvement flows over into the imagination of the reader. Here too the dybbuk motif essentially involves the "cleaving" to a text.

For Gemulah, as for Hanan or Leah, the dybbuk experience is dualistic. She is in the grip of an alien force from which her husband and her friends seek to release her. But, on the other hand, the invasion of her personality is literally a matter of inspiration. It is like the recovery by Blake of the sweet milk and liquid pearl of seventeenth-century divinity. It is while in the agonizing grasp of this force from the past that Gemulah finds the richest release of her personality. Of course, the tragic dilemma is ultimately insupportable. Gemulah falls to her death from a roof in Jerusalem during one of her somnambulistic excursions, and Ginat dies in a vain attempt to rescue her. The ending is nonsentimental: there is no hint (as in Ansky's play) of comfort beyond the grave. But there is a hint of comfort in the ongoing processes of history and in the ongoing history of literary texts. For Ginat's work on the Enamite hymns, in spite of his request that it be destroyed, will in fact be published, and it will have its effect—slow but sure—on the world we know.

> As usual, the dead man's orders were not carried out. On the contrary, his books are printed in increasing numbers, so that the world is already beginning to know his works, and especially the Enamite Hymns with their grace and beauty. While a great scholar lives those who choose to see his learning, see it; those who do not, see nothing there. But once he is dead, his soul shines out ever more brightly from his works, and anyone who is not blind, anyone who has the power to see, readily makes use of his light.[20]

Here, defined allegorically in the characters and their doings, we have spelled out for us the various coordinates so far considered. Gamzu and Ginat are doubles, signifying the conflict of past and future. In the Enamite Hymns, we have the ancient texts on which both these forces must be brought to bear. Gemulah, the woman possessed by the dybbuk (though the term is not used in the story) is the battlefield in whom the struggle is enacted. She will die, there will be suffering and loss, but there will also be a future. And the "light" for that future will be provided by the work of Ginat, the interpreter, the philologist. This achievement, providing the essential link between past and future, is only possible at the cost of immense suffering. Here we have something like the textuality of events themselves. History itself is an aspect of hermeneutics. Sacrifice, revolution, are at bottom a struggle for the meanings embodied in hidden writings that both constrain us and drive us forward. Gemulah's nightly wanderings express just that combination: she is mastered by the voices of the past and yet she is urged forward, driven, charged with a dream. The Jewish character of this dilemma is patent.

The dybbuk in altered form, but still quite unmistakable, continues to haunt the pages of more contemporary Hebrew literature. In Aharon Megged's novel *The Living on the Dead* (1965), the past presses down upon the present in the form of the dead hero, Davidov, a figure from the nation-building, road-making, swamp-clearing era of prestate Israel, whose epic life story a young author, Jonas, has been commissioned to write. The situation is a little like that projected in Henry James's *The Aspern Papers*, and, as in *The Aspern Papers*, the records of the life of the dead man are lost at the end of the story. What binds Jonas to the dead man is the written contract with the publisher, which, while it opens up for the young antihero opportunities for creativity and fame, also depresses and cows his spirit. His problem is to escape from this intolerable burden of obligation. It may be noted that the idea of a precontract, a binding covenant entered into in the past and somehow linking past and present, is central to this work also.

In Ansky, the power of Hanan over Leah derives, as we have mentioned, from a prenatal promise made between the two sets of parents. In "Edo and Enam" the control over Gemulah's destiny is connected with the mysterious leaves of papyrus inscribed in antiquity that pass from the possession of Gamzu to that of Ginat. In the case of Jonas the contract that he has entered into binds him in a more than formal sense to the dead man. His private life becomes disarranged as he, in mesmeric fashion, relives the career of his hero, who becomes also his double. He becomes as heartless to his wife and unborn child as Davidov had been to his wife and family. For in the novel, the heroic world of Davidov, the whole epic image projected by the *halutzic* founders of the state, is savagely pilloried, and yet it is a presence not to be put by. Davidov has constructed the world we live in: it is he who has set up for us the aims and purposes that continue to drive us forward; without them we sink back into emptiness and nihilism, a state represented in the novel by a squalid Tel-Aviv nightclub to which Jones resorts when his responsibilities to Davidov become too much for him.

Jonas never wholly escapes the oppressive grip of the past. At the end, when involved in a court case for breach of contract, he testifies that this paralyzes his creative work. "As long as that case is hanging over my head, I can't start anything new." This may stand as a fitting summation of the mood of a man in the grip of the dybbuk. The past has him in thrall, and until he has come to terms with it, there is no possibility of a new life.

In a comic example, "The Dybbuk from Neve Shaanan" (1966),[21] by Amitzur Eilan, the pressure upon the hero of the presence of his dead father (and of the society that the latter had helped to create) is expressed through the father's last will and testament, from the terms of which the son desperately tries to escape. In the end we witness him simply fleeing from the house on his motorcycle. It is an example of what Frye would call the "low mimetic" version of the archetype.

IV

We are dealing with a structure that, viewed synchronically, brings together among other examples Blake's *Milton*, Agnon's *Edo and Enam*, Henry James's *The Aspern Papers* and Aharon Megged's *The Living on the Dead*. Nevertheless, the differences within the synchrony are more revealing than the similarities. The Jewish writers do not escape the constraint of the past; Blake does. In James's short novel the narrator is obsessed (we might almost say, "possessed") by the spirit of the dead writer whose papers he desires at all costs to acquire. Here, documents belonging to the past take hold of the will and imagination of a young man and shape his life. More correctly, they *almost* shape his life, for in the end he finds he cannot immure himself with the elderly Miss Tina as the price of the precious documents. He escapes, takes his gondola into the middle of the lagoon, and Miss Tina destroys the documents. The past has been allowed to bury its dead. We find him in the end saddened by his loss, but free. Jonas in Megged's novel does not make good his escape. There too, there is a loss of documents relating to the dead man, but the case for breach of contract still hangs over the hero. He is never free.

In "Flood Tide," a short story of the sixties by another Israeli writer, A. B. Yehoshua, a written document from the past, the so-called Manual of Regulations, controls the thoughts and wishes of the narrator, the last warder in a prison threatened by the rising floodwaters. (The story has obvious links with Kafka's "The Penal Colony.") Absurdly bound by obligations enshrined in the Manual, he will remain at his post after all the prisoners have escaped. The long tradition of commentary, "the diaries left by the jailers of antiquity," are enshrined in great tomes "that stand volume by volume, massive and tall in [the] locked bookcase" of the Chief Warder.[22] Yehoshua here wishes to exhibit the grotesqueness of the condition of a man or people held in thrall by an ancient scripture and by the hermeneutic debris that the warders of the prison have, over the centuries, accumulated in order to explain it and give it relevance. The novelist is evidently remembering C. N. Bialik's poem "Before the Bookcase" (1910), which pictures the first-person narrator returning after many years of wandering to stand in front of the serried volumes of ancient wisdom. He is lonely and desolate but drawn nevertheless to seek himself in their pages. Bialik's tone of melancholy and regret at the hopelessness of his quest is here changed to an acceptance of the absurd and the grotesque. Yet grotesque though his situation is, the narrator is bound and held. The Flood Tide itself, a symbol for Holocaust and disaster, is actually predicted and provided for in the Manual of Regulations and its accumulated literature of commentary: "It is from these chronicles that the Chief Warder has learned about the flood tide, about the signs in nature portending it and about the destructive force of the water."[23] Here again we confront the textuality of historical events. Hermeneutics is not adapted to history; it is rather the other way around; events define themselves as modes of understanding. In spite of his tone of detached ridicule, Yehoshua has, in this story, added his mite to the hermeneutic process. The "Manual" continues to master us whether we will or no—that is the meaning of the story. Aspern's biographer in James's novel does not remain bound to his ancient scriptures when the floodwaters threaten: he simply makes off. Like Huck Finn, he lights out for freedom. The Jewish writer, even when he imagines himself to be totally liberated from tradition, finds this option ultimately unavailable.

But it is not only his *relation* to the past that is different. If we examine our paradigms more closely, we discover important differences also in the apprehension of what exactly constitutes the inheritance of the past. Captain Alving's "ghost" in Ibsen's play personifies inherited guilt. The burden of this inheritance lies heavily on Oswald. But more than that, he is a figure inviting to a life of self-indulgence and pleasure. The appeal is to nature and the gods of nature. For the Jewish writer, the figure from the past represents rather trial, responsibility, and effort. Davidov, unattractive though he is in Megged's novel, nevertheless pulls us away from the "den" and its easy pleasures and indulgences. He belongs to the superego. By contrast, Captain Alving, insofar as he points to the past, points back to the Maypole, to the fertility religions that dominated Europe before Christianity got there. We find a similar downward tendency in Conrad's *Heart of Darkness*, another story of enchantment and spiritual alienation. If Kurtz is in the grip of the ancient barbarisms of the Congo, the narrator, Marlow, discovers in himself the same primeval heart of darkness. We sense it, too, in the environment of the River Thames at the beginning of the story, in the memory of the early savageries practiced there nineteen centuries ago, when the Romans came to settle England and bring it painfully into the light. Such a novel reveals to us the seamy side of Western romanticism. It tells us what the Return to Nature is all about. It is not only Wordsworth's heart dancing with the daffodils; it is also Kurtz sinking back into the barbarous and vivid life of the jungle, and it is also Oswald's imbecile reaching out for the sun at the end of Ibsen's play.

To be quite precise, the Western world has two dybbuks: one, which has clear affinities with the Judeo-Christian tradition, generally introduces himself as the burden of the Puritan conscience. We meet him as Blake's image of Milton, inspiring and overpowering at the same time, like the Rock of Sinai. The other, whom we meet in Conrad and Ibsen, represents the pagan past, the downward drag of nature. Both are at work in Western literature in the period with which we are dealing, haunting their victims and seizing them body and soul.[24]

As the most compendious tale of enchantment in both these aspects, we may finally consider Hawthorne's *The House of the Seven Gables* (1851). Never has the Burden of the Past been more emphatically described. It lies heavily upon the two young persons, Holgrave and Phoebe, whose destiny is the subject of the book:

> "Shall we never, never get rid of this Past?" cried he, keeping up the earnest tone of his preceding conversation. "It lies upon the Present like a giant's dead body! In fact, the case is just as if a young giant were compelled to waste all his strength in carrying about the corpse of the old giant, his grandfather, who died a long while ago, and only needs to be decently buried. Just think a moment, and it will startle you to see what slaves we are to bygone times—to Death, if we give the matter the right word! . . .

"We read in dead men's books . . . . We worship the living Deity according to dead men's forms and creeds. Whatever we seek to do, of our own free motion, a dead man's icy hand obstructs us."[25]

The dead hand of the past is symbolized in this novel by "dead men's books" and also by the fathers of the Pyncheon race, in particular the old Puritan Colonel Pyncheon, who seems to threaten the living in the form of an oppressively realistic portrait on the wall of the family mansion, and who is reincarnated in the person of the contemporary Judge Pyncheon, a gloomy figure who casts his shadow over the present inhabitants. He in a manner haunts the house built by his ancestors two centuries before, and will continue to haunt it until his death at the end of the story. Only then will the young people be freed from the spell of the Puritan past and be able to emerge into the sunlight.

But the dead hand of the past also operates through another parallel influence, that of the rustic sorcerer Matthew Maule, another figure from the early period of settlement in New England. In a recalled central episode, we watch his son, a low-born carpenter, casting an evil spell over the beautiful Alice Pyncheon. It is an enchantment involving the invasion and corruption of the latter's personality. "She is mine!" said Matthew Maule. "Mine by the right of the strongest spirit." (Almost the words of the Bleeding Nun to poor Raymond.) Alice becomes subject to somnambulistic fits, like Gemulah in Agnon's tale, during which Maule's power over her has the effect of dragging her down into the abyss, into the Conradian heart of darkness, that wild wood which represents the pagan past of Europe and the Americas. The overriding metaphor is that of abasement.

> A power that she little dreamed of had laid its grasp upon her maiden soul. A will, most unlike her own, constrained her to do its grotesque and fantastic bidding. . . . "Alice dance!" and dance she would, not in such court-like measures as she had learned abroad, but some high-paced jig, a hop-skip rigadoon, befitting the brisk lasses at a rustic merry-making. It seemed to be Maule's impulse not to ruin Alice, not to visit her with any black or gigantic mischief . . . but to wreak a low or ungenerous scorn upon her. Thus all the dignity of life was lost. She felt herself too much abased, and longed to change natures with some worm![26]

Maule's curse lies like a heavy burden upon the Pyncheon race and the curse will not be expiated until Phoebe (the last of the

Pyncheons) marries Holgrave (the last Maule). Then the contraries are made one. It is an ending marked by the imagery of the Garden of Eden, signifying a return to a remoter and more wonderful past than that suggested either by Puritan New England or by the witchcraft of the jig and the Maypole.

Interestingly enough, the image of a written document or contract is central to this tale also. An old roll of parchment (actually a legal contract conveying a tract of land to the first ancestor of the Pyncheons) is hidden in the house. It testifies to the greed of the early Puritan settlers, and it also, in a way, controls the destiny of their offspring and provides the ground for the retribution that overtakes them. Until the document is found, the past will continue to haunt the present. The controlling influence thus given to a record or contract drawn up in antiquity will immediately remind us of the Jewish dybbuk stories we have considered. But there is a characteristic difference. When the past gives up its secret, and the parchment is finally recovered, it is found to be worthless. The past no longer binds.

The Scarlet Letter (1849) obeys a similar pattern. Here the dark inheritance of the past is symbolized by the letter "A" worn by Hester as a sign of her shame. The single enigmatic letter is, in fact, a text subjected throughout the story to multiple and endless interpretation. All the characters try their hand at it.[27] In the end its original meaning will be radically transformed. We can, it seems, opt out of American history and abandon its moral traditions: likewise, we can, if we like, simply leave the House of the Seven Gables and all that it stands for, pack up and retire to a pleasant cottage and garden, as Phoebe and Holgrave do at the end of their story. With the young lovers of the Jewish tales, it is a little different. They feel the same need to escape the dominion of the past, the same need to turn to the light and air of a new age, and yet the roll of ancient parchment is not so easily dispensed with, nor the original signification of its words and letters. Certainly, the process of interpretation must go on, but ultimately our freedom is as much a memory of the past as it is a hope for the future. There is no total rupture.

4

Myths of Continuance

IN ONE OF KAFKA'S most enigmatic fables, we hear of Gracchus, the
hunter of the Black Forest who travels endlessly in his funeral barge
along the shores of all the lands of the earth, not quite alive and not
quite dead either:

> "And you have no part in the other world?" asked the Burgomaster,
> knitting his brow.
> "I am forever," replied the Hunter, "on the great stair that leads up to
> it. On that infinitely wide and spacious stair I clamber about, some-
> times up, sometimes down, sometimes on the right, sometimes on the
> left, always in motion. The Hunter has turned into a butterfly. Do not
> laugh."
> "I am not laughing," said the Burgomaster, in self-defense.
> "That is very good of you," said the Hunter. "I am always in motion.
> But when I make a supreme flight and see the gate actually shining
> before me I awaken presently on my old ship, still stranded forlornly
> in some earthly sea or other."[1]

As has often been said, Gracchus is the archetypal wanderer. He is
Perseus, Ulysses, the Ancient Mariner, Arnold's "Scholar Gipsy,"
and the Flying Dutchman all together, refined to the point where
he displays only the essential outlines of his function. He shares
with the classic wanderers the gift (or curse) of immortality. He
moves incessantly over the face of the earth, shunned and yet hon-

ored (Kafka's story displays both attitudes). There would seem to be a meaning in his fifteen hundred years of voyaging, and yet his ship is rudderless, his comings and goings unexplained and inexplicable. Here, of course, is a powerful and universal structure of the imagination, and yet its most essential feature is its lack of structure. Gracchus tells us that he is always in motion, sometimes up, sometimes down, sometimes on the right and sometimes on the left; he refuses to be contained in any conceptual frame. As well as being a comment on the human condition, this is also—and perhaps more emphatically—a comment on the incoherence and shapelessness of the myth itself of which it is the final distillation. It is myth and antimyth combined. In another fragmentary version of the story, Gracchus submits to a questioner who desires coherence: "Gracchus, one request. First, tell me briefly but coherently how things are with you . . . I'd like to know something coherent about you."² But Gracchus's answer is to reject all such possibility. His story is the denial of all coherence. His is a legend without shape or stasis; it is merely a wavering line, a trace made by that seismograph which records our time on earth. From this point of view, there is just one solid feature to which the story refers us, and that is the earth boundedness of Gracchus. "I only know this, that I remained on earth and that ever since my ship has sailed earthly waters." Though always in motion, he is ever, he tells us, "stranded forlornly in some earthly sea or other."³ Here is perhaps the mark of the wanderer. He is always a Cain, an Adam, i.e., a wanderer *"upon the face of the earth."* Unlike the "Second Self," or the dybbuk, or the devil whom Ivan sees in his nightmare, Gracchus is no shadow or apparition; in his materiality he reflects upon us our bodily existence. It is that which is carried about endlessly and aimlessly upon the river of time.

One particular version of the wanderer archetype that was evidently not far from Kafka's mind in the writing of his tale was the legend of the Wandering Jew. This legend achieved its developed form at about the same time as those other myths of the modern imagination that we have been considering, viz., Faust and the dybbuk.⁴ We read in a pamphlet entitled *Kurze Beschreibung und Erzehlung von einem Juden mit Namen Ahasverus* (1602) of a Jew named Ahasuerus—the reason for the name has never been satisfactorily explained—who is said to have been a shoemaker in Jerusalem at the time of the Crucifixion. According to this account,

Jesus, passing by to the place of his execution, rests for a moment against the wall of the Jew's house, but Ahasuerus drives him away with curses, telling him to "be off to where it was fitting for him to go." Thereupon Jesus pronounces his judgment upon Ahasuerus with the words: "I shall rest, but thou must walk." The curse immediately takes effect as the Jew sets off on his wanderings round the world, where he relates what he has witnessed, and he will live through the centuries denied the consolation of the grave.

Already in the *Kurze Beschreibung* the aspect of physicality is stressed. Ahasuerus is a man like ourselves, whether attractive or unattractive. He is a man of mystery, but a man nevertheless—and his feet are on the ground. Perhaps that is the explanation for his being a shoemaker. There are no wings under his cloak. He is also, as we have noted earlier, a symbol of history. He is the bearer of an historical record, but one never doubts his physicality, just as one never doubts the physicality of the Jews one meets in the street. His power, his deathlessness, his ubiquity do not annul his humanity. Unlike Faust, the Wandering Jew was liable to step out of the pages of books. In 1856 he showed up in New York; in 1868, in Salt Lake City. It is this that makes it possible for us to see in him a reflection of ourselves. Or perhaps it is the other way around: from the beginning, the Western imagination has projected upon the Wandering Jew its own disturbing historical memories. We are held in thrall by the guilt we bear, by the knowledge we have inherited. We too have our knapsack on our backs. It is convenient to make the Jew the repository of that guilt, to see only him as burdened with that knowledge. But ultimately we have to do with a means of envisioning the past itself and our own uncertain, but at the same time inexorable, connection with it.

We are all haunted by remembered episodes and encounters that strangely press themselves upon us when all that seems to connect them is the thread of life itself. Certain memories (what Wordsworth called "spots of time") come to us weighted with significance, and yet they lack the order, the harmony of history as it is normally transmitted. They have rather the startling randomness, the concreteness and—at the same time—the indirection of real historical existence. As old age creeps on, such memories of youth stay with us in odd, troubling details, the meaning of which eludes us, memories in particular of guilt or of imagined guilt.

The past seems to make importunate claims on us. But what

sort of claims are they? And how are they to be satisfied, especially if we regard ourselves as being, in principle, free from obligations based on the traditions of the past? Such is the dilemma of the romantic poets, and it is compounded for Wordsworth and Coleridge by the fact that the action of memory is closely bound up with the processes of the poetic imagination itself. Coleridge's Ancient Mariner, a figure obsessed with the need to communicate his memories of guilt, suffering, and illumination, is a persona of the poet and, more than that, of the arresting and transforming action of the imagination. He also has a close resemblance to the Wandering Jew.[5] If one is liberated, one is also bound. The processes of time itself bind us in a way that calls our spontaneity into question. How are such contradictions to be overcome? One attempt to do just this is reflected in Wordsworth's little poem on the rainbow, the rainbow being, needless to say, the memory symbol par excellence, the sign of the earliest of all rememberings, viz., God's memory of his covenant with Man (Gen. 9.15).

> My heart leaps up when I behold
>   A rainbow in the sky:
> So was it when my life began,
> So is it now I am a man,
> So be it when I shall grow old
>   Or let me die!
> The Child is father of the Man:
> And I could wish my days to be
> Bound each to each by natural piety.

The plaintive tone of this lyric makes it clear that the union of past and present signified by the rainbow is not easily achieved. He could wish that his days were bound each to each! But the sad truth is that such a bonding—such a simple arch of meaning—remains unattainable. We search, we yearn for the overarching sign that links our inwardness with the outwardness of the cosmos, that binds the world together in a visible circle of meaning, that carries us forward confidently from yesterday into tomorrow. But it remains a mere wish, mocked by the transience and impalpability of the rainbow itself.

Only the tangibility of our own endurance remains as the guarantee of the reality of remembered things. The Wandering Jew thus comes to have a special value for the romantic poets. His visible endurance, his earthbound historical pilgrimage make credible

the binding of our days each to each. He becomes expressive of the
possibility of matching our human frailty against the movement of
time itself. For the romantic poets, for Goethe, Schiller, Wordsworth, Coleridge, and Shelley, Ahasuerus becomes an essentially
positive figure with whom the poet can identify. Goethe planned an
epic on the subject of Ahasuerus, and Coleridge likewise planned a
long poem on "The Wanderings of Cain." Cain, we should remember, is a close cousin of the Wandering Jew; he is laden with memory and guilt and granted secret powers of survival.[6] He becomes
likewise a persona of the poet, a savior figure, but also the bearer of
a dark secret. Lord Byron has a drama featuring Cain as its hero.
We should add that there are evident traces of the Wandering Jew
in the typical Byronic hero, that dark, brooding, guilt-ridden figure
of destiny whom Byron popularized for the nineteenth-century
reader. Suffering and alone, he represents, like the Wandering Jew,
a paradoxical combination of wisdom, courage, and despair. But
he too has no definable aim. If he is a figure of destiny, no one can
say what that destiny is. It is a gesture in the void.

Just as the plot or "fable" of the Wandering Jew has no real
shape, no *telos*, so his identity merges with that of many others.
The formlessness of the myth, its tendency to lose its shape and to
be displaced by other myths, is of its essence. We have mentioned
how the Wandering Jew turns into Cain. Edgar Rosenberg points
out how "he adapts himself to the demands of diverse generations
and diverse beliefs." "The Wandering Jew," he says, "can mean all
things to all men and all ages."[7] Just as he shows up in all kinds of
places, so he shows up in many roles. He can assume the role of
Faust, of Shylock, of Christ. Louis Harap reminds us that in Eugene Sue's novelistic treatment of the legend, "the Wanderer is al-
lied with the forces of labor against the rich"—he is a symbol, it
would seem, of the new socialism! He can signify retribution or
rebellion; he can be satanic agent or fighter for freedom. The use of
the Jew in the legend, he concludes, "is remarkable . . . for its extreme flexibility."[8] In Hawthorne's *Ethan Brand* the Ahasuerus figure is identified with the devil; in Shelley's *Hellas* he is a sage and
savior having insight into those truths which remain unchanged in
a world of mutability. We should not think of these innumerable
avatars as the transformations of a basic structure that lies hidden
beneath them. It is rather that the element of transformation is the
essential feature of the structure itself. The Wandering Jew drama-

tizes the lack of pattern that it is the function of his myth to affirm. His is a kind of antimyth. We could put this another way. Here is a myth that reveals its significance precisely along the axis of diachrony. The myth itself wanders and changes in the course of time; it goes underground and comes to the surface revealing each time a different aspect because that is the way that history is apprehended. The wanderer expresses the dialectic of time itself; its predetermined form and yet its lack of determination.

The Wandering Jew is always in a manner a character in search of an author. It is only the literary avatar that momentarily defines him, bestows upon him a temporary entelechy. This is perhaps the true meaning of Edward Arlington Robinson's strange poem on "The Wandering Jew." His eyes he says, "remembered everything."

> Yet here was one who might be Noah,
> Or Nathan, or Abimelech,
> Or Lamech, out of ages lost,—
> Or, more than all, Mechizedek.

The wanderer in Robinson's poem is everyone and no one. He sears all things with his anathemas, finding nothing good "on this other side of death." But one thing preserves him from the extinction of total denial, and that is the presence of the poet, who, as it were, summons him to life:

> Yet here there was a reticence,
> And I believe his only one,
> That hushed him as if he beheld
> A Presence that would not be gone.
> In such a silence he confessed
> How much there was to be denied;
> And he would look at me and live,
> As others might have looked and died.
>
> As if at last he knew again
> That he had always known, his eyes
> Were like to those of one who gazed
> On those of one who never dies.
> For such a moment he revealed
> What life has in it to be lost;
> And I could ask if what I saw,
> Before me there was man or ghost.

The wanderer looks upon the poet and lives; in a deep sense, it is the poet who bestows upon him his immortality. Poetic texts give to the fleeting images of memory a meaningful relation and order. Without the poem we have only the impassioned vibration of consciousness; with the poem, the wanderer achieves a palpable identity, a connection with the living. The legend is thus not only a comment on life; it is a comment on the relation of literature to life, on the dynamics of historical myth-making.

But the earlier avatars fade before the overwhelming centrality of the Wandering Jew in our twentieth century. It is in our time that he undergoes his most important transformation. No longer does he express medieval superstitions and fears, nor does he express the romantic enthusiasm for the outcast. For the twentieth century it may be said that the Wandering Jew has become almost an indispensable symbol for mankind in general: for all are now outcasts, all are wanderers. As Charlie Chaplin or Menahem Mendl (in Sholom Aleichem), he defines for us the human condition. Leopold Bloom in James Joyce's novel *Ulysses* (1922), a kind of unsaintly and unheroic Everyman, is three times linked with the Wandering Jew. He is, of course, also intended to remind us throughout of that other famous wanderer, Ulysses in Homer's epic. But in his unassertive personality, in the essential ambiguity of his role (victim and hero, dreamer and sensual man of the earth, wanderer and homebound petit bourgeois), Leopold is Ahasuerus, the Wandering Jew, enduring and yet struggling in vain to find a unified meaning in life. Homer's wanderer, Ulysses, follows a cyclical plan of homecoming; Penelope's firmness makes his circle just. By contrast, Leopold follows a more uncertain and devious route. There will be a formal ending: the threads (above all, the threads linking Leopold and Dedalus) will come together, but ultimately we are impressed by the formlessness of his path echoed in the formlessness of the genre in which he functions. In contrast to the rounded epic-genre of the Greeks, we have here a meandering narrative, one that images the wayward fashion in which consciousness gathers the earthly atoms of experience and lodges them in the memory.

The question that lurks behind the novel at every stage is the same question as in Kafka's tale of Gracchus: is there a coherent pattern? Mr. Deasy thinks there is. "History," he says, "moves towards one great goal." Stephen, pondering explicitly on Wandering Jews ("Time would surely scatter all. A hoard heaped by the roadside"), is not sure. "History, Stephen said, is a nightmare from which I am trying to awake." Like a nightmare it holds us in thrall;

but like a nightmare its reality is in question. Stephen's doubts here concern not only the goals of history but also the coherence of narrative. *Ulysses* brings together two opposite patterns, the Greek pattern, structured on the archetypes of nature, and the archetype of Ahasuerus. The two do not fuse; their interweaving is the source of multiple ironies directed at the literary enterprise itself. To venture a far-ranging statement about *Ulysses*, one would wish to say that the novel is really about the impossibility of writing a novel (in the old sense of a "comic-epic poem in prose") with the Wandering Jew as hero. Such a novel would be a novel to end novels. It would have neither beginning, middle, nor end.

And yet precisely for this reason, the Wandering Jew is peculiarly adapted to the modern imagination. For we seek literary models lacking in entelechy, forms that deny stasis. The Wandering Jew comes to supply that need. It has been suggested that for this reason, he is now the only possible hero available to the twentieth century after earlier models such as Christ and Faust have largely failed us. He represents a hesitant ideal—the opposite of the self-assertive, godlike hero.[9] And yet, lacking though he is in power or ambition, he symbolizes persistence, the quality of the human. He is "an ever-vibrating perimeter of encounters." The essential things about him—so characteristic of modern man and of modern writing—are his mobility and restlessness: "The archetype of the Wandering Jew—because it is in motion—allows man a recurrent choice; a recurrence of recurrent choices. He can stumble, fall, pick himself up, leap and fall again."[10] This would do as a description of so many typical modern heroes, or rather antiheroes. It is Charlie Chaplin; it is Joseph K. in *The Trial*; it is the characters of Ionesco and Beckett. Vladimir and Estragon in *Waiting for Godot* are true examples of what is here termed the Wandering Jew archetype. Vladimir at one point finds himself unable to rise; Estragon helps him, but he himself stumbles and falls until they move painfully on. Their earthiness is emphasized. All his lousy life he has crawled in the mud, says Estragon; their primary needs are for warmth and shelter and they live on root vegetables. They have wandered far: Estragon has memories of the Holy Land, of the pale blue of the Dead Sea; they remember grape-harvesting in the Rhone Valley; Vladimir recalls the Macon country; they promise themselves to wander on to the Pyrenees. Boots are important for these weary tramps; they pull them on and off repeatedly. They remember odd details from the past, but they forget much more. The problem is to make any kind of connection with the past: one knows that one has suffered but it is hard to know when and where. Men must endure their going hence even as their coming hither—even though the goal of that endurance is unclear and the notion of any "plan" linking past and future, absurd: "To-morrow, when I wake, or think I do, what shall I say of today? That with Estragon my friend, at this place, until the fall of night, I waited for Godot? That Pozzo passed, with his carrier, and that he spoke to us? Probably. But in all that what truth will there be?" All statements relating to the past or the future end with a question mark, and yet the fundamental reality about the existence of the luckless pair is continuance, endurance. They must bear their memories and they must wait for Godot. Whether he will come or not is doubtful, but the waiting is what counts, the posture of expectation, which converts mere biological existence into continuity, into a kind of pilgrimage.

II

While the Wandering Jew in his provenance as well as in his literary history is without doubt a product of the Christian imagination,[11] he appears, not surprisingly, in Jewish writings (or at least in the works of Jewish writers) as somehow relevant to the condition of exile and alienation that the Jews have inherited. Though Kafka does not actually mention Jews in any of his fictions, Joseph K. in *The Trial* and Hunter Gracchus are clearly, among other things, paradigms of Jewish experience. This does not make them less universal; if anything it makes them more so. That is Kafka's special gift. A Jobian touch enters also into these fictions.[12] Joseph K., suffering and yet maintaining his ways, seeking a confrontation with his accusers or at least demanding to know of what he is accused, refusing to take the easy way of suicide at the end, is clearly a Job figure. Here is another of the many avatars of the Wandering Jew.

In more modern Jewish writings, especially in America, Ahasuerus fulfills a central role. He is now something more like the eternal "shlemiel"—victim, humorist, fugitive, survivor. Lacking any sort of grandeur, he nevertheless preserves something of the human image. Bellow provides us with a veritable gallery of such "shlemiels," starting with the "dangling man" of his earliest novel and proceeding to Moses Herzog and Artur Sammler.[13] There is a connection here too with the Wandering Jew of Joyce's fictional masterpiece, for Moses Herzog is modeled on Leopold Bloom, and his name is taken from a minor character in Joyce's novel. Like Bloom, he is a wanderer seeking to affirm a human standard in a world in which it is being constantly eroded. If Herzog only partially succeeds it is because corruption threatens him from within as well as from without. He will stumble and fall and struggle on; when we last see him he has come to a kind of resting place on his journey, and there is just a hint of salvation to provide the "sense of an ending." Artur Sammler is even more than Herzog the quintessential Wandering Jew. Somehow he has been everywhere. He remembers Saint Augustine, the Congo bush, New York, Amsterdam, London. He has been buried alive among the victims of a Nazi execution squad; he has been a partisan in the Zamosht forest; he has been to Israel as a journalist covering the Six-Day War. Above all he belongs to the earth, to "Mr. Sammler's planet." According to Earl Rovit, the Wandering Jew archetype is the key not only to Bellow's fictional world but also to his narrative structure: "the rambling, episodic, picaresque chronicle of jumbled sequential events patterns itself loosely on the myth of the eternal journey or, better, the eternal wandering." There is no real goal; Bellow's typical hero achieves neither damnation nor glorification—"his singular achievement is earthly survival."[14] And yet somehow Artur Sammler hankers after more than that. There is a death at the end of *Mr. Sammler's Planet* and with it a symbolic catharsis, a settling of accounts. It is as though the Wandering Jews of Bellow are looking around for a different kind of myth, which will relieve them of the weight of total aimlessness, which will provide them with meaning, purpose and epiphany—something that Estragon and Vladimir will never achieve. It is as though Sammler and Herzog are not merely disenchanted wanderers; they are disenchanted with the actual role of wanderer. Sammler, in short, is the Wandering Jew who is trying to escape that literary mould: he strives to go beyond the myth and its limitations. He tries to get beyond mere survival. "It was the Sammlers who kept on vainly trying to perform some kind of symbolic task. The main result of which was unrest, exposure to trouble." Sammler is a Wandering Jew, but he is weary of that role. What remains for him, we are told, are "endless literal hours in which one is internally eaten up. Eaten because coherence is lacking. Perhaps as punishment for having failed to find co-

herence. Or eaten by a longing for sacredness." [15] One remembers
Kafka. Gracchus's questioner had also demanded to know about
coherence, and Gracchus's answer had been to say that the wanderer knows no coherence. With this, Bellow's characters cannot
remain quite satisfied.

The desire to go beyond the Ahasuerus model is implicit also in
Bernard Malamud's *The Fixer* (1966). Always in motion, stumbling,
falling, picking himself up, suffering, being unjustly accused like
Kafka's hero in *The Trial*, he will nevertheless survive after the others, such as Bibikov, have died. So far this is the classical formulation of the Wandering Jew. But there will also be something more—
a vindication. This is the Jobian version of the archetype, and Job
here signifies for Malamud not just one more avatar of the Wandering Jew but rather a means of escape from its limitations. Yakov Bok
is a Job figure not only in his suffering, in his trial (as with Kafka's
hero); he is also a Job figure in his ultimate vindication. His survival
is not meaningless: he survives as a witness; he lives to gain a victory, bearing his wounds not as the mark of Cain (in the old Ahasuerus fashion) but rather in the manner of Jacob—his biblical name-
sake—who fought with the angel and prevailed. In this fashion
Malamud is trying to find a myth of continuance that goes beyond
the Wandering Jew and, is in a measure, its antitype.

III

There is, of course, a well-established wanderer who belongs to the
Jewish tradition from within. I refer to Elijah. Elijah the prophet is a
true wanderer and he is immortal. He traditionally moves about the
world to annul evil decrees, to save the individuals in distress, to
heal the sick, succor the poor, and in general perform useful social
services. His surprise visits at any time or place to those especially
deserving his services are the subject of countless tales and legends.
Elijah appears in Islamic folklore too, where he performs the
mythic role of wanderer, and in later Jewish literature he has a cher-
ished place. J. L. Peretz has many delightful Elijah stories, among
them his "Seven Years of Plenty," and then there is also Israel Zangwill's "Elijah's Goblet." In these tales the Jewish imagination sees
Elijah typically as the guest at the Seder table on the eve of Passover,
where he is given a fifth cup of wine to signify his task as the prophet
of redemption. And he is regularly pictured also as the "angel of the

covenant," with a special seat assigned to him ("Elijah's chair") at each and every circumcision ceremony. All this suggests his ubiquity, his deathlessness, and also his readiness to stand by his people in the hour of danger. It also suggests a role model different from that of Ahasuerus. Elijah is a performer of miracles, a harbinger of salvation, a seeker after justice.[16] In short, there is a kind of purpose, or at least a drift, a direction. Unlike Gracchus, he does not sail a rudderless ship. And yet, like the Wandering Jew, he moves without a pattern determinable in advance. His mark is suddenness; his appearances are unheralded, unexpected. This is already established in the biblical account of his doings. He stations himself on the road in the path of Obadiah, the steward of the household of Ahab. Loyal as he is to Elijah, Obadiah finds himself unable to base a policy on these sudden appearances and disappearances. "There is no nation or kingdom whither my lord has not sent to seek thee. . . . And now thou sayest, Go, tell thy lord, Behold, Elijah is here. And it shall come to pass, as soon as I am gone from thee, that the Spirit of the Lord shall carry thee whither I know not . . ." (I Kings 18.10–12). Sporadic movements, violent changes of mood make it difficult to define him in terms of a "signified." He is always a signifier, his myth resisting categorization.[17] And yet we always associate him with a kind of hope. The Spirit that carries him (the word in Hebrew means simply the gust of wind) is carrying him somewhere.

Elijah is not unknown in the Western literary tradition. Joyce glances at him briefly in *Ulysses*. Bloom is handed a tract announcing the visit to Dublin of an evangelical preacher "Dr. John Alexander Dowie, restorer of the Church in Zion." On it are the words "Elijah is coming."[18] Bloom throws away the piece of paper among the gulls in the harbor; we see it later floating away: "Elijah skiff light crumpled throwaway, sailed eastward by flanks of ships and trawlers, amid an archipelago of corks, beyond new Wapping street past Benson's ferry. . . ."[19] "Elijah" here hints at voyages to the east. Bloom will never sail toward the sunrise, but the "skiff Elijah" will, taking with it his hopes and fantasies. W. B. Stanford does well to remind us that Joyce introduces with Bloom a dimension of aspiration unknown to his Greek model Ulysses (and unknown too, we may add, to Ahasuerus).

> Bloom himself retains an ancestral yearning for Zion. . . . Bloom himself is never conscious that he is a metempsychosis of Ulysses: only Joyce knows that. But, in contrast, Bloom is intensely aware of his

Hebraic qualities. He is shaped from inside, as it were, by his Jewish heredity; from outside by the Homeric parallelism. For Joyce and for the instructed reader, the houses and streets of Dublin represent the islands and straits of Homer's wonderland: but for Bloom their ancient analogue is the waters and willow trees of Babylon. . . .[20]

If Bloom is in exile, he is also borne up by the whimsical hope of restoration from exile. The little ball of paper is the vessel of that whimsical hope; it links up with the melonfields north of Jaffa on which he muses early on. Elsewhere, at the close of the "Cyclops" episode, we see Bloom fantastically transformed. No longer is he Ulysses or the wandering Ahasuerus struggling on with his burden on his back; he is Elijah transported to heaven in a fiery chariot, though it is actually a horse-drawn "jarvey."

And they beheld Him in the chariot, clothed upon in the glory of the brightness, having raiment as of the sun, fair as the moon and terrible that for awe they durst not look upon Him. And there came a voice out of heaven, calling *Elijah, Elijah!* And he answered with a main cry: *Abba! Adonai!* And they beheld Him, even Him, ben Bloom Elijah, amid clouds of angels ascend to the glory of the brightness at an angle of fortyfive degrees over Donohoe's in Little Green Street like a shot off a shovel.[21]

The note of bathos here is intended to explode the mock heroism of Bloom, who is running away from the Citizen and his dog; nevertheless a momentary wonder has been shed on him—the wonder of the future as well as that of the past.

Kafka in his surrealistic tale "A Country Doctor" offers us a more dispirited Elijah. He too, like Bloom, has a fiery chariot, but the horses that miraculously whisk him to his destination emerge from a pigsty, led to him by a demonic groom. There are other Elijah motifs: he will be laid by the side of the boy to whose death-bed he has been called in the manner of the biblical Elijah (I Kings 17.21). The biblical figure here is absurdly, even tragically, diminished, but the note of urgency remains. "I had to start on an urgent journey," the doctor declares in the opening sentence.[22]

We find Elijah also in his classical role as a figure of warning. In *Moby-Dick* Elijah is the ragged old sailor who shows up in the path of Ishmael and Queequeg on their way to the *Pequod* to join Captain Ahab on his ill-fated voyage. The biblical scheme is obvious not only in the pattern of naming (Elijah-Ahab) but also in Melville's keen understanding of the sporadic, unpredictable nature of Elijah's movements: "But we had not gone perhaps above a hundred yards, when chancing to turn a corner, and looking back as I did so, who should be seen but Elijah following us, though at a distance . . . it seemed to me that he was dogging us, but with what intent I could not for the life of me imagine"[23] (chap. 19). And later Elijah utters his ambiguous warning as to the fate awaiting Ahab and those who sail with him: "'Morning to ye! morning to ye!' he rejoined, again moving off. 'Oh! I was going to warn ye against— but never mind, never mind. . . . Good-bye to ye. Shan't see ye again very soon, I guess; unless it's before the Grand Jury'"[24] (chap. 21). No doubt the prophet Elijah expresses here something of the notion of retribution (this is also what the name of the vessel *Pequod* signifies),[25] and his warning will remain with Ishmael to the end. Ishmael, whose name is that of the father of the tribe of wild desert-dwellers (Gen. 16.12) is the composite and ultimate wanderer. His immortality is that of Ahasuerus the weary survivor, but also that of Elijah—witness, prophet, and mediator of salvation. Elijah Gadd, the hero's brother in Sinclair Lewis's late novel *The God-Seeker* (1949), is remarkable for his sudden appearances and departures. He it is who utters the gospel of social salvation with which the novel will conclude. It is the new hope for the future.

IV

Both Ahasuerus and Elijah represent attempts to grapple with the meaning of earthly time; they are figures of memory; but the dynamics of the two legends are different. Elijah, as well as bearing the memories and records of the past, signifies liberty, renewal, a future. This is his semiotic function. In ritual he seems to signify the ongoingness of the covenant—hence his presence at every circumcision ceremony; he likewise is invoked on Saturday night at the beginning of a new week; and, as remarked earlier, he has a special and honored place at the festive board on the eve of the Passover, when the Exodus from Egypt is reenacted, thus signifying his part not only in past deliverances but in all new historical beginnings. Old and deathless, he is nevertheless the harbinger of the new. He turns the heart of the fathers to the children, and the heart of the children to their fathers (Mal. 4.6). That is his dialectic. The Wandering Jew, tied as he is to the past and its memories, cannot really fulfill this double role, and it is important to distinguish the two wanderers and their myths from one another.[26]

Of the two, it would seem that Ahasuerus is more congenial to the modern temper than is Elijah. Myths that suggest the absurdity of our continuance are felt to be more authentic than those which suggest hope and deliverance—the latter remind us too much of discredited nineteenth-century ideologies. For this reason modern writers (Bellow and Malamud included) have been attracted to Ahasuerus rather than Elijah. But a careful consideration of the literary evidence suggests that Jewish writers cannot wholly escape Elijah. He haunts them even in the darker periods of their history. C. N. Bialik, the leading Hebrew poet of his time, who had written a fierce elegy for the victims of the bloody pogrom in Kishineff in 1903, sounds again and again the note of exile, of martyrdom. In the last lines of his celebrated elegy "If You Should Know" (1897), he speaks of the life without end that the martyrs and students of the Law—children of the exile—have through their toil bequeathed to us. What he witnesses is a miserable remnant of dwellers in the House of Study, their faces shrunk and wrinkled as they continue, incredibly, to draw life from ancient springs. This death-in-life seems to be for him a fundamental reality. But there is a counterpoint, a certain ambivalence. It seems he cannot exclude the Elijah model even though it enters with much ironical shading and with a degree of whimsy reminiscent of Joyce. In another poem describing the weariness of the exile, he pictures the baby lifting its head from the cradle, the mouse peeping from its hole to see if the Messiah is coming!

> Was that his donkey's bell jingling?
> And the maid blowing on the coals to heat the kettle
> Sticks her sooty face outside to look.
> Is the messiah on his way?
> Was that his trumpet sounding?[27]

This posture of watchful expectation goes somewhat beyond the world-weariness of Vladimir and Estragon. The oddity of the images of expectation—the baby lifting up its head, the mouse peeping from its hole, the scullery-girl's sooty face—all these are in line with the oddity of the phenomenon that Bialik elsewhere calls "the epiphany of Elijah." Oddity and unexpectedness are of its essence.

The ambivalence in Jewish writing toward these two alternate models becomes more marked as a result of the Holocaust. The heroism that the Holocaust yielded was one marked primarily by a Joblike persistence in adversity. The Jew was a survivor, a wanderer who retained the human image while the world receded into barbarism. Simply to survive, simply to remember became the great achievement, the sign of a spiritual victory. His was the dignity of Ahasuerus, the outcast who preserves the human image. Nevertheless, the same historical trauma, and more particularly the rise of the State of Israel that followed it, brought to the fore that other myth of continuance related to the figure of Elijah. The inmates of the concentration camps sang of the coming of the Messiah. Arthur Koestler, though he certainly did not embrace the rise of Israel as an Elijah-type event, declared nevertheless in *Promise and Fulfilment* (1949) that it marked the end of the pilgrimage of Ahasuerus: "Now that the mission of the Wandering Jew is completed, he must discard the knapsack and cease to be an accomplice in his own destruction."[28]

Those who have tried to render Jewish historical experience from within have felt an overriding need to discover myths of continuance that can somewhere be made to stand the strain of contemporary history. And for this purpose both Ahasuerus and Elijah have been found necessary. Elie Wiesel has deeply rendered both these images in numerous writings and has done so with a sense of the dialectical relation between them. Through his pages the figures of Elijah and Ahasuerus flit constantly. We see them in the shadows and we see them in the flickering light. Sometimes they are apart, and sometimes they merge strangely together, grave figures from the past, grave messengers of the future. Elie Wiesel's work runs obsessively about the axis of past and future, and in almost every one of his writings there is a wanderer—a ghost or a survivor who addresses to us the question as to the meaning of Jewish continuance. But if the same question is addressed to him, he can give only an ambiguous answer.

In Wiesel's short story "An Evening Guest," Elijah comes to the Seder table of a Jewish family in Hungary. It is the last Seder they will celebrate before they are deported to Auschwitz. This Elijah tells them, but they refuse to hear. Elijah has shrunk; he has become a pitiful figure. "His movements betrayed his weariness, but his eyes were aflame. One sensed that, for him, the past was his only haven."[29] But rooted though he now is in the past, he alone understands the agony of the present. At the end, he will be seen as a poor refugee on his way to the extermination camp, and only by an incredible leap of the imagination shall we be able to picture him at the end of the journey ascending to heaven in his fiery chariot.

In another Elijah story, the prophet appears to the wretched inmates of the concentration camp, urging them to hope: "It was always of the future he spoke. The truth was that we needed a future."[30] He plays his chosen part even in the darkness of these "last days," offering consolation and encouragement, bringing to each group of sufferers a message of hope in the future. His own past is of no importance: "My past wouldn't interest you. What matters is my future."[31] But having planted the seed of hope, the Prophet is the one ironically chosen for death. They will never see him again.

But there is the other type of wanderer too. One short story of the Holocaust entitled simply "The Wandering Jew" is explicitly based on the Ahasuerus legend. The Wandering Jew is represented as "a hobo turned clown, or a clown playing hobo." His birthplace is anywhere and everywhere—Marrakesh, Vilna, Kishineff, Safed, Calcutta, or Florence. The narrator meets him in Paris after the war and hears from him many things: he discourses on the meaning of the Scriptures and on History. He tells stories of crime and suffering, of the sin of Cain and the sacrifice of Isaac, which prefigures the Holocaust. He fascinates his auditors with his knowledge and insight.

> It was the month of *Av* and, out of respect for the tradition, he spoke to us primarily of the destruction of the Temple. I thought I knew all the legends on this subject, but in his mouth they acquired new meaning: they made us more proud to belong to a people which had survived its own history and still kept it so alive and so athirst.[32]

But in the end he leaves his disciple dissatisfied. The Wandering Jew is changeless, he represents a meaningless persistence. He remains, but for what purpose? What is the meaning of his witness?

> If for him the past is nothing, the future is nothing, then is death nothing either, and the death of a million Jewish children? . . . I am afraid to plunge once more into his legend which condemns us both, me to doubt, and him to immortality.[33]

Wiesel is not here engaged in literary criticism or myth criticism in the ordinary sense, and yet he is not simply telling a story
either. He is weighing up the adequacy of the myth and its relation
to current history. The conclusion he reaches is that he is "afraid to
plunge once more into his legend." The Wandering Jew, it seems,
has come to an end—his legend had not merely been a mechanism
for defining historical situations: it is itself *defined* (in the sense of
"brought to an end") by history. True, he represents survival, a continuity between past and present. But survival itself now becomes
a problem, a matter of oddity, astonishment, and miracle. In these
circumstances, it may be that not Ahasuerus but Elijah will answer
better for the sort of continuance that is now possible. Is not Elijah
perhaps the wanderer of the future?

S. Y. Agnon's short novel *In the Heart of the Seas* (1935) strikes
the precise balance between fantasy and realism necessary to give
credibility to the action of Elijah for the modern reader. Hanania,
as his hero is named, joins a group of enraptured pilgrims on their
way from Galicia to settle in the Holy Land. He is early on identified as the archetypal wanderer—"his clothing torn, his feet
swathed in rags, the hair of his head and beard covered with the
dust of the roads and all his belongings tied in a kerchief which he
held in his hand." Though they have no idea where he has come
from, the pilgrims eagerly enroll him as one of their number, especially as his unexpected and unexplained arrival enables them to
make up the quorum of ten needed for public worship. But after
they have embarked from the Black Sea port of Vilkovo for Con-
stantinople, on the first stage of the sea journey to Jaffa, they are
dismayed to find that Hanania is not on board. He disappears as
suddenly as he had appeared before them in the first place. It transpires afterwards that he had been engaged in bringing a poor
woman evidence of the death of her husband in order to enable her
to remarry (a familiar Agnon motif) and so had become separated
from the rest. However, he decides that this must not stop him
from making the journey to the Holy Land, and so he spreads his
kerchief on the waves and is marvelously transported across the
sea. In fact, the ship's company sight him from the ship during the
voyage without recognizing him. Opinions on board are divided as
to his identity; some think he is the Wandering Jew:

> And what did the gentiles say when they saw a man sitting on his ker-
> chief and riding over the waves? Some of them said, It is a mirage

such as men see when they cross deserts and oceans. And others said: No, he is the one whom Such-and-such a one (i.e., Jesus) cursed, saying that he would never rest. And that is why he wanders from place to place. Yesterday he was on the dry land; today he is on the sea. Gentiles of the seventy nations of the earth were on the ship and all were in commotion and fright at the sight of that figure. There were Jews on one side and gentiles on the other, all staring out in terror until their eyelashes were scorched by the sun. Said R. Shmuel Yosef the son of R. Shalom Mordechai, the Levite: No, it is the Shekhina (Divine Presence) accompanying Israel to its place. . . . [34]

There is even mention of a strange bird that flies near the figure of the wanderer rather in the manner of the albatross in Coleridge's poem. And there is mention of strange and enchanting music (the Sirens?) to which the travelers are dangerously drawn. However, it is clear by the time we get to the end of the story that we have to do with neither the Wandering Jew nor Odysseus, nor the Ancient Mariner. Hanania shows up in Jerusalem, surprising his companions in the middle of the reading of the weekly portion in the synagogue. He is now taller, freshly clothed and with shoes on his feet. He has fulfilled the "covenant with the Land," and now, true to his Elijah role, he will sit beside the doorpost to await the arrival of the Messiah, whose messenger he is. This again is not just a story about wandering; it is about the different myths of the wanderer and the need to discriminate between them. The voyagers looking out from the ship are choosing the myth that is felt to be truest and most appropriate for our time.

Agnon's is a happy tale. But a poem of Uri Zvi Greenberg some years later, under the title of "Elijah the Prophet," gives us an image of a less hopeful Elijah. He will no longer visit the houses of the faithful in Eastern Europe on the eve of the Passover, for their wine has been turned into blood, their homes occupied by their Christian murderers. In this grim version of the Eucharist (we remember that Passover coincides with Easter), Elijah refuses to play the part of the prophet of redemption. The Passover feast will go by in silence, renewal seemingly made impossible by the death of the six million, while Elijah keeps an endless and lonely vigil over their graves.

A sickness without a form
And beneath him the tombs stretching far, far
And choking anger,
For comfort there is none
Nor restitution none. [35]

This, it would seem, is the denial of any future. But such is not the effect of the long, unwearied lyric sequence to which this poem belongs. In its onward sweep of passion, "The Streets of the River"—a collection of some 130 poems—provides the very image of continuance. The poems (it is really one long, continued poem) take their starting point in history and flow back into history. The poet points forward and looks back; admonishes and cries for help. In his prophetic zeal he assumes the very voice of Elijah, who was also, we recall, a wild figure of scorn and anger calling down divine retribution on the followers of Baal.

But the last word is not with Elijah. In the final lines of the last poem, Greenberg looks forward to the visionary terrors of the future. The figure whom he invokes here is Daniel, "a man greatly beloved." It is Daniel, another symbol of futurity, who interprets for us in these closing lines the mysteries of the end of days, their terrors as well as their triumphs and glories, and who speaks of the hour when "the Mighty One, the Life of the worlds, will come to tread his winepress." There is a Blakean note of apocalypse here, and indeed Greenberg often reminds us of Blake. But unlike Blake, Greenberg does not abandon time and place for the region of metahistory. His dream is the Jerusalem of earthly stone and struggle, not Golgonooza, Blake's city of art and vision, which marked the gateway for travelers to eternity.

5

The Binding of Isaac

BEN-BLOOM ELIJAH, we have said, has intimations of salvation. He also turns his heart to the children and turns the hearts of the children to their fathers—a task assigned likewise to Elijah at the end of days (Mal. 4.6). Toward the end of Bloomsday we see Bloom hospitably welcoming the young Stephen Dedalus to his home. The scene, as has often been noted, is meant to recall the reunion of Odysseus with his son Telemachus at the end of Homer's epic, when the epic cycle is completed and Odysseus ends where he began. But the coming together of father and son resonates for Joyce with a wider theme, foreign to Homer, viz., the interaction of past and future. This belongs to the Elijah archetype. In their happy though drunken conversation, Bloom chants for his young friend the Hebrew song of hope in the future, "Hatikvah." (It has since become the national anthem of Israel.) *"Kolod balejwaw pnimah / Nefesch, jehudi, homijah."* But what Stephen hears is different: "He heard in a profound ancient male unfamiliar melody the accumulation of the past." Conversely, what Bloom sees in his young drinking companion is the bright form of futurity: "He saw in a quick young male familiar form the predestination of a future." But Dedalus reciprocates by singing for Bloom the medieval ballad of Hugh of Lincoln, suggestive of antiquity and its terrors. To compound the dialectic, the Jew's daughter in the ballad, "all dressed in green," reminds Bloom of his young daughter, Millicent, and his hopes for her.[1]

The Jew and not just Elijah performs for the human imagination, it seems, the archetypal reconciliation of antiquity and futurity. The hoary semite brings with him the odor of ancient wisdom, but he is also inevitably accompanied by a young son or daughter; he is a figure of memory but also of hope. Shylock is accompanied by Jessica, Barabas by Abigail, Lapidoth by Mirah (in *Daniel Deronda*), Isaac of York by Rebecca, and in Joyce's novel, Leopold acts toward Stephen *in loco parentis*.[2] The Jew and his daughter/son form an archetypal pair that survives, as Leslie Fiedler points out, in Melville, Hawthorne, and later in Herman Wouk.[3] Perhaps the son or daughter represents the tender shoot of the good olive tree, which, in Paul's parable, would be reengrafted in God's good time onto the genuine native stock.

But if youth and age are whimsically reconciled at the end of *Ulysses*, and if the hearts of the children are turned to their fathers, this should not deceive us as to the daunting nature of the generation gap that is here symbolically overcome. On the contrary, what the Elijah model comes to tell us is that the opposition between fathers and sons is so profound that only a prophet supernaturally gifted can overcome it. To this truth literature has always accustomed us. Parents are mortally threatened by their children in *King Lear* and *Hamlet* (we remember Hamlet "speaking daggers" to his mother and only with difficulty restraining himself from using them and thus acting the part of Nero); children are threatened by parents in *Richard II* and *Merchant of Venice* ("would she were hearsed at my foot, and the ducats in her coffin"). It is a seemingly universal archetype. Oedipus is the prototype of the murderous son; Agamemnon, of the murderous father. Chronos devours his children; Medea destroys hers; Orestes kills his mother. There is something inevitable about the pattern, making parricide and infanticide something like a law of nature.

But again it must be insisted that the nineteenth-century situation is *sui generis*; the fear of the devouring father and the oedipal reaction to that fear achieve now an intensity never known before. It begins to look sometimes like the central myth of the age. In America it dates from Charles Brockden Brown's Gothic novel *Wieland or the Transformation* in 1798. Hawthorne provides major examples. A father (or father figure) threatening his child, the rude son striking his father dead (or seeming to do so) as in the grim prediction of Ulysses in *Troilus and Cressida*—these are central compulsions and fantasies in his work.[4] As already noted earlier (chap. 3), *The House of the Seven Gables* dramatizes the notion of the dead hand of the past and its Puritan forefathers threatening the life and happiness of the young. In "Roger Malvin's Burial," Reuben feels himself responsible for the death of his adoptive "father," Roger, and in turn becomes responsible for the death of his own son, Cyrus. In another story of Hawthorne, Rappaccini is a father who perverts nature and poisons his own daughter. Matthew Arnold in England is also preoccupied with the theme. "Sohrab and Rustum" provides the classic treatment. There a Persian father accidentally slays his son. It is also the author's own story, a reflection of his own suffering under the heavy parental sway of Thomas Arnold of Rugby, for Dr. Thomas Arnold was not only Matthew's father, he was also his headmaster. That was Arnold's problem, as it was that of the Gradgrind children in Dickens's *Hard Times*.

The whole ferment of the romantic period in England and elsewhere sometimes seems to resolve itself into a protest against the repressive and threatening father. We remember Goethe's *Poetry and Truth*, with its picture of the stern father, and we remember Shelley escaping into atheism from the father who comes at him with deistic proofs for the existence of God. John Stuart Mill in his moving *Autobiography* recalls how the education he had received from his father James Mill in logic and Greek verbs brought about a spiritual asphyxiation leading to a radical collapse of the nervous system. It was only the fresh air of Wordsworth's poetry that saved him. In Byron's tragedy *Cain* the sin of fratricide is really a veiled form of parricide, the revolt being literally against Adam, our "general Father"! If we have difficulty in growing up, it is his fault for bringing us into the world. Even where there is no violent antipathy, as in Turgenev's *Fathers and Sons* (1861), the sense of an enormous gulf dividing the generations is central. But it is not any two generations; it is stressed that Bazarov, the hero, is the rebel, the cynic, the type of the new man in an age of radical change for Russia and the world. He is a symbol of modernity.

Thus the historical dimension is of the essence. It is not a matter of the generation gap in general, as in the myths of Chronos or Oedipus. Or if it is, this is not the way it is subjectively experienced. It is experienced as a particular historical crisis, a revolt against a "father" who has come to represent the weight of a particular tradition, specifically, the law and custom of Western Europe engrafted on a Christian evangelical past. The French Revolution and the nineteenth-century movements of revolt that followed came to overthrow this, to substitute freedom and light for restriction and darkness. Thus, diachrony is what counts: we do not have here some unchanging, universal structure but rather a "historical archetype" in the strict sense. The young Gosse rises up against his Puritan father in *Father and Son* (1907) in the name of freedom and the pursuit of happiness in a perceived future. Oswald Alving in Ibsen's *Ghosts* and Ernest Pontifex in *The Way of All Flesh* share his revolt. These nineteenth-century examples (and many others) taken together show how a particular historical occasion shapes and structures a very large body of writing. Indeed, the whole tradition of the *Bildungsroman* in Europe, starting with Goethe's *Wilhelm Meister*, continuing through *A Portrait of the Artist as a Young Man*, and culminating grotesquely with Kafka's "The Judgment" and "The Metamorphosis" resolves itself into a mechanism for dealing with this crisis. It is not merely a matter of harsh parental authority and of children desiring to break free, but of a particular cultural inheritance that at a particular moment can be neither accepted nor totally rejected.

Melville's *Billy Budd* (circa 1888) is a peak example of the myth we are discussing. Here a "father," Captain Vere, sacrifices his "son," Billy Budd, on the altar of inherited law and custom; the historical background sketched out in the preface is extraordinarily relevant. It is, we are told, the period of the French Revolution and the fears that make it necessary to offer up Billy are the fears of revolutionary ferment in the British Navy—a challenge to its forms of discipline and authority. Innocent though he is (like "young Adam before the Fall"), Billy represents a freedom new and uncontrolled. The ship from which he had come bears the significant name of *Rights-of-Man*, and the ship into which he is press-ganged and which Captain Vere commands is no less significantly the *Indomitable*. We have here, if you like, a parable of the Western world at the point when the indomitable force of tradition comes into conflict with the "rights of Man" in the new radical form in which those rights now clothe themselves. There is no lack of more general mythological patterning. Vere and Budd are the first two persons of the Trinity, and the story is, among other things, a crucifixion story—as commentators have often noted. Claggart, the snakelike Master-at-arms, takes his place naturally in this archetypal pattern of the "Fall." Vere is also Abraham resolutely offering up Isaac "in obedience to the exacting behest," (chap. XXIII). He is the archetypal father, just as Billy is the archetypal son, and their drama is the reenactment of the ageless war of the generations. The bond of love between them makes the agony of their confrontation the more acute. Here is a universal psychological conflict, but it has been emphatically reordered. Not the myth of Chronos, but that myth realigned as historical rupture, and thereby given a new syntax and a new dynamic function.

We may consider the metapoetics of this work, for as well as speaking about history and its intestinal warfare, it has also something to say about the myth of history and the language of that myth. Vere is essentially a literary figure. He not only symbolizes tradition, he symbolizes tradition verbalized and encoded. The name that has attached itself to him, "the starry Vere" has come out of a poem by Marvell, "Upon Appleton House"—a poem redolent of a disciplined past in which charm and virtue are maintained in an orderly balance. The studied elegance of the verses in which the phrase occurs is the perfect image of that balance:

> This 'tis to have been from the first
> In a *domestick* Heaven nurst,
> Under the *Discipline* severe
> Of *Fairfax* and the starry *Vere*. . . .

Vere thus comes out of a book; he is also surrounded by books. "He loved books," we are told, "never going to sea without a newly replenished library." He is the embodiment of the *logos*, the wisdom of men caught up in articulate speech: " 'With mankind' he would say 'forms, measured forms are everything; and that is the import couched in the story of Orpheus with his lyre spell-binding the wild denizens of the woods.' And this he once applied to the disruption of forms going on across the Channel and the consequences thereof" (chap. XXVIII). The revolutionary events in France are a break with forms of thinking and speaking sanctified by tradition. Vere's authority is very much bound up with this power of formal speech. It is he who verbalizes the nature of the crime and punishment on which the action turns. When Billy strikes Claggart dead,

Vere catches that moment in an aphorism: "Struck dead by an angel of God. Yet the angel must hang" (chap. XX).

Vere's speech, we are told, "both in the substance of what he said and his manner of saying it, showed the influence of unshared studies modifying and tempering the practical training of an active career" (chap. XXII). From this point of view, the confrontation with Billy Budd is the confrontation of speech with speechlessness; for as Billy hears the dreadful calumny spoken by Claggart, he is struck dumb. Vere urges him to speak, but Billy is unable to speak. He is the new man no longer supported by the traditional forms of the *logos*, its balanced utterance:

> "Speak man!" said Captain Vere to the transfixed one struck by his aspect even more than by Claggart's, "Speak! defend yourself." Which appeal caused but a strange dumb gesturing and gurgling in Billy; amazement at such an accusation so suddenly sprung on inexperienced nonage; this, and it may be horror at the accuser, serving to bring out his lurking defect and in this instance for the time intensifying it into a convulsed tongue-tie; while the intent head and entire form straining forward in an agony of ineffectual eagerness to obey the injunction to speak and defend himself, gave an expression to the face like that of a condemned vestal priestess in the moment of being buried alive, and in the first struggle against suffocation. (Chap. XX)

Here is not only the paralysis of language: we may say that in Billy's speechlessness, we have an implicit challenge to the roundedness of the fable itself, whether viewed as a "sacrifice" or as the "inevitable conflict of the generations" or as "a parable of the Fall" or any of the other neat constructions that the author and the interpreter of the novel propose for us. The point about Billy Budd is that he is radically innocent of such constructions. He never understands them: at the moment of his death he understands nothing of its meaning. His last words, "God bless Captain Vere," are, we are told, utterly unanticipated; we may add that they are also absurd. The blow he gives to Claggart is the clearest statement he makes, and this marks not only the death of Claggart but the death of speech. He has no other power of expression—"Could I have used my tongue I would not have struck him." If the work, like so many other works of Melville, is thus a great achievement of myth and structure, Billy represents the challenge to all myth; he represents the anti-*logos*. Billy is the new Adam, born to inherit a wilder garden freed from the forms of speech whereby man has organized and formalized his experience of life in the past. We will, it seems, have to begin to formalize all over again in the radically new environment into which we have been precipitated; or else we will have to begin to think out our myths all over again "from the beginning."

II

Melville refers us to the biblical story of the Binding of Isaac by Abraham (Gen. 22). That is the story that the Bible has provided for expressing (and also "defusing") the battle of the generations. It gives us the threat in all its enormity: "Take now thy son, thine only son, Isaac, whom thou lovest, and get thee into the land of Moriah, and offer him there for a burnt offering upon one of the mountains which I will tell thee of." We may say that here is a crucial difference between Judaism and Christianity. Judaism's sign is the "Akedah," the "Binding"; Christianity's sign is the Crucifixion, i.e., the sacrifice carried out. The ritual equivalent of the akedah is circumcision, i.e., the near miss, not castration. The Father-God of the Hebrews turns out to be a circumcising and not a castrating Father. He calls out of the skies to save the young: "And he said, Lay not thine hand upon the lad, neither do thou anything unto him: for now I know that thou fearest God, seeing thou has not withheld thy son, thine only son from me." It is ultimately the "walking together" (twice mentioned) of father and son that provides the keynote. Savagery is overcome as the generational gap is closed. The flashing knife descends on the ram. Isaac is saved for the future, but he walks toward it hand in hand with his father. This is the Old Testament pattern.

It is remarkable how constantly this scene is invoked in nineteenth-century literature.[5] *Billy Budd* has just been mentioned. There Vere is cast in the role of Abraham while Billy is young Isaac. In *The Way of All Flesh* the akedah model is regularly recalled. Christina Pontifex wonders whether she would have the moral courage to take her firstborn, Ernest, up to Pigbury beacon and plunge the knife into him. She decides she would not be able to manage it, but someone else might possibly do it for her (chap. XXI). Ibsen's Brand is perceived to sacrifice his son to God at the same time as he recalls the sacrifice of Isaac. The theme recurs in our century in Wilfred Owen's grim "Parable of the Old Man and the Young," in Arthur Miller's *All My Sons*, and in many other texts. There is no doubt that this biblical pericope exercised a powerful compulsion over the imaginations of men in the nineteenth century and beyond—for Faulkner it was the Old Testament story he liked best—and yet what is even more remarkable is how often the story is recalled without the happy ending. In the examples just mentioned, the emphasis is on the actual carrying out of the threat. Owen's war poem is the most explicit: the angel calls out to "Abram" and bids him offer a ram instead of his son, "But the old man would not so, but slew his son,— / And half the seed of Europe, one by one." The same antiwar sentiment guides Arthur Miller later on in determining the shape of *All My Sons*: there the akedah idea becomes fused, as in *Brand*, with the crucifixion. Joe Keller is the father who is actually perceived to sacrifice his son Larry to his own narrow family interests: Chris, the surviving son, points (as his name implies) to the Christ role. The world will be saved when the sacrifice has been duly expiated. With the death of Joe himself there is also a suggestion of father slaying, Chris acting the role of Oedipus, who is, of course, both savior and parricide. A jumble of myths! But common to them all is the sense of the inevitability of the completed pattern with its central components—child slaying and father slaying.

Faulkner's "The Bear" (1942) is a partial exception to this— Isaac McCaslin survives, though he repudiates his inheritance and abandons the world of his surrogate father, Sam Fathers. In Samuel Butler's novel too, Ernest Pontifex manages to escape being stifled by his father's evangelical religion. But in nearly all the other examples, there is a seeming need to carry out the threat. Not only that, but strangely, the use of this false or displaced akedah often becomes the occasion for a fierce attack on the God of the Old Testament (this is the thrust of *The Way of All Flesh*). The story attracts the writers as a way of condemning the author of the story! The relation to the story is, in fact, rather like the ambivalent relation to the father himself! We paint him black and yet at the same time he is our "author" and we are bound to him in love and obedience. Similarly, we cannot escape the power and attraction of the archetype. But it is the upside-down version that is chosen. The fact that the Hebrew God had explicitly sought to "prove" Abraham and had intervened to save Isaac is lost sight of; he becomes the dark destroyer who demands child sacrifice. Matthew Arnold exhibits this displaced akedah in "Sohrab and Rustum," and it is central to his social and literary criticism. In *Culture and Anarchy* he expresses the fear that the "devout energy" of Hebraism would confine the free spirit of man that Hellenism ("Sweetness and Light") had sought to liberate. He seems to ignore the fact that if the akedah (with its release of the victim) is typical of Hebraism, the stories of Oedipus and Agamemnon (lacking such a release) are as typical of Hellenism. Blake had even harder words about the God of Sinai in *The Everlasting Gospel*, and elsewhere associated Abraham with the Druids, who practiced human sacrifice.[6] This distortion is a matter of interest to students of literary antisemitism—it goes back at least to Voltaire and the Deists, who felt it their sacred duty to denounce this Judaic barbarity among others.[7] But this is not the aspect that interests us here. A self-deceiving strategy so widespread and so insistent suggests that there is something in the story itself and the way of telling it that causes the fabulist to ignore its explicit tendency and attach himself to another ending, as though the death of Isaac and not his miraculous escape is the consummation devoutly to be wished.

All this, I will argue, is not primarily a matter of social psychology: it is rather due to the magnetic pull still exercised on the reader by the structure that the akedah came to replace. It becomes a matter of difficulty to accept the radical novelty of a story in which the inevitable laws of myth, those which demand child murder and father murder, are suppressed or denied. Such a conclusion is borne out by the Jewish evidence, for it transpires that the "false" or "displaced" akedah is almost as much a part of Jewish writing as of the nineteenth-century works mentioned above. Shalom Spiegel's illuminating study of the akedah in Jewish liturgy and midrash[8] shows how the story is time and again pulled away from its announced direction and takes a sinister lurch into the direction of the myth of Chronos. In one midrash, Rabbi Joshua, a second-century teacher, is reported as saying: "Said the Holy One, blessed be He, to Moses, I can be trusted to reward Isaac son of Abraham, for he left one quarter of blood [the measure needed to sustain life] on top of the altar."[9] There is a persistent reference in many midrashic sources to a wound made in Isaac's neck: he spends three years in paradise being healed of it by the angels.[10] The hint of the resurrection theme in these sources is even more emphatic in the twelfth-century poem by R. Ephraim of Bonn entitled simply "Akedah."[11] There the dead body of Isaac, slain by his father, is brought to life by resurrecting dew:

> He made haste, he pinned him down with his knees,
>   He made his two arms strong.
> With steady hands he slaughtered him according to the rite.
>   Full right was the slaughter.

> Down upon him fell the resurrecting dew, and he revived.
>   The father seized him then to slaughter him once more.
> Scripture, bear witness! Well-grounded is the fact;
>   "And the Lord called Abraham *a second time* from heaven."

The poem thus supposes two acts of sacrifice, the first of which is consummated and is followed by a resurrection, and the second of which is attempted but is prevented by the voice of the angel. In this way Rabbi Ephraim remains true to the akedah as narrated in Scripture but achieves also the actual death and resurrection of Isaac, making the story conform to the "law of the eternal return." This midrashic pattern, which clearly goes back to sources more ancient than this poem, testifies surely to the still-active power of the pagan myths of circularity. Aristotle's preference for a drama that could be comprised in the single circuit of the sun is due not to the difficulty of comprehending an action taking place over a longer period, but to the satisfying senses of inevitability and completeness that such a circular unity of time would bestow on the performance.

The akedah as presented in Genesis 22 trails off into the ongoing and undetermined pilgrimage of Isaac and Abraham and thus notoriously lacks such a unity; it requires that we ourselves find ways of fulfilling its meaning and promise. It is not only Abraham who is tested: the reader is tested also: he must discover in himself the meaning of that survival, its portent and challenge; he must weigh that up against the immense danger that has been overcome on the road to survival. Such a mode of imagining explodes the very structure of mythical time, indeed all fables of circularity. It is no wonder that midrash slips back into more satisfying modes of imagining: a son born, reared, and then sacrificed is a story with a beginning, a middle, and an end; likewise, a son rising against his father, only to be in turn doomed, when he himself becomes a father, to have his own son rise against him, is a myth beautifully adapted to a closed and cyclical notion of time. It is no wonder that King Lear tells us that he is bound upon a wheel of fire and that Edmund the murderous son announces before his own death that "the wheel is come full circle." Shakespeare had a clear sense of the beauty and power of such images: it is the opposite, more untidy notion of a testing and a pilgrimage that, as Kierkegaard says, appalls the imagination. The tragic hero attaches himself to a universal standard; Abraham does not. He is the solitary man who is tested, who is "teleologically suspended"[12] and thus can express himself only in silence, like Billy Budd. Kierkegaard's remarks on his silence are extraordinarily pertinent to our discussion:

> Abraham keeps silent—but he *cannot* speak. Therein lies the distress and anguish. For if I when I speak am unable to make myself intelligible, then I am not speaking—even though I were to talk uninterruptedly day and night. Such is the case with Abraham. . . . The relief of speech is that it translates me into the universal. . . .[13]

Fables such as that of *Billy Budd* introduce such silence and yet they cannot easily accommodate it into the universal language of myth. There will always be a temptation, or, more correctly, a natural tendency of hermeneutics, to round out the akedah, to fill in the gaps created by its silences. Such rounding-out and filling-in has traditionally been the function of midrash.

It is hardly too much to say that the crucifixion and resurrection of Jesus, the primary event in the gospels, is itself a kind of midrash on the akedah. The two stories are linked together in Christian typology, and the link appears to go back to the New Testament. Golgotha and Moriah give us parallel scenes: Isaac bearing the wood for his funeral pyre (Gen. 22.6) becomes the prototype of Jesus bearing his cross (John 19.17). The author of the epistle to the Hebrews, speaking of Abraham and Isaac, seems really to be speaking of Jesus:

> By faith Abraham, when he was tested, offered up Isaac, and he who had received the promises was ready to offer up his only son. Of whom it was said "Through Isaac shall thy seed be called": Accounting that God was able to raise him even from the dead, *and from the dead he did, in a sense, receive him back.* (Heb. 11.17–19)[14]

The resurrection of Jesus on the third day is a further midrashic elaboration based on a hint from Hosea 6.2. The akedah, rounded out in this fashion, does not require a complete break with pagan forms of myth making: we can still remain rolled around in earth's diurnal course with rocks and stones and trees. And that rolling around is what men need constantly to be assured of.

But here we run into a difficulty. It seems that the rewriting of the akedah story in this way (i.e., with Isaac actually being offered up as a sacrifice) is also, collaterally, made necessary by the exigencies of actual historical experience. Ephraim of Bonn's akedah poem has been mentioned. This poem was, in fact, a response to the martyrdom of whole Jewish communities in the Rhineland during the period of the Crusades. Fathers would actually slay their sons and daughters to avoid apostasy and defilement (or simply so as to anticipate their slaying at the hands of the crusaders) before taking their own lives. As they did so, they would actually recall the akedah and call upon God to view their actions as a latter-day binding of Isaac. Rabbi Ephraim had firsthand knowledge of such events. More, therefore, than it is the reconstruction of a primeval myth pattern, his poem is a response to the experience of death and suffering in his own immediate environment. To these he gives a theological meaning by attaching them to the imagery of the akedah. Thus if the poem falsifies the biblical story and lurches into the direction of a real death and a real sacrifice, it is surely from the felt necessity to bear witness to tragic contemporary history.

The same literary displacement occasioned by similar historical exigencies occurs in the literature of the Nazi Holocaust in our own century. Rabbi Zewi Hirsch Meizlisch describes an incident in Auschwitz in September 1944 on the eve of the New Year (the festival during which the story of the akedah is traditionally recited). A father came to him with a grim question in religious law. His only son had been selected for extermination in the ovens. Through some connection with higher authority in the camp it came about that he could have him removed from the group, but it was made clear that if he did so, some other child would be seized to make up the quota. His question was whether the Torah permitted him to save his own son at the certain cost of the death of another. While Jewish law in fact forbids such substitution (on the grounds that one cannot know "whose blood is redder"), the rabbi found himself unable to give a clear answer in the light of the unimaginable horror of the circumstances in which they all found themselves. The questioner preferred to take the rabbi's silence as a negative answer, supposing (with some justification) that had the exchange been permissible, the rabbi would have said so. The only son therefore went to his death, and during the days of the festival that followed the bereaved father prayed that his great act of disinterested obedience to the Torah be accounted as the reenactment of the binding of Isaac, which had likewise taken place on Rosh Hashanah.[15]

What shall be said of such historical consummations? "One cannot weep over Abraham," said Kierkegaard. "One approaches him with a *horror religiosus*."[16] He might have made such a statement even more aptly of the man described in the record kept by Meizlisch. It would seem that the akedah in its naked, original form, where Isaac is saved and the father and child walk together into the future, has to fight not only against the pagan mythical heritage of our culture but also against terrible historical realities that press themselves upon us in life itself. This would challenge the thrust not only of this present chapter but indeed of this entire book. It would make the closed time of myth the proper image of history, rather than its antithesis. This, however, is a conclusion that must be resisted in spite of Auschwitz and its horrors. If we see Auschwitz as the end of the line, we will naturally be driven to mold the akedah event likewise into a pattern of finality: Isaac will have to die. The hardest trial is to insist that the Auschwitz railway junction, in spite of its millions of dead, is not the end of the line, that what counts most in the end is not the ritual of death and sacrifice but that of survival and witness.

One could put this another way. Perhaps the important thing about Zewi Hirsch Meizlisch's record is the record itself. What it signifies in the last analysis is the felt need to preserve a memory of the bereaved father and his only son, for the written word transcends the seemingly terminal event; it breaks the seemingly completed cycle of death and sacrifice. We recall those many doomed victims of the crematoria in Poland and Germany who used their last moments to pen a diary, a poem, or a letter, hiding it very often in the crevice of a wall or burying it in the ground. They saw themselves as witnesses who had something to hand on. History would continue and *theirs was the responsibility for its onward course*. They too were writing their midrash on the akedah event, but, unlike the bereaved father, they were interpreting it not as death and sacrifice but as survival and witness. The written word breaks the vicious circle of mythical time and affirms a future. Or perhaps it is more accurate to say that the future is itself a text, a written word. For if our memory of the past is really no more than an inscription preserved, so our memory of the future is likewise a written missive—an act of faith and witness that makes the future conceivable.

Kafka has been mentioned. The image of the father who is both feared and loved is central to his work: in this he gives us an agonized summation of the nineteenth-century trend we have been discussing. In his extraordinary *Letter to His Father*, he imagines his father saying to him, "You are not fit for life."[17] In at least two of his writings he dreadfully imagines the deaths of two such father-dominated sons as himself. In "The Judgment," Georg, sentenced to death by his father, throws himself immediately over the bridge and into the river. His last words are, "Dear parents, I have always loved you, all the same." In "The Metamorphosis," Gregor again suffers serious injury at his father's hand and, rejected by his family, eventually dies of neglect, hunger, and sickness. For him too hatred and fear are compounded with love. But again Kafka perceived more clearly than anyone that the very penning of the record was his way out of the trap, out of the closed circle of the myth itself. He looked upon his writings as a "long-drawn out leave-taking"—a release from his father. The two works mentioned, more than they are celebrations of the distorted or displaced akedah (that which terminates in the death of the victim) are its *reductio ad absurdum*. In the one story, a helpless, invalid father pronounces a sentence of death on a healthy, vigorous son; in another, the son in order to be slain is literally reduced to the condition of a beetle. These are metaphors that draw attention to their own metaphoric status. They are nightmares that have to be formulated in language in order to be exorcised. Seizing the myth of the father who sacrifices his son in his hands, Kafka grotesquely dangles it before us. In so doing he makes his gesture of freedom: he tells his tale. He survives the syndrome, bearing the missive in his hand relating his trial and sacrifice.

III

But all this suggests something less than the complete meaning of the akedah, which is ultimately a myth of salvation. It is not the binding of Isaac or even his escape that is offered to us ultimately, but something beyond either, namely, the "walking together" of father and son, their reconciliation and reunion. There is a formidable difficulty even in thinking of such possibilities in modern writing, except in the bibulous conclusion of *Ulysses* already referred to. All that Matthew Arnold, or Edmund Gosse or Samuel Butler could perceive down to the end of the road was tragic (or less tragic) separation. And in spite of the deep sense of guilt at his insurrection and the unconquerable need he felt for his father's love and approval, tragic separation is the ultimate meaning also of Kafka's *Letter to His Father*. To find anything nearer to reconciliation, one would have to go back to Shakespeare, who brings Henry IV and his son Prince Hal together when the former is lying on his deathbed. Hal makes his solemn vows as the father passes on his task to his son in a chamber symbolically named Jerusalem. The biblical resonance is clear enough here as the hearts of the children turn to their fathers and those of the fathers to their children. In spite of revisionist readings of Shakespeare's history plays, we are surely to think of a sacred task transmitted. Father and son may be morally flawed (especially the father who carries to his grave the blood guilt of Pomfret Castle), but nevertheless responsibility is transmitted, the responsibility for a future weighted with providential purpose. We are expected to recall such biblical moments as David passing on his kingdom to Solomon (I Kings 2); but above all, there is a sense of a gap being closed as Hal is restored to his father's favor after a youth spent in dissipation and idleness.

But one has only to cite this example to realize how very problematical such a situation is for modern audiences. Such reconciliations can be entertained in our time only in a context of skepticism or sentimentality. Modern producers of Shakespeare are tempted either to slur over the deathbed scene in *Henry IV, Part II*, or to represent Hal as a cynical young man actually coveting the crown and getting out of it by fulsome declarations of loyalty and affection. The father image has been too effectively corroded by all that has happened since the Enlightenment for easy rehabilitation.

This, however, is not quite the last word. I would like to refer in conclusion to a number of modern Hebrew writers who—it seems to me—exhibit the full parameters of our topic. On the one hand, as heirs of all the nineteenth-century intellectual revolutions we have mentioned, they lived the crisis of "fathers and sons" with incomparable intensity; on the other hand, taken together, they do seem to point toward the possibility of a resolution. Both attitudes regularly take the form of a reading, or rereading of the akedah story. Micah Joseph Berdichevsky (Bin-Gorion), at the turn of the century, saw the crisis of fathers and sons as the special tragedy of the writer: "On the one hand he wishes to rid himself of the yoke of the past generations; but on the other hand, he desires that the chain should continue. . . . This is the poetry of heartbreak."[18] Yitzhak Lamdan a little later saw himself as Isaac (his own name, of course) actually being sacrificed or as Isaac's half-brother, Ishmael, in a similar situation (see chapter 6 below). He returned obsessively to this type-scene. Either way, it was the fulfilled rather than the aborted sacrifice that his imagination conjured up. In *Days of Ziklag* (1958), a somewhat high-pitched novel relating to the Israel War of Independence (1948), S. Yizhar seems to see the soldiers of that war as akedah victims, sent to die by their elders. Aharon Megged in *The Living on the Dead* (1965) has his protagonist Davidov, a representative of the nation-building generation, send his son to be killed on the battlefield, and in like fashion Amos Oz in a short story "The Way of the Wind" (1965) presents us with the father, one Shimshon Sheinbaum, a figure made in the heroic mold of the socialist pioneers, who persuades his sensitive, poetically gifted son, Gideon, to join the paratroopers. The boy dies grotesquely from electric shock after his parachute catches in the overhead high-tension cables during an army display to mark Independence Day. A. B. Yehoshua, with a finer ear for the ambiguities of the biblical narrative itself, gives us in "Three Days and a Child" (1968) a sense of the radical menace (heat, sickness, and the threat of snakebite) to the life of the child Yahli during the "three days" of trial, as in the biblical story (Gen. 22.4), but in the end the emphasis will be on survival and escape as the fierce summer heat gives way to the cooler air of autumn and its promise of rain. A shorter tale by the same author, "Early in the Summer of 1970" (1973), is likewise true to the dialectics of the biblical pericope with its balancing of menace and survival. There we have the reported death of a soldier on the Jordanian front during the Six-Day War. The father, significantly, a teacher of Bible, has to identify the body, but when he arrives at the hospital mortuary, he discovers that the body is not that of his son! It is a case of mistaken identity. The reaction of the father suggests brilliantly the problematics of the biblical tale, which is not merely a story of escape but a story of failed expectations, for the expected—and in a mythological sense—desired consummation is denied: "'It isn't him . . .' I whisper at last with infinite astonishment, with growing despair, with the murmur of the water in this cursed room." [19] In a sense the narrator remains a bereaved parent: he returns again and again to the moment when the news of his son's death had first reached him.

All this represents something less than the full understanding of the akedah as salvation myth. There are only the merest hints in Yehoshua, and perhaps it would be unreasonable to look for more than that in a period as inhospitable as our own to myths of salvation. We noted, however, in the previous chapter, that while the Elijah model is out of place in modernity, it may come into its own in the postmodern age. The same may be said of the akedah model; the walking together of fathers and sons is not possible for the children of the Enlightenment, but perhaps it is possible for those who have witnessed the failure of the Enlightenment and are looking for a ground beyond it. I would like to refer at this point to a recent work by the Israeli novelist Aharon Appelfeld, *The Age of Wonders* (1978). Appelfeld is generally regarded as a Holocaust writer, but he is, more correctly, a post-Holocaust writer. He rarely deals with the atrocities themselves: he deals with survivors and the painful recovery by them of a reason for living. In Appelfeld there is neither nostalgia nor sentimentality, but rather a self-lacerating honesty reminiscent of Kafka, whom he resembles and to whom he refers in the novel.

The Age of Wonders is a novel in two parts, sharply divided by a blank page in the middle. In the first part we have a child's growing up in a small Austrian town during the thirties; there are his impressions of people and events, his growing sensitivity, the growth of his sexual awareness. More specifically, we have an estrangement between his father and the rest of the family as his father, a writer, becomes consumed with bitterness—often expressing itself in self-hate—at the approaching catastrophe, for it is the period of the *Anschluss* and the shadows are darkening over Europe and, in particular, over its Jews. Finally, the father abandons his family on the eve of the deportations and the break is complete. Then comes the disaster of 1942–45 symbolized by a blank page.

In the second half of the novel, the protagonist, Bruno, now some twenty-five years older, having by now established a new life for himself in Israel, goes back on a visit to his hometown in Austria in order to seek a connection with the past and with the people he knew in the past. He is at first only partially successful in this, for he has to come to terms with that darker part of himself that belongs to the past. He confronts this past as personified in several characters but most dramatically in a figure who may be thought of as his "Double." This alter ego is one Mr. Brum (the conjunction of names is not accidental), a Jew who had escaped the Nazi dragnet by marrying his gentile housemaid and passing himself off as a beer-swilling Austrian cattle trader. Brum at first refuses to recognize Bruno. "You are mistaken, sir," he says when Bruno hails him by name. However, at a later meeting when Bruno asks him whether he knows him, Brum answers: "Of course, you are the son of the writer A. I used to be one of your father's admirers." At their final meeting, Brum himself initiates the conversation:

> "It's Brum."
> "I'm glad," said Bruno, and his voice sounded as if it came from a transmitter.[20]

But immediately afterwards Brum turns harshly on him and bids him leave them all alone. "You are overstaying your welcome here," he says to Bruno, and proceeds to rail at him and at all the Jews. Hearing this, Bruno throws him down to the ground and strikes him on the face, symbolically laying the demon of his own past. He is now ready to leave the Austrian town of his birth behind and return home.

In close conjunction with these meetings and the memories that they arouse and that they enable him to overcome, we have the narrator's thoughts of his dead father and of the sad history of their separation when the narrator was twelve years old. Bruno begins to feel that perhaps the sense of shame, the tensions, almost the hatred that he felt whenever his father's memory came to him are now giving way to something else: "Now he stood in the place where he had once stood with his father. Now he had reached his father's age, perhaps even a few years more. And like his father's, his own marriage was not happy."[21] Bruno now begins to feel that he can come to terms not only with his past but specifically with the memory of his father. It is a momentous reunion. There is no joy, no pealing of bells, but a certain inner reconciliation that enables Bruno to overcome the past with its great, yawning chasm and to entertain the notion of a future. Jerusalem, the thought of which now comes to him, is the sign of this future, the catalyst that seems to make reconciliation possible:

> And while he was drinking and dozing he suddenly saw everything that had been hidden from him all the time he had spent here: Jerusalem. In Ibn Gvirol Street the trees were casting their shadows on the pavement and a cool breeze was blowing down the street. Two old people were about to turn right at the corner of Abarbanel Street. Mina was standing by the window with her eyes fixed on the elderly couple.[22]

It is under the sign of Jerusalem, as in Shakespeare's play, that the hearts of the children turn to their fathers. Nor is it for Appelfeld the Jerusalem of legend or of dreams, but of everyday, with its cold winds, its aging citizens, its harshness as well as its beauty. Appelfeld's narrator in the story—indeed his fictional characters generally—are in search of a future. But such a future is not entirely separable from their past. The problem is twofold: they must liberate themselves from the demon of the past, but at the same time they must restore communications with it. Such memorializing is a work of paradox and pain. Bruno achieves it on this visit to the sad scene of his youth and with the help of his "memory" of Jerusalem.

There is another, more "literary" way of defining this same process. Appelfeld's problem is to release himself from the overpowering influence of the apprentice novel and at the same time to rewrite it. The first part of *The Age of Wonders* is written in the tradition of the *Bildungsroman*, the type of novel that from Goethe to Somerset Maugham relates the growing up of a young man in his parents' home and his search for freedom and an identity. We watch Bruno in his *Lehrjahre*, learning not only from books but learning about people and about himself, achieving the beginning of maturity as the world opens up gradually before him. He gazes wonderingly at his surroundings and responds to the strange intensities of those around him—parents, relatives, friends, like Stephen in the early chapters of *A Portrait of the Artist as a Young Man*. The narrative method, with its attention to the minute ripples of consciousness, with its sensitive recording of seemingly inconspicuous details, is that learned from the *Bildungsroman* as it had been developed in Europe and marvelously enriched by Proust,

Joyce, Thomas Mann, Theodore Dreiser, and many others. We are held by the inner drama of the child's awakening consciousness; we await what Joyce calls his "epiphany," that moment of fusing of inner and outer reality in which the child's "vocation" will be understood, in which his path forward will be revealed. But instead of that we have the scandal of the blank page: this is the point where the actual deportations will take place. Here is a shattering not only of a life pattern but of a literary genre that can no longer function.[23] In the face of this dark apocalypse, can literature any longer occupy itself with the delicate unfolding of a child's personality? What shall we now make of the image of a sensitive young man learning to know himself in the climate of the European Enlightenment? All this is now seen in a new perspective. What is the meaning now of that "vocation" to which the hero has aspired and to which he has won through in a hundred apprentice novels beginning with Goethe and including the writings of Samuel Butler, Edmund Gosse, and James Joyce? Can that genre any longer be sustained?

And indeed, the second part of the work represents among other things the negation of the genre itself, the abandonment of its basic structure and language. The Bruno of the second half no longer sensitively records his experiences; continuities are shattered; the organicist metaphor (the notion of *growing* that lurks behind such writings from Goethe onwards) no longer works. Speech is broken into staccato utterance, "as if it came from a transmitter" (more literally: a walkie-talkie). The final conversation with the café attendant at the railway station is conducted, we are told, in "words without dress":

> "When does the train arrive?" he asked.
> "At six," said the waitress.
> "On time?"
> "Mostly."
> Strange. The questions and answers sounded to him like words without dress.[24]

Language is naked, consisting of single words thrown out, with gaps in between. Human relations are also abrupt and discontinuous; we are not sure any longer of the identity of the other person from day to day. Is the Bruno of the second part the first-person narrator of part one? As in Beckett's theater, we are not quite sure of the continuing identity of the characters. It is by no means certain that the person one knows as Louise is still Louise when we see her next. Our entire existence is marked by such discontinuities. Fragments have to be pieced together painfully, and sometimes they don't fit. In place of the adjustment to the outer world, the fulfillment that traditionally followed the period of *Sturm and Drang*, we have here the radical difficulty of establishing a stable connection between the self and that which lies beyond the self. The second half of the novel thus marks a sharp break not only in the life of Bruno but in the history of a major European fictional genre; the *Bildungsroman*, it seems, is no longer viable. A new fictional model has to be devised and a new language to match it.

And yet in another sense the *Bildungsroman* has been redeemed. For at the heart of this kind of novel from Goethe onwards had been the issue of the separation of parents and children.[25] It had told of that separation often under the guise of a search for freedom and realization. But what such novels generally left concealed was the wound left by such a separation, by such affirmations of freedom. Here, in Bruno's return to his hometown and his symbolic reconciliation with the memory of his dead father, we have the healing of a wound that is not only that of Bruno but of all his ancestors in the history of the genre. Here in this post-Holocaust novel, father and child, tragically separated since the first brave declarations of the "Rights of Man" (we remember Billy Budd and Captain Vere), come together after a long separation and a long death.

6

The Absent Father

PROUST'S GREAT NOVEL starts off with a fundamental scene that seems to have a special significance for the narrator. It is his going to bed alone in the great house at Combray, denied his mother's good-night kiss. His father, who, we are told, "used constantly to refuse to let me do things which were quite clearly allowed by the more liberal charters granted me by my mother and grandmother," had curtly bidden him to leave his mother alone and run along. The result is that hours later, the child, violently disturbed and quite unable to sleep, waylays his parents on their way to bed. The sacrifice of Isaac is here again invoked, but now with a difference:

> I stood there, not daring to move; he was still confronting us, an immense figure in his white nightshirt, crowned with the pink and violet scarf of Indian cashmere in which, since he had begun to suffer from neuralgia, he used to tie up his head, standing like Abraham in the engraving after Bonozzo Gozzoli which M. Swann had given me, telling Sarah that she must tear herself away from Isaac.[1]

It will be noticed that there is now a new focus of interest—a figure who does not appear in the biblical story at all, namely Sarah. It is to be her sacrifice, and Isaac's ordeal is to be essentially that of the separation from the mother. The rabbis in their day, too, had tried to find a role for Sarah in the akedah story and had done so by sug-

gesting that the death of Sarah recounted in the chapter following
(Gen. 23) came about as a result of shock at hearing of the near
death of her beloved son. She thus becomes the only real victim of
the akedah! Isaac's marriage to Rebekah, which happens next, is
explicitly his way of making up for the loss of his mother (Gen.
24.67). Isaac was thus, like Marcel, a mother's child, though we
cannot quite imagine him having the passional involvement with
his mother of which Proust speaks. The biblical figure was, after
all, "comforted after his mother's death." He was tied to her but not
so completely as to rob him of his emotional freedom and independence. Such "comfort" is evidently not possible for Proust's narrator. The night spent in his mother's arms in the continuation of
the above-cited episode (when his father marvelously withdraws
the ban) will never be matched by the comforts and favors of his
subsequent mistresses. His mother's love was marked by

> that untroubled peace which no mistress, in later years, has ever
> been able to give me, since one has doubts of them at the moment
> when one believes in them, and never can possess their hearts as I
> used to received, in her kiss, the heart of my mother, complete, without
> scruple or reservation, unburdened by any liability save to myself.[2]

Mother love is thus all-embracing, scarcely capable of being displaced later by an emotionally complete union with a chosen wife
who comes to occupy (like Rebekah) the mother's "tent." A similar
triangular pattern, in which the mother's love balances the harsh
restrictive code of the father and totally embraces the child in its
warmth, is common to a great many fictions of the early part of
this century. We think of Virginia Woolf's *To the Lighthouse* (1927),
which starts off with a similar type-scene to Proust's. The harsh
judgment of the father is set off against the milder offices of the
mother. Fulfillment will only come to James after her death, when
her love is symbolically fulfilled in the journey to the lighthouse
and he is symbolically reconciled to the father. In Thomas Wolfe's
Look Homeward, Angel (1929) the mother, Eliza, leaves her husband, Oliver Gant, taking her son, Eugene, with her. Seven years
old, he sleeps with her at nights—"he was riven into her flesh." As
the story of Eugene's life moves forward, father and mother are
alike diminished, but the hold of the mother is the more powerful.

The crucial case is that of Paul Morel in D. H. Lawrence's *Sons
and Lovers*, published in 1913, in the same year as the first volume

of Proust's masterpiece. Here, too, we have the image of the threatening father (with Paul's brother William in the role of Isaac) and of the child who later finds refuge in the arms of his mother. Here, too, the physical embrace is all-important:

> Paul loved to sleep with his mother. Sleep is still most perfect, in spite of hygienists, when it is shared with a beloved. The warmth, the security and peace of soul, the utter comfort from the touch of the other knits the sleep, so that it takes the body and soul completely in its healing.[3]

Lawrence's tone is more hortatory and revelational than Proust's, and the more direct emotions of the Nottinghamshire mining family are in contrast with the more restrained sensibilities of the family at Combray, but the pattern is fundamentally the same— Sarah rescuing the infant Isaac from the knife of Abraham and seizing him in her powerful embrace. In Henry Roth's *Call It Sleep* (1934), the type-scene is repeated. David Schearl is bidden to run from the house to escape his father's violence ("Let me strangle him"), in exact repetition of William's flight from his murderous father in *Sons and Lovers*, and here again the "akedah" victim ends up in his mother's arms. David Schearl runs blindly through the streets and barely escapes death from electrocution after placing a bar between the car tracks on Tenth Street. He is delivered to his house in an ambulance, and the novel ends with the now-familiar scene of the mother-dominated child sleeping in his mother's physical proximity.

> Her dark, unswerving eyes sought his, "Sleepy, beloved?"
> "Yes, mama."
> He might as well call it sleep.[4]

The father, Albert, is seen at the end thoroughly chastised and humiliated. He has gone off to buy medication for David's burnt foot—it will be a long time before he comes back.

As though commenting on the other earlier examples we have cited, Henry Roth is here careful to qualify the absolute peace achieved by the child gripped in the maternal embrace. For D. H. Lawrence writing in 1913, it was what gave the most perfect peace to body and soul—the peace we may say, which passeth understanding; Henry Roth is not so sure. David does not enjoy the perfect repose of Paul Morel sleeping in his mother's bed or the absolute ecstasy of the young Marcel in the same situation; it is rather a matter of weary submission. He feels a "remote pity" for his father as he hears his tread on the kitchen floor, "a kind of torpid heartbreak." It is that which makes his peace and joy less than perfect. His slumber includes a kind of death-wish, "not terror, but strangest triumph, strangest acquiescence. One might as well call it sleep."

We have here a group of examples belonging to a well-defined period of less than twenty years and exhibiting the same very specific motif. It may be that Lawrence's mothers and mistresses, as well as Genya Schearl and Eliza Gant, are in the line of descent from Ceres, Maia, Isis, Penelope, and the tree-goddesses of the ancient world. They are in that sense part of a universal archetype. The devouring, embracing, or castrating mother is as old as time. She is the White Goddess, the Great Earth-Mother to whom, according to Robert Graves, we all owe allegiance. "Her service," he tells us, "is perfect freedom."

> Her habit has never been to coerce, but always to grant or withhold her favours according as her sons and lovers came to her with exactly the right gifts in their hands—gifts of their own choosing, not her dictation. She must be worshipped in her ancient quintuple person, whether by counting the petals of lotus or primrose: as Birth, Initiation, Consummation, Repose and Death.[5]

Repose and death are the blessings she brings, and we are drawn to her because she is as old as time, like Cleopatra in Shakespeare's play: "That am with Phoebus' amorous pinches black, / And wrinkled deep in time" (I.v.27–29). As the human incarnation of Isis, goddess of Nature and fertility, Cleopatra is clearly not simply "Miss Egypt" but rather the eternal feminine—Tiamat, Venus, Aphrodite. She has been known at all times to the race of men, for she is the source of passion, reproduction, and death.

But all this does not really catch the special pathos of Paul Morel's situation or that of David Schearl. They are not reenacting a universal ritual belonging to all time, but responding to a crisis that may quite accurately be charted as belonging to the first quarter of our century. Lawrence himself was later to urge that the special anguish of the oedipal victim (himself included) was a peculiarly modern phenomenon. It was a product of what he defined as contemporary self-consciousness. "The mother-child relationship is *today* the viciousest of circles."[6] His diatribe against "the detestable *love-will* of the mother" as a specific modern poison resembles in its animus the call to throw off the authority of the father, which was sounded at the time of the French Revolution a hundred years or so earlier: it carries the same strong sense of historical exigency. It is time to act for the sake of freedom and the rights of man, Lawrence seems to say. It is time to rid our generation once and for all of "this infernal self-conscious Madonna starving our living guts and bullying us to death with her love."[7]

II

Lawrence did not actually define the myth of mother fixation in its diachronic character; he merely pointed to it as the sickness of his generation—"the actual state of affairs *today*," or "the relation between mother and child *today*," and insisted on this time dimension as against the Freudian reading of the oedipal crisis as a universal law of nature. But we will get no real inkling from Lawrence as to why and how this came about. Why is today—i.e., the first part of the twentieth century—the special day of the White Goddess? Or, to put it differently, how does it come about that even those who look upon her as the universal queen, the power behind poetry and art and religion at all times, turn out to make their discovery of this mighty fact at about the same time? Freud, Jung, I. D. Suttie,[8] Robert Graves, and Erich Neumann[9] all stumble across her during the same few decades. Universal she may be, but it seems that her field day occurs at the moment when the Victorian father is roughly expelled from the household.

And that is, of course, the key to what happened. When the exodus of the Puritan father is accomplished, the mother (hitherto not too prominent) comes back, we may say, with a vengeance. And there is no doubt about her presence and power. Molly Bloom may not actually sit in on the final conversations between Bloom and Dedalus in the "Ithaca" episode, but we feel her presence. She is in bed, of course, but that is where she is most dangerous. In that warm and all-enveloping ambience of Molly Bloom, who is also Gea-Tellus, the Earth-Mother, Dedalus might well have been swallowed up. She becomes, in fact, very interested in him the more she hears of him. He is lucky to escape with his manhood intact. Leopold himself had suffered worse. She is the new woman, the dominating mother figure, waiting to leap out of her covert.

One's problem is thus not solved by eliminating the autocratic father. Ernest Pontifex successfully (so it would appear) rids himself of Theobald, whose life and death are (at the end of the novel) reduced to insignificance; but the vacuum so created is going to be filled by the Mother (with or without an initial capital letter), who will now achieve unprecedented authority. *The Way of All Flesh* must not be thought of in isolation but should be related intertextually with other works. *Sons and Lovers* is in its fashion the sequel to *The Way of All Flesh*. Ernest Pontifex rose up against his father. Lawrence's novel shows us what happens when the rebellion succeeds. Walter Morel has diminished both in social rank and in spiritual stature; he is no longer the head of the family but a beer-drinking, helpless creature. With the disappearance of that moral authority, or rather pseudo-moral authority, which had hitherto been lodged in the Victorian father and husband, we are left with a family dominated by unbridled mother love and mother law. It is the sequel also to *The Doll's House*. Walter Morel is what Thorvald would have become if Nora in pursuit of women's lib had decided to stay at home and take charge of the keys. Thorvald, his moral authority collapsed, would have become an ineffectual drunkard, and Nora would have become the true husband. And to measure the distance we have come in one generation, it may be remarked that if Ernest Pontifex suffered, Paul Morel suffered more. He suffered because his mother left him incapable of growing up into that wholeness of manhood to which Ernest attains at the end of the story.

The true nature of this modern tragedy is best defined in the words of Lawrence himself in a letter to Edward Garnett describing the sons of the Morel family in *Sons and Lovers*:

> These sons are *urged* into life by their reciprocal love of their mother—urged on and on. But when they come to manhood, they can't love, because their mother is the strongest power in their lives, and holds them. It's rather like Goethe and his mother and Frau von Stein and Christiana—As soon as the young men come into contact with women, there's a split.[10]

As Leslie Fiedler has shown, the theme is pervasive in the American novels of the twenties and thirties. The white witch of Fitzgerald, Daisy Fay Buchanan, is also a dark destroyer. She is found at this period in Hemingway and Faulkner also, for whom men are helpless in the hands of their mothers.[11] Fitzgerald's novel *Tender Is the Night* had at one stage of its composition a boy hero and was to have been entitled *The Boy Who Killed His Mother*.

We have thus two parallel and yet opposed myths. The father-son conflict, which is so central in the nineteenth century, resembles in its dynamic character the mother-son conflict, which develops later as its antitype. Both seem to be transformations of a single structure, and yet they are related to one another antithetically along the diachronic axis. Parricidal and infanticidal fantasies are common to both. Matthew Arnold gives us an example of the first myth in "Sohrab and Rustum"; in America, Hawthorne is similarly haunted. In "Alice Doane's Appeal," the hero, Leonard, kills a man in revenge for the supposed violation of his sister. But the face of the dead man "wore the likeness of my father," who had been slain earlier in an Indian raid. Lady Macbeth was inhibited from killing Duncan because he resembled her father as he slept. It would seem that for her nineteenth-century successors this is rather an inducement to homicide. As we move into the twentieth century, the father is largely absent, but we have in his place the castrating or suffocating mother, and the reaction to her takes on a similar form. The parallels are striking. Paul Morel kills his mother by administering a fatal dose of opium during her final sufferings from cancer. But by the same token, she also destroys him. As in Blake's "The Mental Traveller" (a prophetic intuition of the whole historical process we are here considering) she "nails him down upon a rock, / Catching his shrieks in cups of gold." In the end, after she is dead, Gertrude Morel seems to draw Paul toward her. Critics who see Paul drifting toward death and darkness in the final chapter are probably right. We have here the work of *thanatos*, or of Proserpine, the dark goddess of the underworld, whose power, as we have noted, is that of birth, repose, and death.

Considerable irony is created by these two successive myths as writers become aware of the pattern of affinity and contrast between them. In one of Isaac Babel's grotesque and terrible Red Cavalry stories, we hear of one Timofei Kurdyukov, "a big shouldered old-regime village cop," now fighting with the White Army, who deliberately and viciously kills his son Fedor, a member of one of the opposing Red brigades (here we have the familiar confrontation of a father belonging to "the old regime" and a son representing revolutionary novelty, as in the nineteenth-century examples discussed earlier). Some months later the fortunes of war turn and the father falls into the hands of another son, Semyon, who kills him off in revenge. The story is related by a third son in a letter to his "dear mother," which ends with the words: "I remain, Mama, your loving son, Vasily Kurdyukov." We are supposed to measure the worth of the love of the "loving son" against the events related in the letter. The two sets of relations are then ironically juxtaposed by the narrator himself. After reproducing the letter in full, the narrator appends a report on his brief conversation with the writer:

> "Kurdyukov," I said to the boy, "he was mean your pa, wasn't he?"
> "My pa was a dog," the boy said gloomily.
> "And what about your Ma?"
> "Ma's all right. Here, want to have a look? Here's a picture of our family." [12]

We are implicitly invited to speculate on what will happen to the mother (and, by wider symbolic implication, to Mother Russia) now that father Timofei (and the old, tyrannical regime he stood for) has been gotten rid of. In another story in the same series ("Salt"), Babel shows the same cossacks nobly saving the life and honor of a woman who has become the type of the mother. Seeing she has a baby in her arms who may one day be a soldier like themselves, they allow her to sit in their railway carriage unmolested through the night ("cuddle your child the way mothers usually do"). When they discover her baby is not a baby but a bag of contraband salt, they casually shoot her on the roadside. "And so I took my trusty rifle from the wall and I wiped the disgrace from the toiling face of our Republic." [13]

Thus a love-hate dialectic governs the new mother-child relationship as it had governed that of fathers and sons in an earlier generation. In both phases there is suffering, but to judge by Philip Roth's vulgar extravaganza on this very theme, *Portnoy's Complaint* (1967), the dominion of the mother is worse. Sophie Portnoy's authority is harder to bear than the authority of the autocratic fathers of an earlier age. Alex sees his father as no longer a threatening figure but the helpless victim of his wife and son: the main point of the story is how intolerable the new situation is:

> If my father had only been my mother! and my mother my father! But what a mix-up of sexes in our house! Who should by rights be advancing on me, retreating—and who should be retreating, advancing! Who should be scolding, collapsing in helplessness, enfeebled totally by a tender heart! And who should be collapsing, instead scolding, correcting, reproving, criticizing, faultfinding without end! Filling the patriarchal vacuum! [14]

The two syndromes are parallel, but the second, it seems, is harder to bear. Alex Portnoy's nineteenth-century forebears had suffered from a father who laid upon them the heavy weight of the law and the commandments. Mother was, on the whole, not around. Now Father is not around and there is no longer a question of the law and the commandments. All that has gone and has ceased to be a serious option. Alex Portnoy's Jewish mother stands for repression of a different kind: she stands for compulsory biological continuity; she represents a constricting and suffocating warmth; she holds her son in her oedipal grip; the doors are closed and the steam heat is on full-blast. This is the realm of the Furies in Aeschylus. The mother is the source of that authority which binds her son to the obligation of marrying a wife who shall be a reflection of the mother. But at the same time she inhibits him from so doing, from gaining the emotional independence that would enable him to build a home of his own. And all this for his own good! The father had used the rod and it had stung. But the mother's possessiveness, expressed only as concern for the child's happiness and well-being, hurts more than the rod, because it leaves the victim bereaved of his manhood and independence. It leaves him bound fast at his mother's breast.

One could put this difference between the two patterns in a different way, which would reflect more correctly their character as myth. The akedah, as we saw, resting on the intergenerational tension between father and son, retained even in its displaced modern version a faintly perceived release from conflict in the notion of a subsequent "walking together." Father and son ultimately had shared purposes—"so they went both of them together." The roundedness of myth would at some point give way to the more straggling but also more bracing challenge of a pilgrimage, a struggle, an endeavor. D. H. Lawrence in his *Fantasia of the Unconscious* (1922) pleaded for a realm of independence from nature and sex, in which space could be found for purposive, creative goals on the part of fathers and sons. The anti-akedah, however, of which we are now speaking, in which the father is absent and in which the mother sacrifices her son, has no such open-endedness. There is no suggestion of shared purposes to be fulfilled in history. What we have instead is the absolute roundedness of myth, the total closure of the vicious circle of nature itself. No brave new world will be created as the mother directs the passion and creativity of the child toward herself. It is against this inversion that Alex vainly revolts, as do so many mother-dominated heroes in the literature of our time.

Such mother fixation in literature, as in life, is often referred to as a Jewish phenomenon. The "yiddische mama" (of whom Sophie Portnoy is the most notorious example) has become something of an established character, at least in the music hall. But one wonders how Jewish she really is. She is surely anticipated in Lawrence's very un-Jewish Mrs. Morel, in Theodore Dreiser's mother, and indeed in the matriarchal family-pattern that emerged in America, especially among immigrant groups from the beginning of the century. The situation in *Call It Sleep* is not peculiarly Jewish. It can be matched (as far as the emphasis on mother love and mother domination is concerned) in many novels of immigrant life, to say nothing of Negro writing. And one thinks of Faulkner's great novel *As I Lay Dying* (1930), in which the authority of the mother achieves epic proportions. Here is an essential part of the American world in the post-Puritan age. Indeed, Jewish and Hebrew evidences, when properly sifted, point somewhat in the opposite direction. The biblical Sarah—she is, one supposes, the first "yiddische mama" of all— does not seem to mollycoddle her son, Isaac, though he is the only child of her old age. The first, and indeed the only, thing we ever hear of her bringing up of Isaac is that she weaned him and that the weaning was the occasion of a great feast (Gen. 21.8). By contrast, Alex Portnoy never seems to have been weaned. Sophie does not cut him free. Biblical mothers conform to the Sarah type. Rebekah sends her favorite son away from home to suffer privations for twenty long years before he comes back home a grown man with a family of his own. Hannah, the mother of Samuel, does much the same. Jewish mothers in the *stetl* in Eastern Europe often had to manage and control the household in the absence of the father, but they were tough-minded about their sons, frequently sending them away at a tender age to distant academies to earn their spiritual bread and to stand on their own feet. The Hannah-Rebekah model was, in a deep sense, normative. Though this model does not appear much in American Jewish writing today, we do have an occasional protest against the unbridled domination of the White Goddess, who has come to be so much a part of American bourgeois society and literature. Saul Bellow's *Herzog* (1961) tells of Moses Herzog's escape (or attempted escape) from a number of powerful female characters. In a critical scene he morally browbeats his domineering ex-wife, Madeleine, in the police station in Chicago, and finally we see him giving up the others and withdrawing to Ludeyville, there to guard himelf from the tide of nature and sexuality as best he may. In this book, shaped in no small measure by Joyce's *Ulysses*, we have in effect Bloom-Dedalus escaping from the coils of Molly Bloom to achieve a kind of moral independence. The pattern is further developed in *Mr. Sammler's Planet* (1969).

Philip Roth himself in a shorter work, "Eli the Fanatic" (1959), imaged not only the restlessness of the wife-dominated American male but also the restlessness of the writer for whom this pattern has become manifestly inadequate. "Eli the Fanatic" is a story of alienation. The hero is the sick, wife-ridden Jewish bourgeois, but pale and neurotic as he is beside his bouncing wife Miriam (she has more natural bounce because of the baby she is about to bear), he is the only member of the community concerned with saving the human image. He can only do this by withstanding the pressure of the bourgeois comfort-seeking society that surrounds him and the goddess that it serves. Miriam, who keeps reminding him that he needs therapy, is more than anyone else the cause of his disturbance. As Blake said, speaking of Vala, the goddess of nature, who is also the voracious Wife-Sister-Mother: "Her fingers number every Nerve, / Just as a miser counts his gold" ("The Mental Traveller"). In short, it is not the submission to the "yiddische mama" but the attempt to escape her thralldom that is here the issue. And this is the habitual posture of many Jewish fictional characters of the mid-century. Eli's need to escape and liberate himself takes the form of another akedah trial, this time done in comic fantasy. As a lawyer he is charged with the task of ridding the community of Woodenton of a group of alien Jews who bring to the town their ancient superstitions. The most notorious of these, according to Eli's friend Ted, is represented by the story of the sacrifice of Isaac: "Sundays I drive my oldest kid all the way to Scarsdale to learn Bible stories . . . and you know what she comes up with? This Abraham in the Bible was going to kill his own *kid* for a sacrifice. She gets nightmares from it for God's sake! You call that religion?" Eli tries his best to brush Ted's fears aside, but some of them linger in his own mind. Strangely, Eli's unborn son is menaced by the dark aliens. Earlier on, their leader, Tzuref, wishes him peace and good luck on his approaching fatherhood, of which he has mysterious intelligence. Fantastically, the candles go out as he pronounces his wish: "But the instant before, the flames leaped into Tzuref's eyes, and Eli saw it was not luck Tzuref wished him at all." Tzuref has placed his evil eye on the child. Will the child be safely born and, more particularly, will Eli, now succumbing to a nervous breakdown, achieve his identity by becoming a true "father"? That is the trial he must undergo in the "three days" that follow. After the birth, we see him dressed in the dark garb of the stranger, which he has appropriated, "but he knew who he was down to his marrow." He has made his peace with Tzuref, the archetypal father-figure from the past ("I know what it is to have children"), and with himself. Ted meets Eli arriving in his strange dress at the maternity ward and comically supposes that in his mental crisis he has come to reenact the akedah sacrifice:

> Ted tapped Eli's arm. "You're not thinking of doing something you'll be sorry for . . . are you Eli? Eli—I mean you know you're still Eli, don't you" In the enclosure, Eli saw a bassinet had been rolled before the square window.
> "Oh, Christ . . ." Ted said. "You don't have this Bible stuff on the brain—"

Here in the repeated "Eli" we have the call "Abraham, Abraham" done in low mimetic. But Eli has understood the akedah event better than Ted. Isaac will be saved *and so will the father*. Before they plunge the hypodermic syringe into his arm to drown his consciousness, Eli "rose suddenly, as though up out of a dream, and flailing his arms, screamed: 'I'm the father!'" [15] We thus have here a whimsical restoration of the father. Eli at the end enters into the blackness of enforced repose—it is the exact reversal of the typescene from Proust with which this chapter began. But Roth is only playing with the symbolism. The truth is that the power of the father has gone and Miriam will triumph. But at least the story signifies where the need is and the myth pattern that needs to be restored if we are to regain wholeness.

III

Freud tells us that behind the father stands the father God of the Jewish and Christian tradition: he did away with the pagan mother goddesses. Now it seems the process has been reversed. The father

has gone and the mother goddesses have taken over. They are goddesses of the earth and sea, just as the Father God was the God of
the sky.[16] We should, therefore, not be surprised at the new chthonian temper of the age we are discussing. The vigorous upsurge of
mother love and mother authority is related to the earth. (We remember Marcel's grandmother at the beginning of *Remembrance
of Things Past* walking out into the rain and getting covered gloriously with earth and mud.) The Brangwen family, we are told, at
the beginning of Lawrence's *The Rainbow* (1915)

> felt the rush of the sap in spring, they knew the wave which cannot
> halt but every year throws forward the seed to begetting, and, falling
> back, leaves the young-born on the earth. They knew the intercourse
> between heaven and earth, sunshine drawn into the breast and bowels,
> the rain sucked up in the daytime, nakedness that comes under the
> wind in autumn . . . feeling the pulse and body of the soil, that opened
> to their furrow for the grain, and became smooth and supple after
> their ploughing, and clung to their feet with a weight that pulled like
> desire. . . . (Chap. 1)

Earlier on, Whitman had powerfully anticipated the trend:

> Smile O voluptuous coolbreathed earth!
> Earth of the slumbering liquid trees!
>   Earth of the departed sunset. . . .
>   Smile, for your lover comes.[17]

But the mother and bride whom he passionately worships is also
death; lovely and soothing, she is the "Dark mother always gliding
near with soft feet."[18] Again we are in the realm of Proserpine, who,
we should remember, is not only the goddess of nature and the earth
but also of death and sleep. As the male God of the Puritans declines
in authority, becoming a mere "stream of tendency," Demeter and
Proserpine take over. It is a momentous change, and Whitman is its
first powerful witness. For Whitman, the chthonian realm is also
the essential realm of poetry—the coupling of man and earth being
the source of poetic creativity as well as its true emblem and analogy. In "Spontaneous Me," he tells us that what he writes are "real
poems" and not merely pictures; his poems are related to the functioning of the sexual organs and the creativity of the earth itself.
They are essentially "Leaves of Grass." "And this bunch pluck'd at
random from myself, / It has done its work—I toss it carelessly to
fall where it may."[19] Keats had said that poetry should come as

naturally as leaves to a tree. Whitman seems to achieve this. And yet surely the poem itself contradicts his avowed intention. To commit the act of writing a poem and to publish it in durable ink on durable paper is to claim a certain momentousness for what one has said, a momentousness that is part of the saying. Man's days are like grass, says the Psalmist, but the poem that says this is the word that manifestly arrests the process of the decay of all organisms. Using different terms, one could say that while what is signified in Whitman's lines is the evanescence of the poem, the signifiers, through the very gesture of signification, seek to transcend such evanescence. Poetry, inspired by the Muse, who, according to Robert Graves, is just another name for the White Goddess,[20] may express the purest worship of the organism, but the ambition to write a poem is not that of the organism; it is man's defiance of the fleetingness of organic life and his celebration of the power of memory. And the memorializing function of the poem, as we know from Shakespeare's sonnets, ultimately sets itself against death itself: "And death, once dead, there's no more dying then."

In the period we are considering, the archetypal conjunction of Earth-Mother-Bride often defines itself more specifically as the erotic attachment to a particular land, which becomes the mother and the source of poetic inspiration. This is the age of nationalism and populism in Europe and the age of national expansion and consolidation in America. Whitman is, needless to say, the lyric poet of America, expressing his love not just of earth but of the land in its length and breadth with a power hitherto not encountered. His fundamental rhetorical figure is hyperbole, for the grandeur of geography is felt as a vision of the absolute; as such it explodes the ordinary limits of language.

We might express this situation as literature seeking to reflect the new revolutionary nationalism and doing so through the myth of the Great Mother. But would it not perhaps be more correct to reverse the formula? May it not be that political movements are actually generated by the changes in literary mythology, literature preceding history? At the moment when the father image declines and the mother image comes to replace it, we find everywhere the passional devotion to the land becoming more articulate. This is what is meant by speaking of historical archetypes. They shape history and are in turn shaped by it. Nearly all the heroines of the great Russian novels seem to be images of Russia herself and carry with them the power of the love of Mother Russia, which antedates the Revolution and, of course, also survives it. Dostoyevsky wrote the greatest of all novels on the death of the father. ("Who doesn't desire his father's death?" asks Alyosha Karamazov in the court-room.) But he also gives us, in the figure of Sonya in *Crime and Punishment*, something of the dialectic of sin and redemption, which is felt as the reality of Russia herself. The same is true of Tolstoy's *Anna Karenina*. In Pasternak's *Dr. Zhivago* the plot itself in its epic sweep creates an image, mediated through the story of Lara, of the tragic condition of Mother Russia, her beauty and pathos.[21]

No doubt, examples of the application of the mother-son and husband-wife relation to the motherland could be found in many literatures of the late nineteenth and early twentieth centuries. However, I would like to focus in the remaining pages of this chapter on a number of examples from modern Hebrew literature of the love of Zion as mother and bride. While other literatures (including the Russian works just mentioned) might yield better-known examples, it seems to me that the new Hebrew writers have a special interest. They reveal more clearly than others the desperate need for the myth of the mother to support the national movement then in progress, but at the same time they betray the basic inadequacy of that myth. Nietzschean though many of these writers were in temper and ideology, it was no easy matter for them to get rid of the father. They could not bid him farewell quite as readily as did Ernest Pontifex or Alyosha Karamazov. Mother is what they need, but even as they embrace her, they feel the aching void left by the absence of the father. The problem is that the biblical Father God is ineradicably present in the very language they use. It is again the paradox of the signifier and the signified pointing in opposite directions. We are betrayed by the signs we use.

IV

To illustrate the problematics of the love of Zion as Mother-Earth-Bride for the Hebrew poets of our century, I should like to begin by mentioning Yitzhak Lamdan's long poem "Massadah" (1927). Lamdan, who was peculiarly sensitive to myths, which he tended to link directly to historical occasions, designs for us here an "alternate akedah." In this poem he turns to the memory of the heroic defenders of the great fortress of Massadah on the Dead Sea who committed suicide to escape capture by the Romans in the year 73. This he links with the contemporary struggle for Jewish independence and peoplehood in the Land of Israel. In so doing, he visualizes Massadah as a mother seeking in vain to nourish her children at her dry breast:

> How little of God's grace caresses you, Massadah,
> You lonely rejected one between wilderness and sea.
> What will you do, poor mother, for your thirsty defenders,
> As they bury their heads in your lap.
> It is their last refuge. . . .
> . . . why do you still offer me your breast
> When it is parched?[22]

The mother who demands sacrifice—or at least is obliged to witness her child's sacrifice—is then personified in the person of Hagar. It will be recalled that in Genesis 21, i.e., the chapter preceding the narrative of the binding of Isaac, we have the story of the near death of Abraham's other son, Ishmael. There it is Hagar, the Egyptian mother, who is sent with him into the wilderness, where she will be obliged to watch her child perish from thirst. She is said to cast him under a shrub and turn her face away, "for she said, Let me not see the death of the child" (Gen. 21.16). Then, exactly as in the binding of Isaac, to which this story is clearly parallel, the angel calls out of heaven at the last moment and announces that the child will be saved: "Arise, lift up the lad, and hold him in thy hand; for I will make him a great nation." A well of water springs up out of the parched land and Ishmael is saved for the future. But it is Mother Hagar to whom the saving word comes. It is she who will subsequently (verse 21) provide him with a wife, thus ensuring that he will remain under the maternal wing. The two stories are thus typologically related and yet clearly contrasted. Lamdan, writing in 1927, uses this alternate akedah as a key for understanding the trials and sacrifices of his people:

> Why did Hagar weep over Ishmael when he thirsted
>   And the water in the skin dwindled?
>   She had no need to weep—
> Ishmael grew up and he became savage desert-taught,
>   Great distances his bow now threatens.[23]

and he continues:

Where is Sarah to weep over her son Isaac?
Whose every hope has here been ventured
On this fearful desert waste?

Ishmael, securely protected by his mother, would be safe in the desert. But the mother is not so easily accommodated into the myth of Isaac's akedah. There is a plangent note here: if only Mother Sarah could function in the same way as Hagar! If only Isaac's relation to the bleak and inhospitable land could be as simple as that of the savage Ishmael to the desert! Massadah is a mother, and yet she witholds herself, she denies herself; Isaac can establish no easy relation with Sarah-Hagar-Massadah. There is the gesture of passionate embrace, but also the sense of radical isolation. One would like to exchange one myth for the other, the akedah for the trial of Ishmael, but though they are structurally alike—indeed belong to a single homology—they are nevertheless not interchangeable. Ishmael remains Ishmael and Isaac, Isaac. And the role of the father in the latter's story cannot be replaced by that of the mother, however desirable such an exchange might be. The tone of lament that marks the passage is due not only to the absence of maternal comforts, but more particularly—and this is the point that should be insisted upon—to the absence of a myth that would make possible a poetics of maternal comfort. The poets of the Hebrew renaissance sought to establish a relation of easy accord with "Nature," as in the era of European romanticism. But in this poem of Lamdan's and others like it, there is a certain stridency, an intensity in the gesture of erotic communion with the mother that betrays the problematical nature of such communion. In the end, "Mother" turns out to be a dry and barren hillside who will deny her child the fulfillment that was Lamartine's at the lakeside or Goethe's when gazing at the moon or Wordsworth's when seeing the daffodils. The akedah of Isaac with its harsher laws inhibits such untroubled responses: "Here in thirst is Isaac swooning. / Abraham and Sarah's seed"—declares Lamdan.

One can, of course, ignore the akedah and seek a more naked, less "mediated" interrelationship between the land and its restored inhabitants using a simpler mother-son conjugation. This is the drift of several poems by Abraham Shlonsky, the "workers' poet" of a new socialist religion. The following extract from "Jezreel," belonging likewise to the twenties, is strongly reminiscent of the lines from Whitman's "Song of Myself" quoted earlier:

With shirt wide open, like the open temple gates,
With the toes of my feet I will caress the earth of morning.
Here will I stretch out supine, I will lie in mother's lap.
And all the rivers will come to me,
And every tree will strike its roots in me,
And the God of all the world will nestle close to me whispering with
    love—You! You![24]

We note the emphatically masculine character of the figure of the
pioneer or "halutz," who lies supine with shirt open while God approaches him amorously in an unmistakably female gesture. But
Shlonsky's language here betrays him. The verb "mitrapek," translated here "nestles close," is from Song of Songs 8.5, where it refers
not to God but to the Shulamite maiden "leaning on" her beloved.
(Shlonsky is also inevitably "leaning on" or "nestling close" to his
biblical source, for the modern Hebrew poet really has no alternative to the language and image system of the Bible.) But he has
produced an inverted geometry of relationships. No longer does
the "daughter of Zion" follow her male lover into the wilderness or
come out of the wilderness "leaning on" him. Instead, a female
deity "nestles up" to, or "leans on," her erring son/lover. This inverted situation gives to the male protagonist of Shlonsky's poem a
new sense of power.[25] He becomes a kind of Nietzschean superman,
like the pioneers of Whitman's ecstatic "Pioneers! O Pioneers."
Nevertheless, there is a certain uneasiness in the poem revealed by
the ambiguities surrounding the gender of the divine lover/be-
loved. While the *halutz* is lying "in mother's lap," the "God of all
the world" who whispers to him with love in the sixth line of the
extract is grammatically male, and so is the verb "mitrapek". The
poet proceeds to slur over the difficulty: he simply fuses the poetic
"I" with the divine lover together into a single mythic entity:

I will lift up my body in my palms
And beneath the mane of the thick tree
On a throne of green grass I will seat him—
Man-God!

The declamatory rhetoric of the poem serves to erase the awkwardness posed by its various inversions, but that awkwardness
cannot be totally erased. The first line of the passage just cited, "I
will lift up my body in my palms," inevitably (and consciously) recalls Lamentations 3.41—"We will lift up our heart in our palms *to
God in the heavens*"—and the echo of that termination cannot be

wholly suppressed. Like so many others of his generation, Shlonsky sets out to recall the biblical source in order to divert it to a new channel, a determinedly secular or chthonian channel, but the force of the original is too strong for him. Ultimately, it asserts itself in spite of the inversive syntax and the anacoluthon. The omitted words stand out with greater force owing to their very omission.

Other poets face up more directly to the sense of helplessness (and hopelessness) involved in the exegetical void just referred to. C. N. Bialik's poem "Levadi" ("I Alone," 1902) provides a pattern of relationships not entirely unlike that of the Shlonsky poem. Here we have not a *halutz* but a student suffering the stresses of the Enlightenment. His friends have been "swept away by the wind and the light"—the wind of emancipation and the light of rationalism, while he hides himself in the corner of the *Bet Hamidrash*, the House of Study, beneath "the wings of the *Shekhina*." The *Shekhina* —the female aspect of divinity in the rabbinic and kabbalistic literature—"leans on me" (*watitrapek*)—the same precise term from Song of Songs 8.5 as in Shlonsky's above-quoted poem. Her wing is broken, and, more than she protects the forlorn student, she seems to require his protection. The poet vainly seeks to comfort her as she buries her head on his shoulder and her "scalding tear" falls on the folio he is studying. One critic perceptively remarks that the *Shekhina* is sorrowing for the lost male deity, the *Kudsha Berikh Hu* of the kabbalists, without whose masculine authority the *Shekhina* could have no true independent existence.[26] This is the meaning of the "loneliness" referred to in the poem's title. It is the radical loneliness created by the absence of the father. Something similar marks the situation of the meditating subject in Bialik's longer poem "The Pool" referred to in chapter 1.[27] There too, as he gazes into the Pool, the poetic "I" feels himself sheltered by the rustling wing of the *Shekhina* (see line 139). It is within its depths—the psychic depths, we may say, of nature and instinct— that he seeks the ultimate treasure of life. The Pool is, among other things, the White Goddess, the Lady of the Lake; she belongs to the world of romance; she invites us into her dreamy depths, but the price of such absorption is loneliness, alienation, a separation from the "hidden God . . . savior of Israel" of Isaiah 45.15, that male deity whose voice—or rather, the echo of whose voice— breaks the silence of the Pool and the forest glade surrounding it.

It is not difficult to situate the love of Zion in this imagery of the

lonely Jew of modernity in the maternal embrace of Mother-Earth-
Shekhina-Lake. Nor should there be any doubt as to the extraordinary force of the attachment involved. It is, if anything, made more
powerful by the sense of loneliness that accompanies it. To put it
another way, Zion is more than just a mother: she commands the
extra devotion of a widowed mother. That is how she appears for
Matityahu Shoham, writing in 1936. He describes himself "returning" to Jerusalem on a first visit. Jerusalem, and by extension the
whole Land of Israel, is both bride and mother, and to her he returns in love and hope, seeking in her embrace a cure for his intolerable metaphysical loneliness. "O mother of mine, sick and bereft," cries Shoham,

> That you would recognize me, that you would spread over me your
>   mourning wing!
> Be joined fast to me—in the trembling clasp of a first love,
> And silently let us take our fill of embraces,
> And let us listen to the blessing breathed by deserted hills and
>   valleys.[28]

Shoham apologizes for arriving at the Holy City with a group of
camera-toting tourists. But "the mother who hears my heart beat
under my starched shirt" will understand. She will understand
him and receive him in her arms, for his is the true lover's return.
Shoham, we may note (like Bialik), lost his father in childhood.
Here we have the geographical transposition of the theme of or-
phanhood and widowhood, the alienated lonely son seeking spiritual solace in the widowed land from which the male director of
Jewish history is notably absent.

The mother who shelters the lonely son in her trembling or broken wing easily translates into a bride and mistress, thus giving
extra erotic force to the relationship. "Wedge me into the fissure
with each fallen stone. / Hammer me till I grow strong"—cries
Yehuda Karni. Yaakov Fichman, with equal passion and with the
same transparent imagery of the coupling of man with earth and
stones and trees, declares:

> By green of your earth I swear and by your sunlight.
> I inherit the desolation that remains.
> I stand like a tree in stone, by you held spellbound—
> Soul woven with soul, my root in your dry veins.[29]

The sexual image and that of wooing and marriage are fundamental to the poetry of the Return. The young "lovers of Zion," as they were called at the end of the nineteenth century, though often deceptively hard-bitten in appearance and using the idiom of dialectical materialism, were in fact the heroes of a courtly romance, knights come to seek in a journey to the Holy Land the favor of their mistress. And their mistress was no other than the Sleeping Beauty of the fairy tale to be awakened from her spell by the kiss of her destined spouse; she was the Lady of the Lake (one remembers "Rachel"'s poem "My Kinneret"), the imprisoned daughter of a king who is dead. For she too is orphaned and bereft.

Bereavement and love, in fact, go together. The pioneers are liable to find themselves after a night of love awakening on the cold hillside. Somehow, this does not happen in the more truly chthonian poetry of Whitman. His "pioneers" retain their ecstasy to the end of the day. Theirs too is an erotic passion, but it is less clouded by that metaphysical loneliness that we noted in Bialik or Matityahu Shoham. D. H. Lawrence speaks at the beginning of *The Rainbow* of the irresistible sway of the earth, which pulls like desire. It is fulfillment. The Hebrew writers of the very same period feel the irresistible sway of their earth, if anything, more strongly. Israel would lodge, as in Song of Songs 1.13, between the breasts of his beloved. But fulfillment was incomplete; there was a metaphysical loneliness at the heart of the whole enterprise. Typical is the title of Y. H. Brenner's novel of 1920—*Breakdown and Bereavement*. In it he identifies the unrest of his generation as a sex neurosis.[30] It is a deeper loneliness even than that felt by Lawrence's heroes that the men and women of Brenner's generation sought to assuage through contact with the soil of the homeland. Perhaps the loneliness is best caught by Yehuda Amichai in a love lyric nearer to our own day. In the refrain the beloved is addressed in the sad phrase, "Both of us together, and each of us alone." The phrase, taken from the form of legal contract, attaches to itself the pathos of lovers in the latter half of the twentieth century, finding only partial comfort in one another for their existential loneliness. But the key to their loneliness is provided in the haunting first stanza parodying a popular song:

> Another summer has past, my girl,
> The swings go round and round,
> But daddy has not come to the fair.[31]

Amir Gilboa, in a justly celebrated poem "Isaac," likewise darkly imagines the death of the father. It is a nightmare version of the akedah. Isaac and his father take a walk in the woods, "a knife flashes between the trees like lightning," and Isaac calls out to his father to come quickly and save him. But in an ironical reversal of roles, it is Abraham who is killed:

> It's I who am butchered, my son,
> my blood's already on the leaves.
> And father's voice was choked.
> And his face pale.[32]

The orphaned poet becomes an image for an orphaned generation, a fatherless world where all that is left is (as Blake might say) the shadowy emanation of divinity.

The loneliness we are speaking of, therefore, is one brought about through the disappearance of that Father who stands behind the individual father of the individual lonely orphan. (Significantly, in Amichai's novel *Not of This Time, Not of This Place*, 1963, the protagonist is attached to his ancestral faith only through his annual visit to the synagogue where he says *kaddish* for his dead father.) The Nietzschean death of God has bitten deeply into the souls of the writers whom we have been discussing, but it brings them no joy. In the sad emptiness left by his absence, the love-hungry seeker embraces the soil of the homeland, the abandoned widow and bride of Jewish history, the *Shekhina* with broken wing.

V

Why, it may be objected, should the "lover of Zion" in our time be stricken with metaphysical loneliness? Surely Israel as male lover and Zion as wife or bride is essentially biblical. And the biblical sources do not seem to exhibit the union as hiding within itself a root of despair. For Isaiah it is rather separation from Zion that brings despair; union brings delight:

> Thou shalt be called Hefzi-ba [My delight is in her]
> And thy Land Beulah [Espoused].
> For the Lord delights in thee, and thy land shall be espoused.
> For as a young man takes to himself a virgin,
> So shall thy sons take thee to themselves
> And as the bridegroom rejoices over the bride,
> So shall thy God rejoice over thee.

(Isa. 62.4–5)

With this passage in mind, Blake used the name Beulah for the state of fulfilled desire. Later in the same prophet, we have the same unabashed sexual language:

> Rejoice with Jerusalem, and be glad with her, all her lovers,
> Rejoice with her all those who had mourned with her,
> That you may suck and be satisfied with the breast of her
>   consolations. . . .
> As one whom his mother comforts,
> So will I comfort you;
> And you shall be comforted in Jerusalem.

(Isa. 66.10–11, 13)

We would be right in saying that here in these verses and in others like them (e.g., Zechariah 2.10 and Jeremiah 2.2) we have the authentic biblical source for the Zionist love poetry of Fichman, Karni, Shoham, Shlonsky, and many others. And yet there is no hint in those verses of what I have termed the despairing counter-theme. There is a menace in the continuation of the above passage, as the Lord comes in fire to execute judgment, but it is not a menace from within, a failure of nerve of the lover himself. His love remains firm and Zion remains Zion. What therefore has the modern poet missed?

What should be said is that we have here a fractured archetype. For in the biblical uses of the metaphor we have no simple bilateral relationship of Mother : Son or Earth : Pioneer—as in Shoham and Shlonsky. We have instead a covenantal structure involving three functioning partners: God, Land, and People. If we examine the first above-quoted passage from Isaiah, we see that the land is viewed as bride because the Lord (i.e., the male God) has said, "My delight is in her." She can be called "espoused"—*Beulah*—because God has espoused her. The people of Israel partake in this *hieros gamos*, this divine union, because God has admitted them to it. Israel's part in the drama is bisexual. In conjunction with Zion, Israel is the "baal," the lord and bridegroom; but in conjunction with God, Israel is the female partner, the bride. ("As the bridegroom rejoices over the bride, so shall thy God rejoice over thee.") The full experience of covenant involves both roles. It is Israel with whom God dwells; Israel is the sleeping beauty of Jewish history awaiting the kiss of her destined spouse. If the land performs the selfsame role, it is because the words "Zion" and "Jerusalem" are ambiguous—they refer both to people and to land! God in joining himself to Zion is in reality joining himself also to Israel.

This triangle of forces still had a controlling function in the medieval love lyrics of Zion, the "Zionides" of Judah Halevi, Ibn Gabirol, and many others. In one such poem, "The Dialogue of Zion and God" by the seventh-century liturgical poet Eleazar Ben Kallir, Zion is seen as a "mother of sons" complaining to her divine husband, who has abandoned her:

> The mother of sons moans like a dove; she mourns in her heart and complains out loud; she cries bitterly, calls out desperately; she sheds tears, she is silent and stunned.

> My husband has abandoned me and turned away, and has not remembered my love as a bride; he has scattered and dispersed me far from my land; he has let all my tormentors rejoice at my downfall.[33]

Clearly the "mother of sons" is Zion, the city and land, but as the poem proceeds she becomes identified with the "sons" themselves. For it is Israel that has been "scattered and dispersed," and "my love as a bride" takes us back to Jeremiah 2.2, where it is Israel's devotion to her divine lover in the desert that is recalled. In the last half of the poem God responds to Zion's complaint and ends with the words: "My perfect one, I shall not forsake you or forget you."

> My dark one, I shall never desert you; I shall reach out again and take you to myself. Your complaint has come to an end. My perfect one, I shall not forsake you or forget you.

This takes us back to Israel again, for it is Israel in Psalm 137 who vows not to forget Jerusalem—"If I forget thee, O Jerusalem, let my right hand forget her cunning." Likewise Israel enters into the other side of the relationship as the "perfect one" of Song of Songs 5.2. There is thus a dynamic of mutual relationships, a rich ambiguity arising out of Israel's double role of lover and beloved.

When we come to the modern lovers of Zion, beginning somewhere in the nineteenth century, this ambiguity has been suppressed, and with it an essential middle term of the covenant has been lost. Israel forgets her feminine role in the *hieros gamos*, preempting for herself an exclusive male privilege in lordship over the land of promise. This may seem to be no more than an exegetical lapse, a misreading of a literary tradition, but since we are talking about a poetic pattern that has a profound and direct bearing upon

history—indeed the history of our own time—an exegetical lapse
of this kind can be disastrous. When the triangular structure of relationships is abandoned, the union of man and earth may yield a
first, fine, careless rapture, but the danger is that eventually one
may find oneself embracing a stone.

The ultimate stage of disenchantment produced by this fractured archetype may be noted among some recent writers, such as
A. B. Yehoshua and Amos Oz, who take us beyond the poetry of the
Return. In them we may note an anti-Zionist reflex resembling
Philip Roth's revolt against the mother. As we noted earlier, mother
love becomes as unbearable ultimately as the dominion of the father in an earlier day and yields a parallel movement of revolt, for
the oedipal victim has matricidal fantasies. The new iconoclasm of
some present-day writers may be properly characterized as the
rebellion against the mother translated into national and terri-
torial terms. A. B. Yehoshua has nightmares in which his hero
allows a newly planted forest in the Jerusalem hills to burn to cin-
ders.[34] When the father has been banished, the unqualified authority
of the mother too becomes unbearable. Or, to employ our covenant
model, when the triangle of relationships of God : Land : People
gives way to a simple two-way affair of land and lover, both land and
lover will eventually lose their meaning, and finally nothingness
will threaten.

VI

The most tragic statement of metaphysical loneliness, as well as
the most determined confrontation with its cause and remedy, is to
be found in a work by Shin Shalom. He is a metaphysical poet, a
poet of the lonely self, of radical inwardness, but critics have not
always done justice to the tensions and struggles that take place
within his work and that are owed precisely to the strength and
tenacity with which he confronts the challenge of history.[35] Shalom
cannot hide from history in the depths of his selfhood, for in history the "I" does not meet the "Myself": it meets mighty and inexorable events over which it has no control.

In a long poem set in an autobiographical frame and bearing
the strange title of *On Ben Peleh* ("Strength, Son of Wonder," 1940),
Shalom struggles with the classical terms of the covenant—God,
Man, and Land—and with the fundamental terms of Jewish his-

tory—Exile and Return, Past and Future—and strives to wrest a meaning from them. The choice of his biblical title (adapted from the name of one of the rebels against Moses mentioned in Numbers 15.1) suggests that the poem will be marked by rebellion and restlessness but also that its ultimate posture will be one of wonder rather than frustration. There is a mystery at the depths of the "I," but there is equally a mystery at the depths of the people and of the land to which the people is moved to return.

> I knocked at your gates, O Jerusalem
> At midnight, at your Western Wall.
> Eyes stared at me from the Temple Mount.
> Were they God's or an Arab's eyes?
>
> I climbed dead stairs. Upon the wall
> Footsteps are swallowed in the path of the moon.
> Who is it paces at my heels atremble?
> Orphaned here the *Shekhina* mourns.
>
> (III.1)

The same figure of the mourning *Shekhina* whom Bialik had met in the corner of the Bet Hamidrash or near the Pool is here eerily transported to the Temple Mount, and the poet is struck with a sense of oddness and mystery. Is the place empty or is there someone else there? Who is that third who walks always beside him? The imagery of Song of Songs 2.9 is here present: "Behold he stands behind our Wall. He looks in at the windows, he peers through the lattice." But does God indeed peer out of the lattice? Sometimes Shalom is overcome with a sense of an overwhelming presence to whom he can respond and who responds to him in love. And at other times it seems to him that the return to his ancient origins is a return to the grave, to death itself. In the most horrifying episode of all, the narrator appears as a gravedigger on the Mount of Olives. He is burying the pioneers, the Talmud students, the prophets, those torn by holy joy. All the lovers and seekers of Zion are descending into the grave. And he too, the gravedigger, is maddened and doomed by the same frustrated search:

> With hidden scorn the passersby stare
> At my torn garments and my bedraggled beard.
> Once I had a beloved, her name was Zion.
> Endlessly I pursue her shadow through the streets.
>
> (IV.12)

He finally hides himself, like Elijah, in a cave, and a pious woman brings him his daily bread. Until, in his wanderings, he approaches the open window of a hospital and sees within the shrouded figure of a woman. It is the object of his search—"It is she"—the beloved who alone could have cured his intolerable loneliness. He stretches out his hand, supposing the dead figure to be the woman with whom in his travels he had vainly sought comfort and intimacy. But he finally identifies her with the ultimate object of all his tormented yearning, viz., Zion herself:

> Silently, I waited. Her ear was deaf.
> She lay as if asleep under the cover of the sheet.
> I lifted it gently. Naked she lay,
> And I passed my hand over her delicate skin.
>
> "Speak," I implored, "say but one word.
> For you are Zion, yet seem so murderous?
> My life burns away here, and I entreat."
> She gave me no answer, no movement, no stir.
>
> (IV.18)

The erotic gesture is still there, but love is dead. In the vision of the seemingly dead body of Zion, the speaker has reached the lowest point of hopelessness. From now on there will be a slow, difficult, and hesitant attempt to reconstruct the elements of dialogue so that God, Land, and People can function in some kind of mutuality. The remainder of the poem is conducted in a quieter, more thoughtful fashion.

> I shall yet rebuild you, and you shall be rebuilt, O Jersualem, my city.
> I shall yet join my shoulders to the toilers on the wall.
>
> (IV.21)

He moves about the country saddened but also impressed by the "pang of creation, the inhuman pain" of the workers in Jezreel. Joining them he is content to be "like a stone of the field at the edge of the path." And he hears the growth of the grain at the coming of spring. The earth is alive for him, and he feels himself knit to it in the bonds of love. And now, amid the toil and suffering, a child is born to one of the couples among the settlers. A dead land and a dead people is being redeemed as a future is glimpsed.

Here is the first major break in the hard, narrow existence of the speaker in the poem. The next major symbol introduced is that of the watchtower on which the narrator stands guard. On it is a searchlight looking out over a land at war. It is the time when the British mandate was drawing to an end. The tower brings to life in his imagination the watchman of the biblical prophecy who waits for morning and whose soul waits for God. And contemporary history cannot be excluded from this, for the watchtower looks far out to the sea over which the new immigrants come sailing. There is an insistent note of interrogation:

> Why does the heart yearn so for their path,
> And why does that whisper reach back to me?
> "We are your brothers, outcasts of Israel,
> Despised by man, pursued by God Almighty."
>
> (VI.4)

The tower is, as in Yeats, a symbol of the isolation of the poet, but it also signifies the possibility of communication from the prison of the self. Through its beam of light he reaches out to the great congregation of Israel, and at the same time the whisper of the God-hunted, God-driven host reaches up to him. Standing on the tower, moreover, he feels himself marvelously joined to the lord of history, "the lightbearer to the camp. . . . the Ingatherer." And having achieved that sense of communion with the male deity, he is enabled to catch the strange and yet familiar music of that other presence, "the *Shekhina* of the Homeland," as he now describes her, "looking out for her dreaming son" (VI.7). She is that One whom he had thought dead and whom he had vainly sought in the eyes of the world's women. This is the final epiphany, the recovered unity. But even at that moment of seeming clarification, confusion threatens; the crisis of identity is not over.

> What am I, my life, my people, my land?
> In my expanses infinity's horsemen run wild!
> Who battles with whom? It is I with myself!
> The sea with the waves, the there with the here.
>
> (VI.8)

With all his force he clutches once again at the "scarlet thread" of vision:

> I grasp at Being like a scarlet thread
> Whilst the shadow of negation threatens with its hand.
>
> (VI.8)

He ends with a prayer, one wrung out of the heart of modern secularism yet pointing us toward a conceivable future in which the "hidden God" of Isaiah 45.15 might still work his will:

> Great Magician of my depths, increase your forces!
> My heart was sharpened on the stone of despair,
> The torch I hold shall neither fall nor fade.
> Mine is the battle of the God hidden in life.
>
> I sought to bind infinity with my hands
> To hold it in a clod of earth, in the handful of native soil lying near.
> I sought to dress in garments like any man
> Whilst in my veins the scorching fire of wonder burned.
>
> Come to me, stand with me! From far horizons
> Let the light be brought to pierce the darkness.
> My brother, O my brother of the distant generations,
> To you I cry out from the bosom of the dark.
>
> (VI.8)

7

Wastelands and Oceans

THE "VOLUPTUOUS COOLBREATHED EARTH" of Whitman is, as noted above, the archetypal bride and mother. But there are other spatial metaphors that share this function. Even more than the earth, the ocean is the ultimate mother. She provides not only a myth of origins but for many peoples she is the origin of myths. In the ancient Middle East, the primeval ocean is Tiamat (*Tehom*—the "abyss" of Genesis 1.2), regarded by the Babylonians as the primeval female principle out of whose body the world and mankind are made. For Homer, Oceanus is *theon genesis* (*Iliad* 14.201), the origin of the gods. Troy and Venice both emerge from the waves of the sea; Aphrodite rises from the foam of the sea; Andromeda is seen chained to a rock, and her husband, Perseus, is likewise set afloat as a child upon the waves. In this latter example the mythical wanderer is primarily a sea voyager. This seems to hold for the wandering heroes of antiquity and later times also. Arnold's "Scholar Gipsy," of course, haunts the Oxford countryside, which is about as far from the sea as one can get in the British Isles, but the poem ends with him transformed into a "Tyrian trader," in a majestic Homeric simile of voyaging through the Mediterranean to the West:

> And snatched his rudder and shook out more sail;
> And day and night held on indignantly

O'er the blue Midland waters with the gale,
Betwixt the Syrtes and soft Sicily,
To where the Atlantic raves
Outside the Western straits. . . .

Among modern writers, Saint-John Perse, a Whitmanesque French poet, has caught this special quality of the sea with great power. (In French, *la mer* and *la mère* seem to chime particularly well.) The sea is for him not so much a mythical as a premythical presence. In *Amers* (1948), the primordial sea becomes his basic reality, which engulfs all other meanings in its depths. The sea is l'Amante—the archetypal feminine, the mystical conjunction of all that envelops us, gives us being, and beckons us to herself. "Woman" as Pierre Emmanuel very properly remarks in his comments on this poem, "is indivisible from the sea."[1] For the sea is not merely the ultimate female on whose breast we cast ourselves "betwixt the Syrtes and soft Sicily"—she is also the "exultation of fecund life," not merely fertile but the absolute source of fertility, the womb of all swarming and spawning things.

In many languages and cultures deserts seem to have a similar character, so that deserts and oceans tend to become mirror reflections of one another. The camel is spoken of as "the ship of the desert," oases are islands, and the waves of sand are for the desert voyager as impersonal and engulfing as the waves of the ocean themselves. Saint-John Perse himself testifies to this parallelism. In *Anabase* (1924), his long poem of voyaging and world conquest in Asia, the desert seems often to be just that—a reflection of the ocean. What impresses him is the timelessness of the great expanse of desert and steppe, its wonder, its vastness. It is "sans mémoire, l'année sans liens et sans anniversaires." Above all, the desert, like the ocean, releases in him the totality of the experience of sensual love. It is "la terre vaste à mon désir."[2]

However, if the literary evidence is sifted, we shall see that ocean and desert function more often as type and antitype. The biblical desert (and for the Western imagination the desert is primarily a Bible location) is time-laden; it is a place of memory and vision and also a place of lonely trials, privations, and revelations. Another modern French writer, Edmond Jabès, has made this point with great emphasis: "Avec une régularité exemplaire, le juif reprend sa marche volontaire vers le désert; va au-devant d'une parole renouvelée devenue son origine. . . . Qu'est-ce que le désert sinon ce passé dessous, antérieur à notre propre passé; comme aussi notre avenir solidaire?"[3] In the desert we come face to face with the Word, with time past and to come. If for Perse désir-désert is a fundamental paronomasia, for Jabès, following the rabbis, desert (*midbar*) and Word (*dabhar-dibbur*) are the fundamental paronomasia.[4] The desert is the place of revelational encounters, in particular that encounter at Sinai from which Israel traced its historical beginnings as a people. Aphrodite rises from the foam of the sea, but Israel is seen "coming up out of the wilderness, leaning on her beloved." The two situations may seem alike, but Israel, unlike the goddess of love, is the bearer of an historical burden, a commandment. This special sense of place has been caught in words that have been made so familiar by Handel as to constitute almost an archetypal image in themselves: "A voice cries in the wilderness, Prepare ye the way of the Lord, Make straight in the desert a highway for our God" (Isa. 40.3). Here it is not the enveloping ambience of the vast spaces that is invoked. The desert is much rather that place in which we are terribly challenged, exposed, singled out in our individuality. A voice cries out and we are bound to hear; there is nothing to shield us from the word that is there spoken. Adam can hide in the Garden; modern men can hide themselves in their cities amid the "lonely crowd." But there is nowhere in the desert to hide. That seems to be of its essence.

Desert and ocean thus, while seeming alike, are really the spatial aspects of two opposing myths. There is one short book of the Bible, the book of Jonah, where in fact the two myths are set side by side, and the hero is, in a manner, required to choose between them. Jonah is given a command to journey to Nineveh and pronounce a doom upon the city. He seeks to escape his responsibility by taking a ship and putting out to sea. Oddly enough, when the storm comes, Jonah feels comfortable amid the waves and billows and goes down to sleep in the lower parts of the ship. When the mariners ask him what they can do to still the storm, he suggests that they throw him into the depths, where he is swallowed by a fish. The mythological significance of this has often been noted, not least by C. G. Jung himself, who spoke of the "Jonah-and-the-Whale-complex,"[5] which involves the wish to regress into a womblike state, to avoid the "father" and the responsibility he implies, and to disappear into the "ocean" of instinctual life. This interpretation of the episode has been developed in detail by two modern commentators, who point out that Jonah's "descent" into the belly of the ship and his further "descent" into the belly of the fish, where *tehom* (the abyss) is said to be all around him (2.5), is of a piece with all the ancient stories that involve the hero's descent into the netherworld to overcome the forces of chaos. And behind all such stories is the suggestion of the ocean or netherworld as the "primordial milieu where life begins." "Moreover the fish with its connotations of life and fecundity adds to the analogy in representing the motherly womb and takes on a significance that is rooted in the mysterious origins of life. Thrown into the ocean by the sailors, Jonah returns to the very source of his existence."[6]

But the story of Jonah, more than it reenacts this primordial myth, beholds it critically, balances it, and, in an important sense, controverts it. For in chapter 4 of the book, we are given an alternative story of danger and escape from danger. Jonah is cast up now on the dry land, admonished and taught by experience that his prophetic call may not be avoided by way of "regression" into the state of "nature." He sets out on his long overland journey to the city of Nineveh. And there, while he awaits the results of his mission to that city, another scene is enacted. Instead of a ship, Jonah takes shelter now (4.5) in a *sukka* (booth) to shade himself from the heat of the burning sun. The association with the booths in which the Israelites sheltered during their desert pilgrimage after the Exodus from Egypt (Lev. 23.42–43) is patent. The *sukka* here as there symbolizes extreme vulnerability but also miraculous protection. "Can God spread a table in the wilderness?" asks the Psalmist (Ps. 78.19). The verse echoes in Defoe's *Robinson Crusoe* during Robinson's spiritual crisis, brought about by his sickness and the earthquake that precedes it. We may claim Defoe's novel as another Jonah story, a pilgrimage of the covenant type.[7] Robinson is fearfully tried, like Jonah. Moreover here too we have the *sukka*-motif, the hero building himself a house in the desert and, while sheltering in it, alternately complaining of the severity of his ordeal and giving thanks for his marvelous deliverance. His corn grows miraculously, like Jonah's gourd.

Thus, against the "Jonah-and-the-Whale complex," we have "Jonah-and-the-*sukka*" and "Jonah-and-the-gourd." The gourd (*qiqayon*), which grows miraculously overnight and withers just as

rapidly the following day (4.6–7), symbolizes likewise the polarities of the desert experience, with its unbelievable manifestations
of grace and its unendurable hardships. For the desert is, above all,
a place of trial, the trials associated with history and the tensions
of history. In the story, *sukka* and *qiqayon* are syntagmatically related to Jonah's prophetic mission to Nineveh, with Jonah in his
capacity as the instrument of *Heilsgeschichte*. The storm and stress
of history, its potentiality for unexpected advances and reverses,
are beautifully caught by this image of the frail hut in the wilderness and the worm that blasts the sheltering gourd followed by the
hot east wind. Jonah submits (albeit with some reluctance) to
the desert option. He is, we may say, presented with two parallel
but opposing myths (the same verb *vayeman*—"and He appointed"
—used both of the fish and the gourd, indicates the parallelism),
and he is called upon to choose between them. But it is difficult to
choose, and Jonah shows no great enthusiasm for his exposed condition at the end of the story. Nor are we told what further trials
may be in store for him. The book ends on a note of divine interrogation, with Jonah discomfited. Unlike Robinson Crusoe, he will
evidently not end in prosperity. The biblical lack of closure is in
contrast here with the comforts at the end of the road provided by
the Puritan middle-class imagination of Defoe. Jonah will have to
accept the problematical kind of hope represented by the booth
and the gourd as the condition of that covenant destiny in which he
is involved.

II

It is worth looking a little more closely at the desert as presented in
the biblical texts. Often it loses its identity as a spatial metaphor
and seems to function more exclusively as an historical archetype.
It stirs memory and desire, especially the memory of the great desert crossing at the time of the Exodus:

> He found him in a desert land, and in the waste howling wilderness;
> he led him about, he instructed him, he kept him as the apple of his
> eye. (Deut. 32.10)

It will be seen from this passage that the desert scene is dialectical
in character. While it is associated with punishment and ruin (a
"howling wilderness"), it is also the focus of our most exalted mem-

ories. It is a place of intimacy and wonder. He kept Israel there as "the apple of his eye." In spite of its emptiness and desolation, there is in the desert a kind of excitement always in the air. It is not only where something great has once happened, but it is where something of great moment is always potentially about to happen. Milton too had a sense of this. In *Paradise Regained*, he seizes on the notion of Christian hope and salvation under the rubric of a trial in the desert, basing himself on the gospel of Luke. The desert purges but also exalts. From it salvation comes through trial and suffering.

For the Hebrew prophets, the desert is where we have the clearest vision of beginnings and endings. This gives it its fundamentally historical orientation. We traverse the desert not only to move from point to point in space, but to make a voyage through time, in fact through the time of salvation history. It takes us back and it brings us forward. It brings into the present something of the polarities of the exodus event, its dialectical combination of suffering and wonder. We noted this combination in the poem of Shin Shalom discussed in the previous chapter. We may add now that it is the peculiar property of the desert scene in the Bible. Hosea threatens the self-satisfied and idolatrous inhabitants of Samaria that they will be exiled and reduced to the condition of tent dwellers in the desert as they were at the time of the exodus from Egypt (Hos. 12.9). In one way this is a threat, but it is also a promise, for there in the desert the God of Sinai will renew his love affair with his people: "Therefore, behold I will allure her, and bring her into the wilderness, and speak comfortably unto her" (2 : 14). We return to the desert in order to call to mind the memory of youth and love: "Thus says the Lord, I remember the devotion of your youth, your love as a bride, how you followed me in the wilderness, in a land not sown" (Jer. 2.2, RSV).

Here in the desert, then, is a peculiarly Hebrew landscape: to forget the desert scene is to forget the ground of one's true identity: "Neither said they, Where is the Lord that brought us up out of the Land of Egypt, that led us through the wilderness, through a land of deserts and pits, through a land of drought, and the shadow of death, through a land that no man passed through, and where no man dwelt?" (Jer. 2.6).

Modern writers have responded to many aspects of this biblical desert archetype, but they have rarely if ever exhibited it as a whole. Even T. E. Lawrence, who was drawn to the desert powerfully both as scene and symbol, does not give us much in the way of prophetic hope. The desert addresses itself chiefly to his morbid side: "The essence of the desert was the lonely moving individual, the son of the road, apart from the world as in the grave."[8] T. S. Eliot finds grave moral meanings in the desert in some of the choruses from "The Rock." In *Ash Wednesday* (1930) it is occasionally seen as the way to the Promised Land:

> Under a juniper-tree the bones sang, scattered and shining
> We are glad to be scattered, we did little good to each other,
> Under a tree in the cool of the day, with the blessing of sand,
> Forgetting themselves and each other, united
> In the quiet of the desert. This is the land which ye
> Shall divide by lot. . . .[9]

The scattered bones of Ezekiel's vision undergo here "the blessing of sand" and seem to be destined for a kind of resurrection. But the tone of the poem is more often than not one of renunciation: if there is a revival it is a problematical one, one that will leave the world as we know it relatively unchanged.

But the most intense exploration of the desert archetype in modern literature is in Eliot's earlier poem, *The Waste Land* (1922). Of course, it is the negative side that is chiefly exhibited. As the title of the poem indicates, the desert is above all things a *wasteland*, not a trysting place or a scene of hope reborn. As in *Ash Wednesday* later on, here too he echoes Ezekiel's vision of the Valley of Dry Bones. The prophet had been asked: "Son of man, Can these bones live?" and had then witnessed the miracle of their rebirth. *Ash Wednesday* was to recall the question and answer it with a qualified yes. But here in *The Waste Land*, the echoing is ironical, for there is no hope of anything growing "out of this stony rubbish":

> What are the roots that clutch, what branches grow
> Out of this stony rubbish? Son of man,
> You cannot say, or guess, for you know only
> A heap of broken images, where the sun beats,
> And the dead tree gives no shelter, the cricket no relief,
> And the dry stone no sound of water. Only
> There is shadow under this red rock,
> (Come in under the shadow of this red rock),
> And I will show you something different from either
> Your shadow at morning striding behind you
> Or your shadow at evening rising to meet you;
> I will show you fear in a handful of dust.

The biblical echoes in *The Waste Land* are more pervasive and detailed than is generally thought. The above passage recalls not only Ezekiel's prophecy but Isaiah's vision of the suffering servant "who grew up like a root out of the dry ground" (53.2). And in lines 8 and 12 the passage reminds us of the same prophet's warning to the wicked of the house of Jacob: "Enter into the rock and hide in the dust from the terror of the Lord" (2.10). The poem gives us a fundamentally biblical assembly of stage properties: rock, sand, bones, fire, water, and the absence of water. There is a biblical resonance about the "wasteland" itself: both the term and the landscape that it signifies are everywhere in the Bible. Ruth Nevo has correctly noted that "the wasteland is the main, the central, the key symbol in the prophetic books; there is scarcely a page of the major prophets, from Amos the shepherd and sycamore-picker of Samaria, to the Deutero-Isaiah in Babylon on the eve of the Return, on which wasteland imagery does not appear." And she goes on to insist that the series of biblical symbols centering on the wasteland "are to be found equally and in a corresponding sequence, in Eliot's poem."[10] Not only does this apply to the landscape of desolation, but we may note that the very characters of the poem and their doings have often a closer association with the biblical wastelands than is generally recognized. Eliot himself has obscured this by directing attention elsewhere. It should be noted therefore that the vision of the land that is to be made desolate and the cities laid waste in the Old Testament prophecies has special reference to (a) faithless women, (b) futile or helpless kings, and (c) sorcery or soothsaying. There is no point at this time of day in going over the familiar ground of the myth of the Fisher King, of Madame Sosostris, famous clairvoyante, or of the casual fornications that form the matter of "The Fire Sermon." Let it be said simply that the biblical resonance here is probably as important as the Grail legend. The central landscape of desolation, moral and physical, is essentially part of that type-scene regularly conjured up by the prophets when imagining the destruction that awaits a sinful people: "He is gone from his place to make the land desolate, and thy cities shall be laid waste without an inhabitant" (Jer. 4.7).

III

However, caution is needed. One student of this poem has argued that "Eliot is among the prophets."[11] What one would want to say is that the density of the biblical imagery actually lights up the fundamental departures from the prophetic model. Those who wish to read the last section of Eliot's poem, "What the Thunder Said," as a vision of revival have to consider the fact that while it echoes chapter 31 of Jeremiah in its reference to Rachel weeping for her children ("murmur of maternal lamentation"), it does not embody the vision of the returning exiles "walking by the rivers of waters" and "singing in the height of Zion" from that same chapter. To the contrary, the speaker at the end (the Fisher King?) is seen "upon the shore / Fishing, with the arid plain behind me." The note of disenchantment remains. As we have already noted, the echoing of Ezekiel in "The Burial of the Dead" is in essence ironical:

> What are the roots that clutch, what branches grow
> Out of this stony rubbish? Son of man,
> You cannot say or guess, for you know only
> A heap of broken images. . . .

The dry bones do not come to life as they do in Ezekiel's vision. The Hebrew prophets had a sense of striving toward a future and of the miraculous possibilities that future might bring with it; in the midst of the wasteland there is a hope of historical fulfillment. This Eliot finds it difficult to affirm. It is easier to adapt oneself to the archetypal wastelands of the Grail legend (the Grail, we may remember, is a female fertility symbol). This is the mythological pattern that Eliot had absorbed from Jessie Weston's book and other sources. Here the questing hero is called upon to perform rituals of propitiation, which will have the effect of healing the waters and restoring fertility to the land. The pattern, based on the annual cycle of the year, the burgeoning of spring after the death of nature in the winter (or, in middle-eastern countries, the annual rains that fall in Tishri after the desolating summer heat of Tammuz), looks toward the goddesses of the Earth, the Great Mother. Primitive men were able to feel themselves united with this cycle of nature, their natural rhythm keeping time to the rhythm of the seasons of the year. Sir Galahad or Sir Perceval functions essentially in such a world, oriented not to History but to Nature.

The truth is that the two sets of imagery, the biblical and the pagan, are set off against one another with a measure of dialectical tension between them that prohibits the embracing of either in its totality. Madame Sosostris is "the wisest woman in Europe" when viewed as a purveyor of those mysteries intimated by the Tarotpack; she is a symbol of corruption when viewed as one of the soothsayers excoriated in Isaiah 2.6—hence the "wicked pack of cards"—for she bids us look for the cause of our troubles in our stars rather than in ourselves. The two systems do not merge. If Eliot treats the biblical myth ironically, then it is also true to say that the fertility religions have become problematical in the extreme. Modern man, cut off from the sources of Nature, exposed as never before to the storms of History, is left with a heap of broken images.

Eliot's real problem is not ocean versus desert, even though that pattern exists in the poem (we remember the drowned Phoenician sailor on whom the death imagery of the poem is focused), nor is it even a question of the pagan versus the biblical, although that pattern too is central, as we have just seen. The real issue is time versus timelessness, historical consciousness versus a poetics of transcendence, in which the tensions of history are ignored or sidestepped. From this point of view Eliot's work is profoundly ambiguous. In one way, he is the most history-conscious of modern poets. For him past times constantly echo in the memory. Our lives are the result of historical process, of tradition. He is deeply sensitive to the special atmosphere of the time he lived in. *The Waste Land*, for this reason, has become a crucial statement of the modern condition. And yet the poem ostentatiously resists these implications. Far from reflecting and seeking to resolve a particular historical crisis, it urges upon us a vision of a mythologically governed universe, one governed by "the law of the eternal return." In the *Four Quartets* (1943), he was to make a theoretical statement of this. "History," he declares, "is a pattern of timeless moments." We seek the "still point of the turning world," where historical time is somehow abolished and only a pattern of stillness remains:

> At the still point of the turning world. Neither flesh nor fleshless;
> Neither from nor towards; at the still point, there the dance is,
> But neither arrest nor movement. And do not call it fixity,
> Where past and future are gathered. Neither movement from nor
>   towards,
> Neither ascent nor decline.

The repetitions in this passage enact the notion of a circling dance movement. The aim is to find the dialectical balance between movement and stasis both in poetry and in life (for the *Four Quar-*

tets is exercised with the art of poetry itself): "at the still point, there the dance is."

Such a nondynamic approach to time and art is certainly to be found in *The Waste Land*. We are encouraged by the author himself (especially in the notes appended to the poem) to discover in it a universally valid design, a timeless universe such as that surveyed by Tiresias, who had foresuffered all and is simultaneously present in ancient Thebes and in modern London with the typist and her lover. In this unlocalized landscape, the Grail legend, Dante's *Inferno*, Buddha's Fire Sermon, and the Hindu scriptures all converge. We are, it would seem, as in the *Four Quartets*, at a place "where past and future are gathered." It is that area of the mythical imagination beloved of Eliot's friend Ezra Pound, and we may assume that it was under his influence that the poem received this decided emphasis. Philip Rahv has rightly pointed to the tendency of Pound's *Cantos* to reduce the ancient, medieval, and modern world to "an unhistorical miscellany." "The historical imagination," he says, "is transformed into a mythical imagination for which historical time does not exist."[12]

And yet, while Eliot likewise seeks to raise his conception to the nonhistorical, mythical level of pure aesthetic consciousness, we may rightly question, with Rahv, whether Eliot really is, at bottom, so very antihistorical. For in the end, the dominant tone is surely not that of stasis or harmony but of anxiety and alienation. The horrors he experiences are not in the end to be assuaged by mythology, however accurately drawn from Sir James Frazer or Jessie L. Weston. The world, it seems, is too much with us. "The present decay of eastern Europe" to which Eliot alludes in his notes to the final section of the poem, is not likely to be cured by the ritual gestures associated with the journey to the Chapel Perilous.

> In this decayed hole among the mountains
> In the faint moonlight, the grass is singing
> Over the tumbled graves, about the chapel
> There is the empty chapel, only the wind's home.
> It has no windows, and the door swings,
> Dry bones can harm no one.

The details of the sinister abode in which the questing hero is required to spend the night are supplied by the Grail legends. But here it seems that these details operate as a poetic metalanguage for defining the present status of the Grail images themselves. They are no longer as vital as they were: they are decayed, dry, and empty. Here in the scene of emptiness and ruin we have a series of phrases that carry with them a sense of the limitations of mythology itself: "There is the empty chapel, only the wind's home." No longer shall we find a rich poetic meaning in the Chapel Perilous; no longer will it provide us with a path of initiation into the mysteries that guarantee fertility either in life or art. It is somehow too late in the day for Sir Perceval and his quest. We are up to our necks in history.

IV

From this point of view, we may consider a rather obvious aspect of *The Waste Land* but one that has been little discussed. I refer to the evocations of the First World War and its aftermath, especially in the first section of the poem entitled "The Burial of the Dead."

> Unreal City,
> Under the brown fog of a winter dawn,
> A crowd flowed over London Bridge, so many,
> I had not thought death had undone so many. . . .
> There I saw one I knew, and stopped him, crying: 'Stetson!
> 'You who were with me in the ships at Mylae!
> 'That corpse you planted last year in your garden,
> 'Has it begun to sprout? . . .

The reference to the Punic Wars ("the ships at Mylae") rather than to Jutland or Gallipoli and the references to the third Canto of the *Inferno*, where Dante meets the lost souls at the entrance of Hell ("I should ne'er / Have thought that death so many had despoil'd"), as well as echoes of Baudelaire and Webster to which the author directs us in the notes, operate as a smokescreen. They have prompted Cleanth Brooks to remark that "All the wars are one war; all experience, one experience."[13] But is that true? Does our twentieth-century experience confirm the notion that "all the wars are one war," that there is nothing uniquely terrible about our modern wars beginning with that of 1914–18? And more to the point: does the poem in the end require us to transcend history in this fashion, or does it not rather dwell obsessively on the dreadful disenchantment of the years that followed the first of the great modern holocausts? The above-quoted passage indeed seems to rest on a very particular memory of the First World War. Bertrand Russell recalls a typical scene: "After seeing troop trains departing from Waterloo, I used to have strange visions of London as a place of unreality. I used in imagination to see the bridges collapse and sink, and the whole great city vanish like a morning mist. Its inhabitants began to seem like hallucinations." He adds: "I spoke of this to T. S. Eliot, who put it into *The Waste Land*." [14] The same phenomenon described by Russell is recalled later in the fifth section of Eliot's poem:

> What is the city over the mountains
> Cracks and reforms and bursts in the violet air
> Falling towers
> Jerusalem Athens Alexandria
> Vienna London.
> Unreal

The poem, it may be claimed, is in a deep sense mimetic. It catches not the generalized "Inferno" of some transhistorical literary archetype, but the agony of a particular inferno, a unique vision, that of a war in which the scope and manner of the destruction were without precedent. Eliot had a sense of this. [15] He had given six extension lectures at Oxford in 1916, and the last of these had been concerned with "the Influence of the War." In a later poetic statement (prompted, in fact, by the Second World War), he states: "War is not a life: it is a situation, / One which may neither be ignored nor accepted." [16]

Other holocausts have been perpetrated in this terrible century of ours, and perhaps as a result of this, we have tended to forget the special apocalyptic horror of World War I, a war that destroyed an entire European generation, that scarred the very earth itself over a vast territory between the North Sea and the Alps, leaving it a wilderness of desolation and decay. Verdun, the Somme, Ypres, the Pripet Marshes—these with their millions of dead were the fundamental images with which the literature of the postwar era had somehow to come to terms. It is, says Eliot in the continuation of the lines just quoted, "A problem to be met with ambush and stratagem, / Enveloped or scattered." *The Waste Land*, with its "broken images," with its evocation of the first spring flowers "breeding out of the dead land," with its conversation in the pub about the demobilized soldier coming back to a dingy home and a prematurely aged wife, is such a stratagem.

V

Thus, while we do well to point out the classical and biblical origins of the wasteland or desert archetype (I take the wasteland to be the negative face of the desert), and to be aware also of its provenance in the medieval legend of the Grail quest, it should be insisted that here again, as in the earlier archetypes we have discussed, we have a modern structure of the imagination. Like the Faust legend, the akedah, the dybbuk, and the Wandering Jew, the wasteland too may be traced back to premodern sources, but it reaches its apogee in the nineteenth century, when it serves as a way of dealing with the crisis of that age, and it reaches its dreadful consummation in our own time, when we awaken from the nightmare to find it truth. Here we have again a crucial example of that intersection between history and literary myth that is the subject of this book. In a way, it is also the subject of Eliot's *The Waste Land*.

Eliot had originally chosen the last words of Kurtz from Conrad's *Heart of Darkness* as the epigraph to his poem.[17] There, Kurtz, "lying in the dark waiting for death," has a final vision, which he sums up in the words "The horror! The horror!" This text is particularly relevant to our subject. Conrad's book, coming at the beginning of our century, gives us an image of evil spatialized into a landscape of nightmare. Its theme is the collapse of the moral values of the West, but this interior collapse is given symbolic force in the dreadful scenes that confront Marlow as he makes his voyage up-river. Death is the ultimate reality dominating the scene. Mister Kurtz, deposited with little ceremony into a muddy hole on the banks of the Congo, is the prototype of the millions of dead of 1914–18 who had, in dying, uncovered "The Horror" within themselves and within the world they knew. Though Eliot (at the suggestion of Ezra Pound) finally rejected this text in favor of a passage from the *Satyricon* of Petronius, which gives us a less historically determined vision of death and horror, Conrad remains a presence in the poem.

Another text that Eliot had in mind as a prefiguration of our contemporary urban wasteland was Dickens's late novel *Our Mutual Friend* (1864–65). (From it he had originally drawn the title for the first two sections of the poem.) In that novel we have constantly before us the image of "a suburban Sahara, where tiles and bricks were burnt, bones were boiled, carpets were beat, rubbish was shot, dogs were fought, and dust was heaped by contractors" (Book I, chap. 1). The warehouses and offices of the city have an air of death, and the whole drab landscape is dominated by the great heaps of dust, which provide the central visual image of the book. "Coal-dust, vegetable dust, bone-dust, crockery dust, rough dust, and sifted dust—all manner of dust" (chap. 4). We are reminded of the verse that says: "All are dust, and all turn to the dust again." All is vanity and hopelessness. Such sights were to be seen in Dickens's London for those who had eyes for them, and yet Dickens is writing for an age that knew no wars of any magnitude and that prided itself on its technological progress and architectural magnificence. *Our Mutual Friend* and *Bleak House* are, from this point of view, deliberately inversive novels giving us a nightmare vision, a dark simulacrum of reality as normally received by a hopeful generation.

There are other such dark intimations throughout the literature of the nineteenth century. Behind the façade of elegance of upper-class British society, Trollope in *He Knew He was Right* (1868–69), likewise reveals an image of squalor and madness. Louis Trevelyan is rather like the Fisher King himself. Dying in the isolated Italian country dwelling of Casalunga, he discovers a world suited to his mental and physical condition.

> The soil was parched and dusty, as though no drop of rain had fallen for months. The lizards, glancing in and out of the broken walls, added to the appearance of heat. The vegetation itself was of a faded yellowish green, as though the glare of the sun had taken the fresh colour out of it. There was a noise of grasshoppers and a hum of flies in the air, hardly audible, but all giving evidence of the heat. Not a human voice was to be heard, nor the sound of a human foot, and there was no shelter; but the sun blazed down full upon everything. (Chap. 92)

What in Trollope was an image of individual degeneration, the mental and physical collapse of the hero of his story of jealousy, becomes for Eliot the key to an epic vision of a whole civilization. The world as we know it becomes a kind of Casalunga,

> where the sun beats,
> And the dead tree gives no shelter, the cricket no relief,
> and the dry stone no sound of water.

According to George Steiner, "the vision of the city laid waste" so prevalent in literature and painting from 1830 onwards, is a European "counter-dream," the obverse of romantic pastoralism.[18] From Balzac and Charlotte Brontë to Emile Zola and James Thomson, we have increasing evidence of this counterdream, which gains force almost in precise ratio to the growth of confidence in the new science and industry. We have here an antimessianic nightmare to match a messianic dream of progress.

As time goes on it becomes grimmer and darker. Zalman Shneour, a Hebrew poet writing in Paris in 1913, predicts European civilization's descent into war and chaos. An enraged medieval monster emerges from the ruins of the world to hatch an egg bigger than the earth itself. We cannot tell when and where the calamity will come, but wherever we turn, it will eventually overtake us, "For the dark ages draw near."[19] The same notion (conveyed in almost exactly the same imagery) is expressed a few years later by W. B. Yeats in "The Second Coming" (1921). He too sees a desert landscape, and, traversing it, a monstrous apparition:

> A shape with lion body and the head of a man,
> A gaze blank and pitiless as the sun,
> Is moving its slow thighs, while all about it
> Reel shadows of the indignant desert birds. . . .
> And what rough beast, its hour come round at last,
> Slouches towards Bethlehem to be born?

It is the vision of a dark apocalypse, of a messianic age in reverse.

Yeats knew nothing of Shneour, but the "rough beast" of Yeats, slouching across the desert to be born, and the "dragon of the dark ages" of Shneour, basking like a reptile in the sun and reviving "after ten jubilees of slumber," are clearly of the same species. The two images intersect at the midpoint between 1913 and 1921, revealing a relation of reciprocity between the World and the Word that literary critics are generally loath to acknowledge.

How shall we understand such reciprocity? It is not only that poetry bears witness after the event; it also seems to warn and prophesy. It predates the events. The wasteland lives in the imagination of poets but not as a static mental content indifferent to time and history. It waits its hour, gaining in urgency and expectancy, becoming more insistent as the crisis approaches. From this point of view it may be suggested that in Yeats the "rough beast" refers not only to apocalypse but also to the literature of apocalypse. "Its hour come round at last" suggests that the signs, the language for dealing with this radical situation, have now come into their own. The poem of Yeats is about the dynamics of literature and history, about the way in which literature anticipates and responds to events. The word lives within us, but it seeks a union with the world. From twenty centuries of stony sleep, the image of the wasteland is finally vexed into wakeful existence "by a rocking cradle." This is the "second coming" of which the poem speaks, the rebirth of images made real by the harsh exigencies of history.

A whole anthology could be prepared of poems that anticipate the First World War, that bear witness to the imminent stirring of the long-sleeping monster. In Germany, Georg Heym wrote a poem in 1911 entitled simply "Der Krieg." In it he too visualized a monster arising:

> He that slept long has risen, risen from the deep vaults far below. He stands in the dusk, huge and unknown, and crushes the moon to pulp in black hands.

And further down in the same poem, we have the inevitable imagery of the wasteland, as Heym accurately describes for us, in advance, the landscape of hysteria over which the god of war presides:

> A great city sank into yellow smoke, hurled itself without a sound into the belly of the abyss. But vast he stands above the glowing ruins and brandishes his torch three times into the wild heavens above the reflected glow of storm-torn clouds, into the cold deserts of dead darkness, to dry up the night afar with the conflagration, and he pours fire and brimstone down upon Gomorrha.[20]

Paul Fussell has drawn our attention to Hardy's collection of *Satires of Circumstance* (1911, 1914), which in tone and mood anticipate, one might even say predetermine, much of the poetry of the war.[21] Siegfried Sassoon saw in Hardy the chief model for his satirical and bitter war poetry. Strangely, Hardy's collection is full of cemeteries, graves, and even battles. One poem entitled "Channel Firing," written in April 1914, pictures the dead stirring in their graves at the sound of gunnery practice at sea. "We thought it was the Judgment-Day / And sat upright." It turns out to be not yet Judgment-Day, but there is madness in the air: "All nations striving strong to make / Red war yet redder." One cannot imagine a poetic language more sharply focused on events—in this case, coming events. The word and the world intersect at all points; poetry will fit itself to coming events, serving to give them shape and meaning, and then in turn, when they have occurred, the poet will memorialize them, trying through language to come to terms with them. In both cases the poem is an act of remembering; and perhaps poetry has no higher function. Such memorializing we may claim as the very ground of poetic communication, for the reader is deeply involved in poetry of this kind. The reader too has known these things. In his dreams or with his waking senses, he has felt the monster stirring. It is the poet who articulates that reality for him, who makes it possible for him to know and recognize, who provides him with the indispensable verbal signs needed to make sense of the past and the future.

VI

Judging from the examples just noted, we would look in vain at this time of day for a fuller and more positive rendering of the desert archetype in modern literature. It seems as though, like some of the earlier archetypes we have studied, the desert archetype too has established itself in a fractured form. It is the "hopeless desert" of Charlotte Brontë's "hipochondria"—"tawny sands with no green fields, no palm tree, no well in view" (*Villette*, chap. 15). A displaced or negative desert, a mere wasteland, to match a displaced akedah, a hopeless wanderer and an absent father. All that is left of the fuller vision is the wish expressed by Eliot: "If there were rock / And also water." "But" he adds, "there is no water." This, however, is not quite the last word. The desert as a place of excitement and even hope still lives in the imagination to balance the darkness and desolation of the wasteland, and perhaps its time too will come round at last! In *Arabia Deserta* (1888), C. M. Doughty gives us a scene of desolation, of "mountains looming like dry bones through the thin air"[22]—and yet somehow his Arabian nomads (whom he pictures romantically in the image of "the Hebrew Patriarchs") are near to heaven in their simple faith and dignity, and the naked land where they dwell becomes a transparent medium for communication with the unseen. There is a kind of promise in the air, though one wonders whether it does not belong more to Doughty than to the reality that he encountered in his desert wanderings. C. N.

Bialik, in a long epic-style poem entitled "The Dead of the Desert" (1902), is likewise not exempt from a measure of romantic idealization, but, as one would expect from a Hebrew poet writing at the turn of the century, he also feels the weight of history, past as well as present, so that the desert becomes the scene of a vivid historical drama in which his own generation is seen somehow to participate.

"The Dead of the Desert" is based on a rabbinic legend, according to which the Israelites who died in the wilderness during the forty years of wandering from Egypt to Canaan are still to be found lying supine in the sand, awaiting their hour.[23] We are presented with a mystic landscape, in which the six hundred thousand warriors lie in sleep, their weapons at their side; the scene is one of splendor, beauty, and terror:

> And the sun rises and sets, whirls in its jubilees;
> the desert subsides and stirs, the silence returns as before.
> Cliffs lift their heads in wonder at the dark abyss of time,
> arrogant in their silent splendour, proud, eternally alone.
> For league upon league no voice, no syllable breaks the stillness;
> oblivion has swallowed forever the victories of a bold generation.
> Whirlwinds have razed the footprints of the terrible warriors of the
>   wasteland;
> sand has piled up around them, rocks thrust out through the dunes;
> the desert holds its breath for the brave sunk in endless sleep.[24]

It will be noted that the emphasis is on timelessness, eternity, the unceasing circuit of the sun, the changelessness of a scene that takes us back somehow beyond history. This mythical character is picked out by the procession of symbolic, larger-than-life creatures who approach the dead but are unable to harm them: the magnificent eagle, whose "shadow floats across the arid sands," the great snake, "flaunting the gold of his scaly coat," and the lion, whose "bellowing roar" "reverberates in a hundred thunders to the very edge of the plain." In the shadows we seem to see the shapes of "gigantic primordial beasts." Here we have a wasteland which is emphatically that of mythology: the mighty dead have been there seemingly since the beginning of time. The cycle of nature holds sway and we are humbled before its might and terror.

But as in other sagalike poems of Bialik (in particular "The Pool"), we have here a sharp break, a momentary shattering of the stillness of the timeless continuum, as well as a break with the long hexameters. The dead come to life in a great act of insurrection:

In that hour
seized by a vibrant impulse the mighty phalanx awakes.
They suddenly rouse themselves, the stalwart men of war
lightning ablaze in their eyes, their faces aflame, hands on swords.
They raise a great shout with one voice, the voice of the six hundred
    thousand,
a voice that tears through the tumult, vies with the desert's roar.
Encompassed by furious storm, resolute, unyielding, they cry:
                    We are the brave!
                    Last of the enslaved!
                    First to be free! . . .[25]

Here the explosive coming to life of the dead warriors (even if it lasts only for a brief hour) signifies the revolutionary phase of history. It is what he calls elsewhere "the epiphany of Elijah": it has nothing to do with the mythological cycle of death and rebirth. It is, rather, its antithesis. We have here instead an historical cycle of exile and return structured by the modalities of historical time. There is a linear scale dating from the Exodus and looking toward a climax when the dead will arise to assert a new life. But this life is felt to have been always potentially present, hidden though it was in the desert sand. The eagle, the serpent, and the lion, symbols of royal power, pay tribute to a host whose power will ultimately eclipse their own. There in the desert, the great story began. And there it is felt to be somehow appropriate that it should reach a consummation. The desert is a place of death, but it is also, paradoxically, a place of rebirth. However extravagantly conceived, the wasteland of Bialik's poem preserves this essential biblical dialectic.

"Canopy in the Desert" (1970), a long and impressive poem in twelve "Gates" by Abba Kovner, was inspired by the return to Sinai—the original source of the Jewish people's historic memories—in the course of the Six-Day War. Here is the hard and in some ways painful materialization of what for Bialik had been high-flown invention. Chimera gives way to commonplace. As against the legendary wilderness of Bialik (which Kovner's poem ironically recalls) is the sand, which gets under the fingernails, which drifts into the lungs and the liver. As against the magnificent dead of Bialik, their eyes ablaze, their faces tanned and strong, watched over by lions, are the pathetic remains of the Egyptian soldiery, strewn among the dunes:

I gave up my shoes on the white mound.
The coat was left in the canyon.
(I will bring you copper buttons, my son, my orphan)
Copper buttons
May Allah pity the well
that tricks me!

See me, my loved ones, in a nightmare
not in a dream.[26]

The narrator sees all around a terrible emptiness and dryness, like the dry rock of Eliot's poem but without the Dantesque cadences; the sand moves about restlessly like the pages of a long debate,

A long terrible
debate

and the blue is canopy

And the red
is bloodred.[27]

Recollections of T. S. Eliot are probably not accidental. Kovner's poem shows not an imaginary wasteland but the thing itself, an unaccommodated wilderness. To this we have returned after centuries of commerce with the fabulous and the legendary. Nevertheless, the past is not to be avoided: it mocks us from every stone. The six hundred thousand of the generation of the Exodus still "breathe in the cliff," and the narrator finds his face among them, chiseled in profile.[28] This wasteland seen in the purging pitiless light becomes a place where the past meets the present; it is a place of encounters:

From this bugged thicket
To winding gorges in a dry cloud
To a ravine our canyon
where the sky is clear as the path of knowledge

to return to the valley of the lost!
To come together again [29]

—literally, "to come once more to the meeting."

Seemingly void of human presence, the desert is, nevertheless, haunted by memories. One has the sense of someone, something shrouded in the silence, like the "third who walks always beside you" in Eliot's poem:

Behind seven veils
There is
There surely is some dune
that isn't a fable. To clutch at.
To fasten down.[30]

The barren landscape is a place of emptiness and yet of assignation:

Perhaps the divine is hidden
In a place where no one waits.[31]

"Perhaps the divine is hidden." The return to Sinai becomes inevitably a spiritual event, a challenge to the latter-day Israelite to
seek his true identity. It is an identity not easily found but also not
easily avoided. One does not seek the biblical echoes, but they find
us whether we will or not, in particular the memory of that marriage, so weighted with tragedy and promise, once contracted in
that selfsame wilderness. "A Canopy in the Desert"—it is, of course,
a marriage canopy—takes us back to the "primal scene"—to which
all Hebrew prophecy refers—when Israel gave herself as a bride to
her divine bridegroom, as in Jeremiah 2.2 or Ezekiel 16.8. Genders
have become a little mixed in Kovner's poem. It is not clear whether
the bridegroom is Israel or Israel's God. Identities are mysteriously
confused, but a bridegroom there is, and he goes out to meet his
bride in the scorching light of the desert. The wedding is prepared,
the marriage contract drawn up. The wedding guests are strangely
appareled; they ride in half-tracks using the code names of army
units. Finally the moment for the long-awaited reunion arrives:

a bridegroom toward a bride
walks
in the desert.
The glass shattered. The ring closed
and the cry of happiness. Candles burn.
In a shining circle my ushers
embrace a silk canopy
my love is not at my side.[32]

The ritual accompaniments of a Jewish wedding are provided for
the occasion, but the revelation fails to materialize: "my love is not
at my side."

The agonized search for meaning, it would seem, has failed. No
sacred marriage will be reenacted in the desert, and yet the desert

remains filled with mystery, its very nakedness an invitation to the lover:

> Make me grow, my love, in soil as naked
>
> as it was created . . .

> Naked soil is the way to my beloved.
> I came to her like someone coming to a tryst.
> I quietly try to rebuild
> a city, transparent.[33]

Among the many paradoxes in this wasteland poem is that connected with the image of growth. The desert is by definition a place where nothing grows, and yet Kovner remarkably transfers to it the notion of organism, of a people planting and being planted:

> I heard that you know how to plant a tree
> And make a whole celebration for it
> With a little soil and many words.
> Watch! honest people from the north, come
> and watch![34]

We are reminded for a moment of the happy tree-planting cere-monies of an earlier day of national effort—of the drying of swamps and the planting of orchards. But this is ironically belied by the continuation, for the speaker is a seller of balloons!

> I planted young balloons in the sand
> they grew
>
> balloons
> without water. Without intricate
> tools without ceremony
> only a salt wind. With sky[35]

The balloon-seller is (as Kovner himself has noted)[36] the central figure in the poem. He is also a persona of the poet, or rather a sym-bol for poetry itself. Colored, transparent, fragile, filled only with breath, the balloons that grow in the sand are the true flora of the desert, miraculously taking root in the air, belonging to the sky rather than to the earth. For when we speak about our connection with the desert as being a way of moving from point to point in time, a voyage into the past or a striving toward a future, what we really mean is a reunion with the words of the past and a first en-counter with the words of the future. From this point of view, the desert beckons us forward, offering us the "first flowers from the King's garden."

> Since the day has come the day
> has come! And they are transparent. They are light
> and not yet ripe
>
> —for a quarter. Very first flowers from the King's garden
> two for a quarter. . . .[37]

Ultimately, what the spirit seeks is an identity, a language. We do not live by bread alone. We crave not vegetation, but metaphors of vegetation. It is these which the desert can provide.

Metaphors of light are also powerfully present. The desert is a place of light, and yet of light that purges and burns, that has more in it of terror than of joy. Above all, it is a place of love, haunting us with a love that once was but that eludes us in the present. And yet the very intensity of the search, the very force of the yearning, bear witness to a continuing covenant. Through the same desert as that in which the first Israelites wandered, we make our way, in dust and pain, to build the city of the future.

8

Myth and Antimyth

THE SUGGESTION was made from time to time in the preceding discussion that in the modern and the postmodern era something like a reintegrated historical archetype becomes possible. The figure of Elijah is whimsically reconstituted for us by Joyce and later by Agnon; the desert reveals a meaning once again in Kovner's poem; fathers and sons achieve a wintry reconciliation in Appelfeld; when the Faustian myth has released all its destructive energy, a kind of future seems once again possible. But all this needs some qualification, for postmodern writing reveals more often than this the *reductio ad absurdum* of all archetypes, including the archetypes of history that we have been examining. In *Giles Goat-Boy* (1966) John Barth takes the myths of salvation and explodes them one by one—the Goat-Boy revelling in his animal nature is the messiah figure, the Grand Tutor. Two World Wars and a Holocaust leave modern man in a state of computerized impersonality. His world is now dominated by the incomprehensible ambience of WESCAC. Barth leans heavily on ancient myths and on patterns derived from the Old and the New Testaments (Old Syllabus and New Syllabus), but his technique is extravagantly reductive, after the manner of Swift. The richness of myth is retained but in the form of fantasy, in a system of allegorical contrivance, whereby the archetypes themselves are scrutinized and deliberately dissolved.

Our modern sensibility includes a lively awareness by writers themselves of the very archetypes we have been discussing. But this awareness can undermine their viability as myth. Borges's "The Other" (*The Book of Sand*, 1975) is based on the archetype of the double with explicit reference to Dostoyevsky and Conrad; moreover, it is the historicized version that he gives us. Sitting on a bench in Cambridge, Massachusetts, the narrator meets his earlier self as he was fifty years previously; the name of the Other is also Jorge Luis Borges, and they exchange "reminiscences." To confirm his veracity, the narrator shows his double a dollar bill bearing the date 1964. It is, of course, an investigation of the nature of time and the passage of time (significantly, the narrator's reveries open with Heraclitus's image of the eternal flow of time), but with the difference that the impossible involutions of the archetype tease us ultimately with their absurdity and their impossibility. If we remember our previous self, then why doesn't one have a memory of oneself fifty years ago as meeting one's later self? And so on. Fantasy takes the place of vision. In the end, the narrator and his double arrange to meet again, but almost by consent neither shows up for the meeting. "We said goodbye without having once touched each other. The next day, I did not show up. Neither would he."[1] It is, Borges seems to say, too late in the day for the myth of the double. The story ends on a note of bathos. "The other man dreamed me, but he did not dream me exactly. He dreamed, I now realize, the date on the dollar bill."[2] It is not so much that for the aging Borges the future (as well as the past) has become a dream leading in no particular direction, but that the archetypes themselves, and indeed all literary contrivances of this sort, seem at this time of day to ask to be turned on their heads.

Bellow's *Henderson the Rain King* (1959) is from this point of view a great comic masterpiece. Faustian and wasteland imagery are evoked in order to be exploded in mock-epic fashion. The hero makes his way to darkest Africa to find everywhere he turns analogies with the life of the modern city. This is the persistent comic strategy. Henderson bounds and screams and cavorts naked in the mud, performing his ritual dance to bring the rain as in some fertility wasteland ritual: "After the gust of breeze came deeper darkness, like the pungent heat of the trains when they pass into Grand Central tunnel on a devastated day in August." It is the last section of *The Waste Land* and the vision of the final abominations in *Heart of Darkness* turned on their heads. In F. Scott Fitzgerald's *The Great Gatsby* or in some other writings of Bellow himself, the same collocation might have been developed into a perception of the modern city as a jungle—with all the implications of such imagery. In *Henderson* this is avoided; the juxtaposition of New York and deepest Africa is rather a matter of burlesque. We have gone beyond the mythical consciousness by knowing too much about it and too much about the texts in which it is revealed. The trick of juxtaposing the world of myth with the image of the modern city and its inhabitants as a way of burlesquing both the literature of alienation and the literature of myth, has become something of a subgenre, in particular among present-day American Jewish writers belonging to the New York City area. We saw it in Philip Roth's story "Eli the Fanatic," with its evocation of the akedah against the trivializing background of the modern American bourgeoisie. Total seriousness is avoided. Bernard Malamud's "Angel Levine" (*The Magic Barrel*, 1958) turns Elijah (or a figure akin to him) into a black and places him in the middle of New York. The result is a delightful extravaganza. Allen Hoffman's *Kagan's Superfecta* (1981) likewise brings Elijah the Prophet to the West Side of Manhattan to save his hero from his lifelong addiction to betting on the races.

A rich comic effect, achieved by setting the archetypes against the trivializing background of the life of a great modern city, also characterizes the work of Cynthia Ozick. In "Puttermesser and Xhanthippe" (*Levitation*, 1982), she has her heroine create a "Golem" from the earth of the plant pots in her New York apartment. The Golem legend is a variant of the Faust myth, its modern history beginning at about the same time as that of Faust, in a version related of the sixteenth-century Rabbi Judah Loew of Prague. The Golem is a manikin or homunculus brought into existence by magical contrivance (usually by permutations of the letters of the divine name). Originally created to make the world a better place, it runs amok and endangers people's lives. When this happens it has to be returned to the dust by obliterating a letter that turns the word for truth (*emet*) into death (*met*). Ozick revives the tale with an admirable touch of fantasy, giving us, so to speak, the scherzo movement only. However, such lightness of touch does not exclude a keen intellectual perception of the nature of the myths and their working. "Puttermesser and Xhanthippe" is among other things an exploration of the way in which myths of salvation revert to, or degenerate into, myths of nature. "Xhanthippe," the Golem (and also the narrator's "double") originally called into being in order to serve the cause of truth and advance history in a messianic direction, sinks back into the grossness of the instinctual life, becomes, in short, a timeless "biological" myth of nature. There is nothing left then but to bring her existence to an end.

Ozick, in fact, here and elsewhere in her writings, grasps the dialectical interplay of the myths of nature and of history with which this book is concerned. In "The Pagan Rabbi" (1966) she brings her hero—a theological student from New York—into the wildwood in search of the lost Dryads (in reality the grove of the nymph is a fetid inlet where the city's sewage is discharged). Rabbi Isaac inherits the history-oriented tradition of Moses but is tempted by the timeless world of nature. It is Pan versus Moses. In his infatuation, he inscribes three curious words in his notebook: "Great Pan Lives." Ironically (and this is the central irony of the story), it is the modern-day disciple of Moses, with his sense of the past, who keeps the memory of Pan alive. But in the end Isaac will pay the price for his dereliction. He will die, monstrously hung up on the branch of an oaktree by his own prayer shawl, while the soul of Israel will survive in eternal hostility to the Greek gods of nature. The sense of the archetype of history is well caught in the vision of the soul of Isaac as a Wandering Jew trudging up the road at the end of the tale: "He is half bent over under the burden of a dusty old bag. The bag is stuffed with books. . . . Such antique weariness broods in his face. . . . I asked if he intended to go with his books through the whole future without change, always with his Tractate in his hand, and he answered that he could do nothing else."

A rich array of archetypal motifs is to be found in the writings of I. Bashevis Singer, among them many of those we have been discussing in this study. In his hopeless persistence, Asa Heshel, the hero of *The Family Moskat* (1950), is the Wandering Jew all over again. Jews, he says, are "a people who can't sleep themselves and let nobody else sleep." The sense of historical continuance is impressively caught in this novel. But mainly Singer, like Roth, Malamud, and Ozick, seems to exploit the archetypes for the purpose of fantasy and extravagance. His writings are full of dybbuks and demonic bargains (e.g., *Satan in Goray*, 1935) and of images of the past revisited (e.g., *Shosha*, 1978). In "The Admirer" (*Passions*, 1975), we are taken into a past that, for the alienated modern city-dweller in search of sensations, has become both fascinating and unreal. Elizabeth Abigail de Sollar tries to find her way back to the world of her Polish grandfather, but it is a juxtaposition for the sake of ironic whimsy. Rupture (which Singer is strongly aware of) is here perceived not as a wound to be healed but as a focus for playful invention. In "Sam Palka and David Vishkover" from the same collection, he uses the motif of the double as an amusing cliché. Sam Palka belongs to the American, materialistic middle-class world; David Vishkover, his other self, represents his existence prior to the Holocaust. Palka finds in New York a young woman straight out of the *stetl*, beautiful, pious, and unaffected by the reality of today. She is even reading an old-fashioned Yiddish storybook: "I had read it years before on the other side. I thought I was dreaming and I pinched myself." And so he proceeds to live a double life, one with his own American wife and family, the other with Channah Basha, whom he promises to marry one day when he is free. But, of course, he never will be free from the present. There is no way of bringing these two modes of reality together, and we are left with mere fantasy. The action of memory has become a matter of nostalgic chimera.

Singer enjoys letting the archetypes loose in a medium of free fantasy, often free erotic fantasy. There is always the action of memory, but it is not memory to be painfully reconstituted for the sake of the future, as in the writings of Aharon Appelfeld. Singer immures himself in the past rather as Yasha (in *The Magician of Lublin*, 1960) immures himself in his hermitage. That is in fact one image for his fictional strategy; another is provided by his heroine Shosha (in the novel of that title)—a Peter Pan figure arrested at a certain point in history before the rupture occurred. In short, Singer sentimentalizes the past, extravagantly reinvents it for us, at the same time that he shows how impossible it is to relate it to the world we live in.

II

To entertain the archetypes quizzically, sentimentally, or fantastically is still a kind of tribute to their power. Even as the modern writer smiles at himself and the object of his quest, he acknowledges that there are, nevertheless, objects, and there is a quest. But we may note a much more radical tendency in other modern or postmodern writings, a tendency to something approaching nearer to nihilism. In a tone that varies from world-weariness to despair, the archetypes are beheld as meaningless and deluding. Instead of being comically entertained, they are rejected, and as a result we find ourselves in the region of antimyth. *Giles Goat-Boy* has been mentioned. In another fiction of the same period, "Night-Sea Journey" (1966; in *Lost in the Funhouse*, 1968), Barth abandons mock epic for a more direct negation of the myths of history. The quest and the pilgrimage alike are summarily dismissed; life is viewed under the metaphor of a swarm of fish swimming blindly in the water toward an imaginary shore. Like the narrator himself, they will all die and achieve nothing, neither goal nor insight:

> Arguments from function and design don't impress me: granted that we can and do swim, that in a manner of speaking our long tails and streamlined heads are "meant for" swimming; it by no means follows—for me at least—that we *should* swim, or otherwise endeavor to "fulfill our destiny." Which is to say, Someone Else's destiny, since ours, so far as I can see, is merely to perish, one way or another, soon or late. The heartless zeal of our (departed) leaders, like the blind ambition and good cheer of my own youth, appalls me now; for the death of my comrades I am inconsolable. If the night-sea journey has justification, it is not for us swimmers ever to discover it.

The objects of Barth's particular barbs are the students of mythology, in particular Carl G. Jung, Joseph Campbell, and Lord Raglan, who perceive our lives and thoughts as governed by archetypes, permanent and uplifting. Barth dismisses outright the notion of heroism, of a purpose for which the hero may strive, a love to which he may attain. All is delusion. We are spawned and perish— that is all. "The horror of our story has purged me of opinions, as of vanity, confidence, spirit, charity, hope, vitality, everything—except dull dread and a kind of melancholy, stunned persistence." In spite of the comic reduction (fish swimming = men living), the Swiftian note of despair is patent. And it is not merely despair of life: it is despair of the literary structures that were long thought to bestow meaning on life and history. It is not merely the pilgrimage that sickens but the literature of pilgrimage, the "inventing [of] rules and stories and relationships." Even the literature of protest itself (of which the work is an example) becomes a meaningless gesture, for the narrator fails to do what he says he ought to do, viz., "terminate this aimless brutal business."

Of course antimyth is almost as old as myth itself. Certainly in the modern period it has been its shadowy accompaniment. We recall Macbeth's great "walking shadow" speech. His destiny has been shaped by the modalities of tragedy. The Faustian hero has greatly dared and greatly sinned; the wheel having come full circle, his fortunes having fallen into the sere, the yellow leaf, he will now be magnificently eclipsed and the devils will come and take his soul. But before he performs these final gestures of his role of tragic hero, he seems here to pause and question the very role itself. His striving and dénouement become a meaningless passage (as meaningless as a night-sea journey), for life is no more than

> a poor player,
> That struts and frets his hour upon the stage,
> And then is heard no more.
> (V.v)

The onward pilgrimage and the tragic quest are dismissed; time has neither *telos* nor circularity. Tomorrow, today, and yesterday merge together as meaningless succession, as death finally blots out all distinctions between them. As in Barth's fiction we all "perish one day or another, soon or late."

> And all our yesterdays have lighted fools
> The way to dusty death.

Art and literature are also in Shakespeare's mind in this speech. The "poor player" image is a reflection not only on life but on the play, on this very play, in fact, which, in its mythical patterning, would seem to provide a regulative structure, a necessary system of order. That too is revealed as no more than so much strutting and fretting. The nihilistic conclusion looks both ways—to life and art:

> it is a tale
> Told by an idiot, full of sound and fury,
> Signifying nothing.

Not only is life a tale told by an idiot; all tales are told by idiots, and they too signify nothing.

As a matter of fact, there is an even more august prototype than Macbeth's speech for Barth's story with its nihilistic thrust. "Night-

Sea Journey" proves to be a gloss on two verses from the biblical book of Ecclesiastes. "For man also knoweth not his time; as the fishes that are taken in an evil net, and as the birds that are caught in the snare; so are the sons of men snared in an evil time, when it falleth suddenly upon them" (9.12). Here, too, man's life and death are seen under the figure of fish swimming and perishing in the sea. Death, for the Preacher, levels man with beast and insect—a simple thought but staggering if we allow ourselves to take it steadily and take it whole: "As the one dieth, so dieth the other; yea, they have all one breath; so that a man hath no preeminence above a beast: for all is vanity" (3.19). Or Barth: "Chance drowns the worthy with the unworthy, bears up the unfit with the fit by whatever definition, and makes the night-sea journey essentially *haphazard* as well as murderous and unjustified."

Ecclesiastes has found an echo in more than one product of the modern consciousness. In Saul Bellow's *Mr. Sammler's Planet* (1969), it is a pervasive presence. The world-weariness of Artur Sammler is straight out of *Koheleth*, and this picked out also by direct quotation. Sammler is musing ironically on the new vistas opened up by the notion of travel to the moon: "Wasn't it the time—the very hour to go? For every purpose under heaven. A time to gather stones together, a time to cast away stones. Considering the earth itself not as a stone cast but as something to cast oneself from—to be divested of. To blow this great blue, white, green planet, or to be blown from it." The idea of escaping from our life on earth to some other planet proves itself to be another vanity in the preacher's catalogue of vanities. "New worlds? Fresh beginnings? Not such a simple matter . . ." muses Sammler. The Preacher had said that there is nothing new under the sun. That being so, space travel offers no essential novelty, and, as Sammler frequently reflects, the literature of space travel has also long been with us in H. G. Wells and other writers. That too has brought us nothing but an illusory sensation of freedom. In the end there is nothing for us to do but to stick to where we are on this planet. ("He hath set the world in their heart"—Koheleth had said.) The aging Sammler, who had seen and suffered all and had then decided that all is vanity, both the squalor of the modern city and the glory of the past, precisely echoes the mood of Ecclesiastes, a book, according to the rabbis, that was written by Solomon in his old age.[3]

Another major work of the modern imagination should be mentioned here. It is Borges's story "The Book of Sand" (1975), which develops and sharpens an idea he had adumbrated many years earlier in "The Library of Babel" (1941). These fictions seem to represent the working out to its monstrous conclusion of another verse from Ecclesiastes which says "Of making of many books there is no end and much study is a weariness of the flesh" (12.12). (We may note that the modern "deconstruction" of the literary work is evidently not so modern after all. The Preacher's reflexive concern here with the vanity of writing reduces the enterprise of the composition of his own book to a sorry and meaningless tale.) In "The Book of Sand," Borges's narrator comes into the possession of a book that has no beginning and no end, a Book of Sand as meaningless and appalling in its infinity as the desert sands themselves: "He told me his book was called the Book of Sand, because neither the book nor the sand has any beginning or end."[4] The number of pages is infinite; one can never isolate the first page or the last; the contents of the book defy every principle of order; never can one find the same page twice. It is, in fact, a devilish book, representing the very antithesis of the notion of the literary work as that which introduces rhythm and order into the flux of existence. In particular the Book of Sand represents the antitype of that Book which boasts the most majestic of beginnings and endings. In Borges's tale the Book of Sand is brought to the narrator by a seller of Bibles who had come into the possession of it during a journey to India. When he sells it to the narrator, he receives in exchange a valuable rarity —a black-letter Wiclif Bible. The Book of Sand is thus the dark counterpart of the Bible itself. We might even say that it lights up the yawning vacuity that is darkly hidden in that book also. The Book of Sand is something like the Aleph of the Kabbalists, the primary letter in which all words are contained, the symbol of nothingness (*ayin*) and everything.[5] Indeed, in one of his most famous early tales, "The Aleph" (1945), Borges sees in that initial letter of the Hebrew alphabet (which is also the mathematical sign of infinity) the shapelessness of infinity itself; he sees in it an unstructured emptiness—"convex equatorial deserts and each one of their grains of sand."[6] "The Aleph" too had represented an attempt to grasp the dialectic of myth and antimyth, of which "The Book of Sand" is the ultimate summarizing statement. In all these fictions the sandy desert from which salvation comes, whence the Shulamite goes up leaning on her beloved, reveals its other visage—the visage that

Shelley too had glimpsed in "Ozymandias of Egypt." It is a vista that defies and confounds all meaning, swallowing up our ends in our beginnings. Historical archetypes, we may say, imply their antithesis.

But, paradoxically, the Preacher too had perceived this before either Shelley or Borges. To say that of the making of many books there is no end is to perceive the futility of nonbeing, which even the Book of Books cannot annul, and which it even, in a manner, comprehends and darkly signifies for us.

III

Another biblical text has powerfully supported the modern imagination in its search for the antimyth. I am referring to the Book of Job. The author of Job was, it would seem, haunted by the image of a monstrous world in which defiant power would threaten, a world of eerie shapes and nightmares (4.13f), of unimaginable gulfs, of the Pleiades and Orion (9.9) in their infinite spaces, and of the great creatures of the deep (40.15f) that lie far beyond our human perception and that, unlike the creatures of Genesis 1 and 2, refuse to submit themselves to man or enter into a covenant with him (41.4).[7] Here we have the world of *Shadday*, the God of impersonal and immeasurable power, who rules over a mighty cosmogony in which man is all but totally eclipsed. *Shadday*, in fact, is mentioned some thirty times in Job, more than in all the rest of the Bible put together.

It may be argued that the world of *Shadday* has its own structure, its own dark, inverted order. We could fit it into the Table of Demonic Imagery, which Northrop Frye proposes to match the Apocalyptic Imagery of the Bible,[8] where we have Satan instead of God, demons of the tempest instead of *seraphim*, and the wasteland instead of the Garden of Eden. Job, in fact, with its frequent substitution of darkness for light, death for life, provides a complete "demonic parody" of the luminous cosmogony of Genesis; it offers a myth of Creation, but of Creation in reverse. This, it seems, is what Milton was looking for in the first books of *Paradise Lost*—a diabolical Trinity to balance the holy Trinity of heaven, "a universe of death" and of "darkness visible" to balance the universe of life in paradise. He found it in Job.

But Job introduces a more radical antimyth than this, viz., a questioning of all stability and order whatever. Job introduces to our imagination the notion of an abyss without form, an unstructured phantasmagoria,[9] resistant to the very idea of myth, having the formal shape neither of a "U" nor even of an inverted "U." What we have is *tohu*, chaos itself—the antithesis of all pattern. It is Job's friends who urge on him myths of different kinds, patterns of punishment or redemption, or testing, or seeking. These, they claim, are reliable patterns, secure, repetitive, and built into the order of the universe. It is precisely against this that Job seems often to be inveighing. Bildad tells him in chapter 9: "Though thy beginning was small, yet thy end will be very great." Job counters this by saying: "I go whence I shall not return, to the land of darkness and the shadow of death. A land of gloom as darkness itself, and of the shadow of death *without any order* and where the light is as darkness" (10:21–22). In the absoluteness of his death, he sees not a parody of the myth of Creation, but a total absence of pattern and order. What Job glimpses is nothingness. "He stretcheth out the north over the empty place, and hangeth the earth upon nothing" (26.7).

Melville in *Moby-Dick* was among the first to glimpse this dimension of Job. He meditated deeply on Leviathan, "king over all the children of pride" (41.34), and, though his work is a great achievement of mythology, indeed of many mythologies, it also powerfully suggests in the whiteness of the whale the denial of all meaning and pattern. Leviathan attests to a universe emptied of significance: "It is that by its indefiniteness it shadows forth the heartless voids and immensities of the universe, and thus stabs us from behind with the thought of annihilation."[10] In his most fearful passages, Melville catches the existential horror that comes upon us when we confront a world without myth or even without a secure parody of myth—a universe of fearful immensity and emptiness, comfortless in the eternal silences of its infinite spaces. Echoing Psalm 8.4, Job asks in chapter 7, "What is man that thou shouldst magnify him? and that thou shouldst set thine heart upon him?" His answer is not that man is a little lower than the angels or a little higher than the devils, but that he is a burden to himself. Rejecting all mythological consolations in disgust, he mutters, "Let me alone till I swallow down my spittle." He wishes to sleep in the dust: "Thou shalt seek me . . . but I shall not be." The last word of this terrible chapter is not-being. Mr. Sammler reflects on these verses from Job when he tries to suggest to his Indian visitor, Dr. Lal, the unimaginable reality of Auschwitz.

A great deal has been written about the test or the wager—that between God and Satan—as the controlling myth of Job. The test or trial, as we have seen, is fundamental to the whole notion of historical archetypes. As such, the Jobian test has appealed to many poets from Goethe to MacLeish. But what must be insisted upon is that from Job's point of view—and his is the point of view that dominates the greater part of the book and with which we deeply identify—there is neither test nor wager. He knows nothing of these things. Even after his long-drawn-out agony is over, God never tells him why he has suffered. There remains something unfathomable, uncommunicated about these dealings between God and Man. It has been well said that the God of Job is one "who eludes creation, revelation, communication. . . . He is the *God beyond dialogue*. . . . without an echo, without yesterday and without tomorrow, the God of absolute Silence."[11] This would do very well as a summary of the world evoked for us by Macbeth's "Life's but a walking shadow" speech, which we glanced at earlier. And indeed that speech echoes Job in more than one phrase. Bildad had said, "We are but of yesterday and know nothing, because our days upon earth are a shadow" (8.9). And as for life's being a "brief candle"— that too had evidently been suggested by "The light shall be dark in his tabernacle, and his candle shall be put out with him" (18.6). The despair of meaning is the mark of Macbeth's speech, as it is of these terrifying intimations of death and silence in Job.

Frye has pointed to the writings of Kafka as "a series of commentaries on the Book of Job."[12] He points in particular to *The Trial* as "a kind of 'midrash' on the Book of Job."[13] Here is a valuable insight. *The Trial* is surely very Jobian, especially in the sense that the hearing is held with the defendant absent and without his ever knowing of what he stands accused![14] There are, in fact, many parallels. Nevertheless, *The Trial* is not like Job in the sense we are now considering: it is an organized fable with a beginning, a middle, and an end. But other writings of Kafka betray a more radical incoherence. "The Hunter Gracchus," it has been earlier suggested, belongs to the Wandering Jew archetype. But that archetype, more than it is an expression of myth, is very often, as in this case, an expression of antimyth. What it gives us essentially is the wavering line of persistence itself, little more.

Likewise, many of Kafka's fictions, such as "A Hunger Artist" or "In the Penal Colony," give us simply naked suffering—surely an essential dimension of Job. Suffering has become meaningless, without pattern, and as such cannot be given the shape of tragedy or of myth. The tragic hero obeys a rhythm, belongs to a cycle: Kafka's Hunger Artist does not. He belongs neither to myth nor to tragedy. If myth is, as Frye maintains, the protective skin that marks the boundary between ourselves and that which is beyond ourselves in history or nature,[15] then these sufferers are, like Job himself, men without a skin. Their vulnerability is absolute. They have perceived in the universe a realm of indifference that cannot be assuaged by myth and for which the proper response is very often . . . silence. This is Job's conclusion when, after hearing God's unanswerable demands, he declares: "Behold I am vile; what shall I answer thee? I will lay mine hand upon my mouth" (40.4).

Through silence, the modern imagination confronts myth with antimyth. We saw earlier (chap. 5) how Billy Budd, the handsome sailor, is at the critical moment in his fable struck dumb. In this he represents something like the anti-*logos*, the antithesis of that formal speech which Captain Vere has so completely at his command. But the silence of Billy Budd also challenges the roundedness of the very fable to which he belongs. For historical archetypes, in contrast to timeless myths, point toward historical rupture, and rupture forces us eventually toward the silence of antimyth. In his horrifying novel of Eastern Europe during the Nazi occupation, *The Painted Bird* (1965), Jerzy Kosinski's boy protagonist is struck dumb as he suffers the ultimate indignity at the hands of his persecutors. And corresponding to the muteness of the hero is the almost total absence of dialogue in the novel as a whole and the formlessness of the narrative, which turns out to be radically unstructured, a mere string of picaresque episodes. Here we have a narrative that is little more than the wavering path of persistence in the face of unendurable things. It is the archetype of the wanderer reduced to mere continuance.

Silence has become a fundamental modern category. In the later works of Samuel Beckett ("Film," for instance) we arrive at a theater without words. We are left with a silence more eloquent sometimes than speech as the characters make their gestures of hopelessness and terror. Nelly Sachs has also captured this in her poetry. In a poem simply entitled "Job," in memory of her father, she writes:

> Your eyes have sunk deep into your skull
> like cave doves which the hunter
> fetches blindly at night.
> Your voice has gone dumb,
> having too often asked *why*.[16]

Job is the most eloquent of biblical books, certainly the richest of all the creation poems in the Bible, and yet it is also, as Nelly Sachs has discerned, the celebration of silence. That is its irony. It takes us to the ultimate verge of what in this study have been called "historical archetypes." At that point, no avowals of ends and purposes are possible.

Again Shakespeare has anticipated the moderns. One critic has spoken of *King Lear* as a pantomime version of Job.[17] He was thinking of the Jobian sufferings of Lear and Gloucester and of the grotesqueness that often accompanies this suffering. But we may add that the silences in *Lear* give to the play a Jobian dimension also. Silence is often the only way we know of responding to a world that has either been mythologically falsified or has become intolerably emptied of significance. In Act I, Cordelia, observing the ritual exchange of vows and promises between the King and his false daughters, Goneril and Regan, withdraws into silence: "What shall Cordelia speak? Love and be silent." Her "Nothing" in reply to Lear's direct invitation—"what can you say to draw / A third more opulent than your sisters?"—reminds us of Job, chapter 7. Gestures of grandeur, questions that presuppose an established rhetoric, an orderly arrangement of human affairs, are answered by an invocation of nothingness. Cordelia, as one perceptive student has observed, "destroys the ceremony" being enacted between Lear and his daughters.[18] She too comes to us (like Job) against the background of a test or wager staged by Lear without her knowledge, and she too is looking for a form of dialogue less organized, less symmetrical, less predictable than this setting would seem to require.

Lear, for his part, will also learn a human wisdom different from that implied in the formalities of royalty. Instead of seeing himself as just a little lower than the angels, he will learn to say in effect: "Let me alone till I swallow down my spittle." For him too the final note will be silence, as he gazes speechlessly on Cordelia's dead body. We are not to know whether he dies of grief or perhaps of joy thinking that Cordelia still lives. The play provides no answers, only questions and silences, or else it turns the questions over to the spectator, inviting him to test them out in his own life, unsustained by the preordained responses of mythology.

Myth and antimyth are built into the Shakespearean dramatic pattern to a greater extent than is realized. King Lear is, for the most part, the tragic hero as we have always known him. His tragedy is defined by the "wheel of fire." The wheel is a major metaphor in the play; Lear's fall is felt to exhibit the fatal cyclical movement of tragedy, and as such it has an inevitability about it that belongs to the very laws of nature, the operation of those orbs from which we do exist and cease to be. When men become old and weak they are pushed aside by the young and powerful as in a universal cycle of change. But Gloucester's fate is somehow different. As against the circular form of Lear's tragedy, we have here an uncertain movement forward, that of the archetypal pilgrim. Staff in hand, Gloucester finds his way, with the help of Edgar, across the wilderness of this world. The environment of Gloucester's tragedy is in this sense very much more biblical, very much more Jobian, even than Lear's. There is a weary onward striving, a meeting with an unrecognized son who seeks his blessing (Isaac and Jacob?), and there is the painful acquisition of wisdom. Gloucester, like Job, wishes above all things to be dead, to be with the infants that never saw the light, but, like Job, he is made to endure, to go on living even though life has lost its savor. Gloucester would have liked to get into a grand tragedy of the Greek kind. He seeks to die in tragic fashion by literally falling perpendicularly from a cliff. But he is denied the steep tragic horror of such a dénouement. Instead, he will fall flat on the boards to be picked up by Edgar and gently persuaded to continue his journey through further trials. His question on rising to his feet, "But have I fall'n or no?" articulates precisely the ambiguous structure of the play, its balancing of myth and antimyth. One would like to resolve its contradictions in the manner of Lévi-Strauss, seeing them as part of a mathematical equation that could be expressed as the balance between the raw and the cooked, nature and culture, born of one or born of many. But we have something more like form versus formlessness, where formlessness is not part of an equation at all, but rather a protest against all equations.

I V

For two major Hebrew writers of our times, the Jobian archetype is central, and they too have sensed its dimension of formlessness, seeing in Job a frustrated quest-poem, a radical antimyth. First, there is Uri Zvi Greenberg, whose *Rehovot Hanahar* (Streets of the river, 1954), already referred to in an earlier chapter, is a great collection of elegies devoted to the Holocaust and its aftermath. Like Job itself, it has a kind of frame story exhibiting the curve of redemption and retribution—retribution for the criminals and a kind of wintry redemption for the victims. Taken together, the poems of this collection testify to Israel's myth of history. There is destruction, exile, and return: a fiery pillar guides the survivors; a fiery sword devours Amalek. On the last page, God repents and saves mankind from the flood that threatens. And yet, set off against all this is the sense of the unique, unstructured horror of the Holocaust, the sense of a typologically unanticipated disaster, of a silence that defies all pattern, of a universe of death without form, of a word hanging over the void. Within *Streets of the River* we have what comes near to being a negation of the very structure of the poem itself. The individual poems in their metalanguage often point toward formlessness. Elijah becomes "a sickness without a form."[19] "Martyrs of Silence" starts with a reference to the poet's birth and to the moon as a central symbol of his poetry. There is a close-knit pattern of intimacy: we see in the first stanza mother, father, newborn child, and the moon in the window. But the parents have now disappeared into silence; all that is left is their unfulfilled yearning; and the moon is no longer an organizing focus for his poetry, but merely a shadowy gleam across the waves of a world no longer whole.[20]

Finally, I would like to refer to S. Y. Agnon's posthumous novella "The Covering of the Blood," belonging to the early sixties.[21] Formlessness is here a function of the narrative technique. There is a multiplicity of narrators; a nameless organ-grinder dies, and his task passes on to one Adolf, a Jewish survivor from the Austrian army in the First World War. Years later, after the Second World War, Adolf arrives in Jerusalem, tells his tale, dies, and hands on the organ-grinding business, together with a parrot and a monkey, to one Reb Hillel, who tells his tale to the narrator of the story, who tells the tale to us. There are thus at least three enclosed narratives; all are marked by the same meaningless wandering and by the shapelessness of a career of organ-grinding that passes from one narrator to the other. Dominating the whole, however, is a quest, but a frustrated quest, for Reb Hillel is charged by an American Jew—himself a Jobian figure of tragic disappointment—with the task of finding one survivor from the township in Eastern Europe where he had been born. All his own family have disappeared in the Holocaust, but his hope is that some fellow townsdweller has nevertheless survived and can be located. Reb Hillel searches unsuccessfully for a survivor who might have found his way to Israel. He discovers too late that his friend Adolf was indeed from the same *stetl* as his American friend. But now Adolf is dead and the only possible candidate is a nephew of Adolf's who had been taken captive by the Syrians while working in the fields of a kibbutz on Israel's northern border. But it is an empty hope; there is little or no chance of his being alive and returning to claim the money that Reb Hillel has been charged to deliver. Moreover, the money itself has now lost its value, having been changed from dollars to Israeli currency through the bad advice of a bank manager. It will hardly be enough, we are told, to buy a swaddling garment for an infant, if ever an infant qualifying for the prize were to be discovered.

There is a famous verse in Job that says, "Though he slay me, yet will I trust in him" (13.15). However, this is only one way of reading that verse. The written consonants (*ketiv*) point in the opposite direction and can be rendered: "See, he slays me: I have no hope!" Both readings are preserved in the Masoretic tradition, and we are supposed to keep both in balance.[22] Myth and antimyth, we may say, are intimately related by this homonym. Agnon's story—a kind of modern gloss on Job—seems to point in the direction of the latter reading—"See, he slays me; I have no hope!" But the other reading is present also. Reb Hillel has the last word in the book. In his weary persistence he symbolizes a kind of hope: he carries out the terms of his contract, as though to say, "Though he slay me, yet will I trust in him." But his contract, now emptied of value, is viewed in a perspective of irony. His world is desolate. Twice married but now widowed, his children all dead by sickness, war, and Holocaust, he will, unlike Job, never raise a new family. The last sentence of the book speaks of questions for which there are no answers, and of the heavens that are impenetrable to human inquiry:

> I have said too much, said Reb Hillel. But anyway I spoke about the Jews and if the good they do is a little more than the evil, that is certainly a good thing to talk about. I once read in a book that God in heaven looks severely on those who speak badly of the people of Israel. I don't know how that author learnt this and who told him about what goes on in heaven! But it makes sense that when it comes to people who have suffered so much, one shouldn't rub salt on their still-bleeding wounds.[23]

There is a strong element of foregrounding here. It is not only the wounds that remain unclosed in this tale of unmitigated suffering: the tale itself denies closure. And yet the very absence of closure implies a kind of hope. To tell the tale that Reb Hillel tells to the narrator and that the narrator tells to us is, we may say, a speech act of a particular kind. There is faith in the gesture itself. The sign has continuing value even when the signified suggests hopelessness and horror. That we go on reading Job and those modern fictions which catch its severe dialectic means that we go on. If there were no going on, there would be no texts and no readers. The survivor in the text speaks to us as one survivor to another. Edgar in Shakespeare's play, like Reb Hillel in Agnon's tale, is a survivor. He lives on to draw his breath in pain, to tell the story of Lear and Gloucester—a comfortless story of intolerable suffering followed by death. And yet the very retelling of it implies a kind of hope, a kind of future. As in Job, there is endurance, even if one endures only to bear witness to the fate of those who did not and could not endure. Those who live on have seen the worst of their time, but they live on nevertheless to testify, to bear in their hands the remembered word for a future telling.

Notes

A number of earlier studies by the present author are partially incorporated into this book. They are:

"Historical Archetypes: Notes Towards a Definition" (in Hebrew), *Bikkoret Ufarshanut* (Criticism and interpretation), no. 17 (March 1982): 57–63; "The Pact with the Devil," *The Yale Review*, LXIX (1980): 520–32; "The Figure of the Dybbuk," *Commentary* LI (April 1971): 70–75; "Elijah and the Wandering Jew," in *Rabbi Joseph H. Lookstein Memorial Volume*, ed. Leo Landman (New York: Ktav, 1980), pp. 125–35; "Job as Modern Archetype," *HSLA* 11, 1 (1983): 102–14.

Acknowledgment is hereby made to the publishers and editors concerned.

In addition, the book makes use of and develops ideas formulated over the past twenty years or so in a variety of essays and longer studies. The numbers in brackets after the following items refer to chapters in the present work. No further reference to these materials will be made in the notes.

LONGER STUDIES

Jerusalem and Albion: The Hebraic Factor in Seventeenth Century Literature (London: Routledge and Kegan Paul, 1964) [1 and 3]; *The Dual Image: The Figure of the Jew in English and American Literature*, 2d ed. (New York: Ktav, 1971) [3 and 5]; *Hamlet and the Word: The Covenant Pattern in Shakespeare* (New York: Ungar, 1971) [1 and 8]; *S. Y. Agnon* (New York: Ungar, 1975) [2].

SHORTER STUDIES

"Israel Zangwill: Prophet of the Ghetto," *Judaism* XIII (Fall 1964): 407–21 [3]; "The Hero as Jew: Reflections on *Herzog*," *Judaism* XVII (Winter 1968): 42–54 [4 and 6]; "Blake's Miltonic Moment," in *William Blake: Essays for S. Foster Damon*, ed. A. Rosenfeld (Providence: Brown University Press, 1969), pp. 36–56 [3]; "Antony and Cleopatra: The Limits of Mythology," *Shakespeare Survey* XXIII (1970): 59–67 [1 and 6]; "Fathers, Mothers, Sons and Lovers," *Midstream* XVIII (March 1972): 37–45 [5 and 6]; "The Absent God," *Judaism* XXI (Fall 1972): 415–27 [6]; "Introducing Cynthia Ozick," *Response* VIII, no. 2 (Summer 1974): 27–34 [8]; "Shakespeare and the Puritan Dynamic," *Shakespeare Survey* XXVII (1974): 81–92 [1 and 2]; "Bialik and the Greater Romantic Lyric," *Mélanges André*

Neher (Paris: Adrien Maisonneuve, 1975), pp. 227–36 [1 and 6]; "Three Motifs in the Literature of the Hebrew Renaissance," *Encyclopaedia Judaica Yearbook 1977–78* (Jerusalem: Keter, 1979), pp. 85–89 [6 and 7]; "A Time to be Silent and a Time to Speak: On A. Appelfeld's *The Age of Wonders*" (in Hebrew), *Zehut* I (May 1981): 150–54 [5]; "Ruth and the Structure of Covenant History," *Vetus Testamentum* XXXII (1982): 425–37 [1]; "Creation in Reverse: *The Book of Job* and *Paradise Lost*," in *Milton and Scriptural Tradition*, ed. James H. Sims and Leland Ryken (Columbia: University of Missouri Press, 1984) [8].

CHAPTER 1: HISTORICAL ARCHETYPES

1. Leslie A. Fiedler, "Archetypes and Signatures," in *An Introduction to Literary Criticism*, ed. M. K. Danziger and W. S. Johnson (Boston: D. C. Heath & Co., 1960), p. 271.

2. Maud Bodkin, *Archetypal Patterns in Poetry* (London: Oxford University Press, 1934), p. 310.

3. Northrop Frye, *Fables of Identity* (New York: Harcourt, Brace and World Inc., 1963), p. 31.

4. Ibid., p. 21. Italics added.

5. Geoffrey H. Hartman, *Beyond Formalism* (New Haven: Yale University Press, 1970), p. 363.

6. There is no agreement about the use of the terms *myth*, *archetype*, *motif*, and *structure* and the boundaries between them. Mircea Eliade seems to keep *myth* for the larger organizing vision (e.g., "the myth of the eternal return") and *archetype* for more particular functions, gestures, events, or paradigms (see *The Myth of the Eternal Return, or Cosmos and History*, trans. W. R. Trask, Princeton: Princeton University Press, 1965, Preface). For others it is rather the other way around. In this study I shall use *myth* for fables and thought patterns belonging to large classes of men, and corresponding more or less to Cassirer's "Symbolic Forms." It points toward *ritual*. *Archetypes* (or occasionally *motifs*) are mythic formulations or parts of myths to be found in literary texts, where they may or may not have a dominant role. They point toward *theme*. The term *structure* is reserved on the whole for the dynamics of texts themselves, the formal properties that the *myth* or *archetype* seems to require. *Structure* therefore points away from thematics to literary and linguistic systems as such. But some overlapping is unavoidable.

7. Northrop Frye, *Anatomy of Criticism* (Princeton: Princeton University Press, 1957), p. 192.

8. Naturally, folk literature and romances are full of such tests as the slaying of dragons, tests of identity and feats of endurance (like Orlando's defeat of the champion at the beginning of *As You Like It*). These go back to the trials of Hercules and forward to J. R. R. Tolkien's various quests and trials in *The Lord of the Rings*. A great number of such feats and ordeals as well as suitor-tests (such as that of the three caskets in *The Merchant of Venice*), tests for cuckolds and murderers etc., are classified by Stith Thompson (*Motif-Index of Folk Literature*, Bloomington: Indiana University Press, 1966, H 300–499). And see also John Stevens, *Medieval Romance: Themes and Approaches* (New York: Norton, 1974), pp. 78–89. What I am trying to isolate here, however, is something different—the sense of life itself as a test, or of crisis situations that test our moral fiber (for this

latter one thinks not of Portia's suitors but of the crisis undergone by Angelo in *Measure for Measure*). The test in this sense seems to be not particularly a feature of romance.

9. "Hamlet and Orestes" (The British Academy, 1914; revised 1920).

10. Cf. Ernst Cassirer, *The Philosophy of Symbolic Forms*, vol. II (New Haven: Yale University Press, 1955), pp. 119–20, 240.

11. Ibid., p. 120.

12. Cassirer, *The Philosophy of Symbolic Forms*, vol. III (1957), p. 171.

13. Ibid., p. 182.

14. Paul Ricoeur, *The Conflict of Interpretations: Essays in Hermeneutics* (Evanston: Northwestern University Press, 1974), pp. 81, 82, 84, 85.

15. Ibid., p. 84.

16. Ibid., p. 384.

17. Cf. Babylonian Talmud, *Shabbat*, fol. 119b: "R. Elazar said, How do we know that speech is like a deed? It is because of the text which says, 'By the word of the Lord the heavens were made' (Psalms 33.6)."

18. Walter Benjamin, *Reflections*, trans. Edmund Jephcott (New York: Harcourt Brace Jovanovich, 1979), p. 319.

19. A. J. Greimas, "Structure et Histoire," *Les Temps Modernes*, vol. 22 (1966), reproduced in *Structuralism and Biblical Hermeneutics*, ed. A. M. Johnson, Jr. (Pittsburgh: The Pickwick Press, 1979), pp. 70, 71.

20. Frank Kermode, *The Sense of an Ending: Studies in the Theory of Fiction* (New York: Oxford University Press, 1967), passim.

21. Ibid., p. 141.

22. Ibid., p. 148.

23. On this, see at large the writings of Martin Buber, especially his *Königtum Gottes* and *Moses*; George E. Mendenhall, *Law and Covenant in Israel* (Pittsburgh: Biblical Colloquium, 1954); W. Eichrodt, *Theologie des Alten Testamentes*, vol. I; and, for a briefer summary, G. E. Wright, *The Old Testament Against Its Environment* (London: SCM Press, 1950), pp. 54–73. The relevance to Shakespeare is noted by T. F. Driver in *The Sense of History in Greek and Shakespearean Drama* (New York: Columbia University Press, 1960), pp. 38–40.

24. Fiedler, "Archetypes and Signatures," p. 276.

25. Cf. W. J. Bate, *The Burden of the Past* (Cambridge, Mass: Harvard University Press, 1970), p. 133 and passim.

26. On visionary history in Herder and Coleridge (with reference also to biblical Apocalypse and Prophecy), see E. S. Shaffer, *'Kubla Khan' and The Fall of Jerusalem* (Cambridge: Cambridge University Press, 1975), pp. 19, 21, 89, 125, etc.

27. See Thomas Mann, "Freud and the Future," in *Essays of Three Decades*, trans. H. T. Lowe-Porter, reproduced in *The Modern Tradition: Backgrounds of Modern Literature*, ed. R. Ellmann and C. Feidelson, Jr. (New York: Oxford University Press, 1965), p. 676.

28. Cf. Marthe Robert, *From Oedipus to Moses: Freud's Jewish Identity* (London: Routledge and Kegan Paul, 1977), p. 11 and passim. Also cf. David Aberbach, "Freud's Jewish Problem," *Commentary* LXIX (June 1980): 35–39.

29. Cf. Geoffrey Hartman, "Romanticism and 'Anti-Self-Consciousness,'" in *Romanticism and Consciousness: Essays in Criticism*, ed. Harold Bloom (New York: Norton, 1970), p. 51. Hartman sees this new interest as reflecting the "perilous nature of consciousness" in this period.

30. Trans. HF. For further comment, see below, chap. 6, p. 120. A full

translation of this poem is included in *Chaim Nachman Bialik: Selected Poems*, trans. Ruth Nevo (Tel-Aviv: Dvir, 1981), pp. 120–33.

31. The genre has been well defined by M. H. Abrams in his essay "Structure and Style in the Greater Romantic Lyric," first published in *From Sensibility to Romanticism*, ed. Frederick W. Hilles and Harold Bloom (London: Oxford University Press, 1965), pp. 527–60.

CHAPTER 2: THE PACT WITH THE DEVIL

1. *The Birth of Tragedy*, Chapter XVIII, trans. Francis Golffing (New York: Doubleday, 1956), p. 109.

2. *The Decline of the West*, trans. Charles Francis Atkinson, vol. II (New York: Knopf, 1938), p. 301.

3. Ibid., p. 298. T. K. Seung argues plausibly that Faustian man is first clearly discerned in the writings of Boccaccio, with their this-worldly emphasis, their literalism, and their emphasis on power as the ultimate value of knowledge. See *Cultural Thematics: The Formation of the Faustian Ethic* (New Haven: Yale University Press, 1976), pp. 247, 258, etc.

4. *Faust*, Part I, trans. Walter Arndt (New York: Norton, 1976), p. 42.

5. Ibid., p. 41.

6. Cf. Exod. 31. 16–17.

7. The linking of the Sabbath day with the millennium of history is a Jewish commonplace (cf. Babylonian Talmud, *Sanhedrin*, fol. 97a). It is also well established in Christian typology from the seventeenth century onwards, especially in America. Cf. Mason I. Lowance, "Typology and Millennial Eschatology in Early New England," in *Literary Uses of Typology*, ed. Earl Miner (Princeton, N.J.: Princeton University Press, 1977), pp. 247, 253, 254f.

8. Thomas Mann, *The Story of a Novel: The Genesis of Doctor Faustus* (New York: Knopf, 1961), p. 191.

9. Cf. J. W. Smeed, *Faust in Literature* (London: Oxford University Press, 1975), p. 120.

10. For thoughtful comment on this quasi-Hegelian scheme, cf. Stéphane Moses, *Une Affinité Littéraire: le Titan de Jean Paul et le Docteur Faustus de Thomas Mann* (Paris: Éditions Klincksieck, 1972), p. 132. Moses discerns a final comforting synthesis involving the reconciliation of opposites. My own reading of Mann suggests a more pessimistic conclusion.

11. Robert N. Bellah, *The Broken Covenant: American Civil Religion in Time of Trial* (New York: Seabury Press, 1975), pp. 14–16, 139.

12. See *Works* (1612), I, 39.

13. *The Devil and the Jews* (New Haven: Yale University Press, 1943), passim.

14. Cf. Paul N. Siegel, *Shakespeare in His Time and Ours* (Notre Dame, Indiana: University of Notre Dame Press, 1968), pp. 238–46.

15. Smeed quotes a number of German writers of the Nazi period on this subject. One Georg Schott speaks of "jüdisch-mephistophelische Teufelei." Smeed, *Faust in Literature*, pp. 124–25.

16. Cf. Leslie Fiedler, *Love and Death in the American Novel* (New York: Criterion Books, 1969), 415f.

17. Cf. Bellah, *The Broken Covenant*, pp. 8–9, 26.

18. Mann, *The Story of a Novel*, p. 91.

19. See Gustaaf van Cromphout, "*Moby-Dick*: The Transformation of the Faustian Ethos," *American Literature* 51 (1979): 21, 28.

20. Joel Blocker and Richard Elman, "An Interview with Isaac Bashevis Singer," in *Critical Views of Isaac Bashevis Singer*, ed. Irving Malin (New York: New York University Press, 1969), p. 23.

21. Cf. Evelyn Torton Beck, *Kafka and the Yiddish Theatre* (Madison: The University of Wisconsin Press, 1971), pp. 70–97.

22. From the Hebrew version of R. Kalonymos (Jerusalem: Senunit, 1915), p. 85.

23. *The Age of Enormity* (Cleveland: World Publishing Co., 1962), p. 274.

24. *Two Tales by S. Y. Agnon*, trans. Walter Lever (New York: Schocken Books, 1966).

CHAPTER 3: DOUBLES AND DYBBUKS

1. Cf. Otto Rank, *The Double: A Psychoanalytic Study*, trans. Harry Tucker, Jr. (Chapel Hill: University of North Carolina Press, 1971), pp. 69f. 85.

2. Ibid., p. 60.

3. Fyodor Dostoevsky, *Notes From Underground*, trans. Constance Garnett, in *The Continental Edition of World Masterpieces*, vol. II (New York: Norton, 1966), p. 764.

4. Ibid., p. 771.

5. Friedrich Nietzsche, *The Birth of Tragedy*, chapter xx, trans. Francis Golffing (New York: Doubleday, 1956), p. 124.

6. Cf. C. E. Keppler, *The Literature of the Second Self* (Tucson: The University of Arizona Press, 1972), chap. 8 (pp. 161f), "The Second Self in Time."

7. *The Short Stories of Henry James*, ed. Clifton Fadiman (New York: Random House, 1945), pp. 610, 612.

8. For further discussion of the Wandering Jew, see below, chap. 4.

9. W. J. Bate, *The Burden of the Past* (Cambridge, Mass: Harvard University Press, 1970), p. 133.

10. *The Poetry and Prose of William Blake*, ed. David V. Erdman (New York: Doubleday, 1970), p. 114. (Subsequent quotations from the same edition.)

11. Cf. Plate 29.22.

12. The descent of Milton in Blake's poems is evidently intended to recall the descent of Raphael in Milton's *Paradise Lost* V, 266f; this episode in turn is based on the well-established motif of the descent of Hermes in Vergil, Homer, etc. On the significance of this motif for the epic tradition, see Thomas Greene, *The Descent from Heaven* (New Haven: Yale University Press, 1963), pp. 374f.

13. Jorge Luis Borges, *The Aleph and Other Stories 1933–1969*, trans. Norman Thomas Di Giovanni (New York: Dutton, 1977), p. 110.

14. See Gershom Scholem, s.v. "Dibbuk," in *Encyclopaedia Judaica*, vol. VI, pp. 19–20; also Gedalyah Nig'al, "The Dybbuk in Jewish Mysticism" (in Hebrew), *Daat* (Ramat Gan: Bar-Ilan University), no. 4 (Winter 1980): 75–101. (English summary, pp. 62–63.) For the sixteenth-century provenance of these tales, see Nig'al, *Dybbuk Tales in Jewish Literature* (in Hebrew) (Jerusalem: Rubin Mass, 1983).

15. Babylonian Talmud, *Hagigah*, fol. 16a.

16. Cf. M. Kohansky, *The Hebrew Theatre: Its First Fifty Years* (New York: Ktav, 1969), pp. 32–47.

17. S. Ansky, *The Dybbuk: A Play in Four Acts*, trans. H. G. Alsberg and Winifred Katzin (London: Benn, 1927), p. 43.

18. A Russian critic, M. Zagorsky, saw in *The Dybbuk* an image of the Soviet Revolution; in Palestine, among the Jewish settlers, on the other hand, it was sometimes criticized as being a glorification of the life of the ghetto and its superstitions (see Kohansky, *The Hebrew Theatre*, pp. 45, 94).

19. *Two Tales by S. Y. Agnon*, trans. Walter Lever (New York: Schocken Books, 1966), pp. 143–233.

20. Ibid., pp. 232–33.

21. Successfully produced by the "Zavit" Theatre, Tel-Aviv, 1966. Published in the collection *Emptied House* (in Hebrew) (Tel-Aviv, 1970).

22. A. B. Yehoshua, *Three Days and a Child*, trans. Miriam Arad (New York: Doubleday, 1970), pp. 184, 177.

23. Ibid., p. 177.

24. I. Bashevis Singer in many of his novels, notably in *Satan in Goray* (1935) and *The Slave* (1962), also portrays the power of nature in a form resembling the Conradian Heart of Darkness as operating in decided opposition to the pull of the "Jewish" superego. But in this and other respects Singer's work is not to be taken as characteristic of the Jewish literary tradition.

25. Chap. 12 (emphasis added).

26. Chap. 13.

27. I am indebted for this thought to Mrs. Sharon Baris of Bar-Ilan University's English department, whose ongoing study of the Daniel theme in American literature sheds much light on the hermeneutic quest in this novel.

CHAPTER 4: MYTHS OF CONTINUANCE

1. "The Hunter Gracchus," in Franz Kafka, *The Complete Stories*, ed. Nahum N. Glatzer (New York: Schocken Books, 1946), pp. 228–29.

2. Ibid., pp. 232–33.

3. Ibid., p. 228.

4. For a full account of the history of the legend, see G. K. Anderson, *The Legend of the Wandering Jew* (Providence: Brown University Press, 1965), passim. See also Edgar Knecht, *Le Mythe du Juif errant* (Grenoble: Presses Universitaires de Grenoble, 1977).

5. On the poem's link with the Wandering Jew legend, see John Livingston Lowes, *The Road to Xanadu* (London: Constable, 1930), pp. 249–55.

6. Cf. Ibid., pp. 257–60. On the analogue with Cain generally, see Hyam Maccoby, "The Legend of the Wandering Jew: a New Interpretation," *The Jewish Quarterly* (London) XX, no. 1 (Spring 1972):5.

7. Edgar Rosenberg, *From Shylock to Svengali: Jewish Stereotypes in English Fiction* (London: Peter Owen, 1961), pp. 188, 189.

8. Louis Harap, *The Image of the Jew in American Literature* (Philadelphia: The Jewish Publication Society of America, 1974), p. 241.

9. Somewhat to the contrary, Joseph Campbell sees the Wandering Jew as part of a "monomyth" relatable somehow to mother fixation, or else as an example of "Cosmic Man" who has access to ultimate wisdom. (*The Hero with a Thousand Faces* [Princeton: Princeton University Press, 1968], pp. 63, 237). Once again, it seems to me that the Jungian or Freudian approach proves singularly unhelpful in regard to the "archetypes of history." What is lost in Campbell's formulations is the *wandering* itself.

10. From an unpublished paper by Earl Rovit, "Notions of the Hero in Contemporary Literature." (With kind permission of the author.)

11. At the same time, an interesting analogue to the original legend is to be found in the rabbinic story of Rabbi Judah the Prince, who once refused his protection to a calf being led to the slaughter and suffered miserably for many years as a punishment. (Babylonian Talmud, *Baba Mezia*, fol. 85a; *Bereshit Rabba*, chap. 33.)

12. Northrop Frye remarks with his customary insight that Kafka's work "from one point of view, may be said to form a series of commentaries on the Book of Job." (*Anatomy of Criticism* [Princeton: Princeton University Press, 1957], p. 42).

13. Cf. Ruth R. Wisse, *The Schlemiel as Modern Hero* (Chicago: University of Chicago Press, 1971), pp. 79–107. Regrettably, Professor Wisse does not touch on the link with the Wandering Jew tradition except in a brief reference at the end (p. 126) to Adalbert von Chamisso's tale of *Peter Schlemiel*, which Dov Sadan has properly related to the legend of the Wandering Jew.

14. Earl Rovit, "Saul Bellow and the Concept of the Survivor," in *Saul Bellow and His Work*, ed. Edmond Schraepen (Brussels: Vrije Universiteit Brussel, 1978), pp. 95, 96.

15. Saul Bellow, *Mr. Sammler's Planet* (London: Weidenfeld and Nicolson, 1970), pp. 91, 92.

16. Cf. Aharon Wiener, *The Prophet Elijah in the Development of Judaism* (London: Routledge and Kegan Paul, 1978), p. 137.

17. Henri Meschonnic speaks interestingly of the Jew (indeed the Wandering Jew) as a "wandering signifier" having an elusive status somewhere in between poetry and history. (*Jona et le signifiant errant* [Paris: Gallimard, 1981], pp. 95–112, 128).

18. J. Joyce, *Ulysses* (New York: The Modern Library, 1940), p. 149.

19. Ibid., p. 246.

20. W. B. Stanford, *The Ulysses Theme* (Oxford: Basil Blackwell, 1968), pp. 220–21.

21. Joyce, *Ulysses*, p. 339.

22. For suggestive comment on these aspects of the story, see Hillel Barzel, "The Biblical Layer in Franz Kafka's 'The Country Doctor,'" in *Biblical Images in Literature*, ed. Roland Bartel, James S. Ackerman and Thayer S. Warshaw (Nashville and New York: Abingdon Press, 1975), pp. 90–99.

23. Herman Melville, *Moby-Dick* (New York: Norton, 1967), p. 88.

24. Ibid., p. 91.

25. Pointed out by David H. Hirsch in *Reality and Idea in the Early American Novel* (The Hague: Mouton, 1971), p. 209.

26. Aharon Wiener makes the distinction (*The Prophet Elijah*, p. 137), but others have sought to conflate the two legends (e.g., Kaufman Kohler in *The Jewish Encyclopaedia* [New York: Funk and Wagnall, 1901–1906], s.v. "Elijah"; H. Loewe in C. G. Montefiore and H. Loewe, *A Rabbinic Anthology* [New York: Meridian Books, 1960], p. 257; and H. Sinsheimer, *Shylock: The History of a Character or the Myth of the Jew* [London: Gollancz, 1947], pp. 116–18). While it should be insisted that the two legends are phenomenologically distinct, Elijah seems nevertheless to shadow the Wandering Jew in some of the Ahasuerus tales. See, for example, Miles Wilson, *The History of Israel Jobson*, 1757 (discussed by Anderson, *The Legend of the Wandering Jew*, pp. 133–36). An interesting example is C. F. D. Schubart's famous and influential poem "Der Ewige Jude" of 1783. Critics

do not seem to have noted the significance of the situation of Ahasuerus: he is found in Elijah's most characteristic location, i.e., a cave on Mount Carmel! Moreover, we see him at the end of the poem begging permission to die—just as Elijah does in I Kings 19.4. And finally he sleeps in the care of an angel, as does Elijah in the verse following. Schubart concludes with the words:

Ein Engel trug ihn wieder ins Geklüft,
Da schlaf nun, sprach der Engel, Ahasver,
Schlaf süssen Schlaf; Gott zürnt nicht ewig.

27. "If the Days be Long," 1909, trans. HF.

28. A. Koestler, *Promise and Fulfilment* (London: Macmillan, 1949), p. 335.

29. Elie Wiesel, *Legends of our Time* (New York: Holt, Rinehart and Winston, 1968), p. 24.

30. Ibid., p. 55.

31. Ibid., p. 56.

32. Ibid., p. 101.

33. Ibid., pp. 108–109. In a later novel, *The Oath* (1973), Wiesel continues to grapple with these dualities. The central character, Azriel, is haunted by the records of the past and by an oath laid on him by an Ahasuerus figure named Moshe the Madman. But he lives to break the oath and transmit the burden to a younger man, who becomes a messenger for the future. In consequence Azriel becomes not only a witness and survivor but a savior as well.

34. Trans. HF. R. Shmuel Josef is Agnon himself, who appears as a character in the story. The translation by I. M. Lask (New York: Schocken Books, 1948) unfortunately fails to register the allusion to Jesus.

35. U. Z. Greenberg, *The Streets of the River* (in Hebrew) (Tel-Aviv: Schocken, 1954), p. 285, trans. HF.

Chapter 5: The Binding of Isaac

1. James Joyce, *Ulysses* (New York: Random House, 1946), pp. 673–76.

2. Cf. E. Rosenberg, *From Shylock to Svengali* (London: Peter Owen, 1961), chap. IV.

3. L. A. Fiedler, *Love and Death in the American Novel* (New York: Criterion Books, 1969), pp. 251–52.

4. Cf. Frederick C. Crews, *The Sins of the Fathers: Hawthorne's Psychological Themes* (New York: Oxford University Press, 1966), p. 29 and passim. While Crews seems to me to give the right emphasis to the central importance of the conflict of fathers and sons in Hawthorne, he underrates the historical aspect of this struggle and treats Hawthorne's attitude to the past as "metaphorical of individual mental strife." In other words, he looks at it (in Freudian fashion) as part of a universal psychological structure. The thesis of this chapter—indeed of this book—is different.

5. For a discussion of this *topos* in the writings of Ibsen, O'Neill, Faulkner, and Arthur Miller, see Shelly Regenbaum, "The Sacrifice of Isaac and Related Archetypes" (Ph.D. diss., Bar-Ilan University, 1978). For some American examples, see E. Miller Budick, "'American Israelites': Exegetic Literalism in the American Imagination," *HSL* 10 (1982): 69–107; for some remarks on the contemporary meaning of the akedah, see R. Drai, *Le Pouvoir et la parole* (Paris: Payot, 1981), pp. 161–65.

6. See *Jerusalem*, plate 27, and a *Descriptive Catalogue*, no. V.

7. See J. Katz, *From Prejudice to Destruction: Anti-Semitism, 1700–1933* (Cambridge, Mass: Harvard University Press, 1980), pp. 29, 38, and Notes thereon.

8. Shalom Spiegel, *The Last Trial: On the Legends and Lore of the Command to Abraham to Offer Isaac as a Sacrifice: the Akedah*, trans. Judah Goldin (Philadelphia: Jewish Publication Society, 1967), pp. 31–32, 47, 58, 64–65, 75, etc.

9. Quoted by Spiegel, ibid., p. 46.

10. Ibid., pp. 6–7. References to the akedah are frequently introduced into the synagogue liturgy as part of the benediction for the resurrection of the dead.

11. Reproduced in full as an Appendix to Spiegel's work, trans. Goldin.

12. Cf. S. Kierkegaard, *Fear and Trembling and Sickness unto Death*, trans. W. Lowrie (New York: Doubleday, 1954), pp. 71, 72, 122.

13. Ibid., 122.

14. From the NEB translation, which gives the sense of the last phrase here more strikingly than AV or RSV (emphasis added). Examples of the akedah-crucifixion analogy in patristic literature are listed by E. Wellisch, *Isaac and Oedipus* (London: Routledge and Kegan Paul, 1954), p. 72. Wellisch interestingly views the "Akedah Motif" as a mechanism for resolving the tensions of the Oedipus complex (p. 78).

15. Zevi Hirsch Meizlisch, *Responsa for Martyrs* (in Hebrew) (Chicago: International Printing Company, 1955), vol. I, p. 8.

16. Kierkegaard, *Fear and Trembling*, p. 71.

17. Franz Kafka, *Letter to His Father*, trans. Ernst Kaiser and Eithne Wilkins (New York: Schocken Books, 1966), p. 123.

18. Micah Joseph Bin-Gorion, *Selection* (in Hebrew), ed. Y. Erlich (Tel-Aviv: Am Oved, 1955), pp. 22–23.

19. A. B. Yehoshua, "Early in the Summer of 1970," trans. Miriam Arad, *Commentary* LV (March 1973):45.

20. Aharon Appelfeld, *The Age of Wonders*, trans. Dalya Bilu (Boston: David R. Godine, 1981), pp. 202, 253, 266.

21. Ibid., pp. 209–10.

22. Ibid., p. 263.

23. Alvin H. Rosenfeld has noted this reversal of the *Bildungsroman* in Elie Wiesel's *Night* and in Primo Levi's *Survival in Auschwitz* (*A Double Dying: Reflections on Holocaust Literature* [Bloomington: Indiana University Press, 1980], p. 29). And see also Lawrence Langer, *The Holocaust and the Literary Imagination* (New Haven: Yale University Press, 1976), pp. 82, 84.

24. Trans. HF.

25. Cf. Susanne Howe, *Wilhelm Meister and his English Kinsmen: Apprentices to Life* (New York: Columbia University Press, 1930), chap. IX, passim.

CHAPTER 6: THE ABSENT FATHER

1. Marcel Proust, *Swann's Way*, trans. C. K. Scott Moncrieff (New York: Modern Library, 1928), p. 44.

2. Ibid., p. 238.

3. D. H. Lawrence, *Sons and Lovers* (New York: Viking, 1968), p. 67.

4. Henry Roth, *Call It Sleep* (New York: Avon Books, 1964), p. 441.

5. Robert Graves, *The White Goddess* (1947; London: Faber, 1961), p. 485.

6. D. H. Lawrence, *Fantasia of the Unconscious* (1922; New York: Viking, 1960), p. 174.

7. Ibid., p. 173.

8. I. D. Suttie, *The Origins of Love and Hate* (London: Kegan Paul, 1935), chap. IX.

9. Erich Neumann, *The Great Mother* (London: Routledge and Kegan Paul, 1955).

10. D. H. Lawrence, *Selected Literary Criticism* (London: Heinemann, 1956), p. 13.

11. Cf. Leslie A. Fiedler, *Love and Death in the American Novel* (New York: Criterion Books, 1960), pp. 300–306.

12. From Isaac Babel, "A Letter," in *Lyubka the Cossak and Other Stories*, trans. Andrew R. MacAndrew (New York: New American Library, 1963), p. 140.

13. Ibid., p. 136.

14. Philip Roth, *Portnoy's Complaint* (New York: Random House, 1969), pp. 41–42.

15. Philip Roth, "Eli, the Fanatic," in *Goodbye, Columbus* (New York: Bantam Books 1963), pp. 200, 194, 215.

16. On the symbolism and worship of the Earth-Mother in primitive societies, see Mircea Eliade, *Myths, Dreams and Mysteries*, trans. Philip Mairet (London: Harvill Press, 1960), pp. 164–74, 185–87.

17. Walt Whitman, "Song of Myself" (1855), section 21, in *Walt Whitman's Poems*, ed. G. W. Allen and C. T. Davis (New York: New York University Press, 1955), p. 89.

18. "When Lilacs Last in the Dooryard Bloom'd" (1865), section 14, in ibid., p. 228.

19. From *Leaves of Grass* (1856), in ibid., p. 171.

20. Robert Graves, *The White Goddess*, pp. 446, 448.

21. I am grateful to Dr. Ellah Belfer, who pointed out to me this dimension in the characters of Lara, Sonia, and Anna Karenina.

22. From the translation by Ruth Finer Mintz, in *Modern Hebrew Poetry: A Bilingual Anthology* (Berkeley and Los Angeles: University of California Press, 1966), p. 132.

23. Ibid., p. 134.

24. Ibid., p. 176.

25. Cf. Robert Alter, *After the Tradition* (New York: Dutton, 1969), p. 220.

26. Cf. Adi Zemach, *The Hidden Lion* (in Hebrew) (Jerusalem: Kiryat Sefer, 1966), p. 175.

27. Cf. Mary Catherine Bateson's thoughtful essay, "A Riddle of Two Worlds: An Interpretation of the Poetry of H. N. Bialik," *Daedalus* (Summer 1960): 740–62. Miss Bateson argues that the dreaming depths of the Pool are feminine while the oak tree (and elsewhere the forest) is masculine. The union of the two is the attempted union of the male and female aspects of divinity, the active and the passive. But I would wish to dissent from her view that we are finally offered a way of reconciling the "riddle of the two worlds" through poetry itself. There seems to me no such final reconciliation in the poem.

28. M. Shoham, *Ketavim* (in Hebrew) (Jerusalem, 1964). Trans. HF. And cf., for comment on this aspect of Shoham's writing, Ruth Kartun-Blum,

From Tyre to Jerusalem: The Literary World of Matityahu Shoham (Berkeley and Los Angeles: University of California Press, 1969), p. 128.

29. *Anthology of Modern Hebrew Poetry*, ed. S. Y. Penueli and U. Ukhmani (Jerusalem: Israel Universities Press, 1966), I, 105 (trans. Robert Friend).

30. Cf. Y. H. Brenner, *Breakdown and Bereavement*, trans. Hillel Halkin (Ithaca: Cornell University Press, 1971), pp. 142, 210.

31. First appeared in 1955. Trans. HF.

32. *The Light of Lost Suns: Selected Poems of Amir Gilboa*, trans. Shirley Kaufman (New York: Persea Books, 1979), p. 26.

33. "The Dialogue of Zion and God" by Eleazar ben Kallir, ed. and trans. T. Carmi, in *The Penguin Book of Hebrew Verse* (Harmondsworth, Middlesex: Penguin Books, 1981), pp. 223–24.

34. Cf. A. B. Yehoshua, "Facing the Forests," in *Three Days and a Child*, trans. Miriam Arad (New York: Doubleday, 1970).

35. Here I would wish to dispute the view of Baruch Kurzweil that Shin Shalom, through "the deification of the I as God-Man," gives us a "meeting with the Nothing." See "Shin Shalom's Explorations in the Depths of the I," prefixed to Shin Shalom, *On Ben Peleh*, trans. V. E. Reichert and Moses Zalesky (Jerusalem: Youth Department of the Zionist Organization, 1963), p. 20. The first three extracts cited from this poem are from the translation of Reichert and Zalesky; the remainder are adapted by HF.

CHAPTER 7: WASTELANDS AND OCEANS

1. *Saint-John Perse: Praise and Presence* (Washington, D.C.: Library of Congress, 1971), p. 18.

2. This and other quotations from *Anabase* as edited by T. S. Eliot (London: Faber, 1959). For comment on this aspect, see Shlomo Elbaz, "T. S. Eliot et Saint-John Perse: Face à Face et Face au Désert" (Ph.D. diss., Hebrew University, Jerusalem, 1975), pp. 282, 333, 576.

3. Edmond Jabès, *Le soupçon. Le désert* (Paris: Gallimard, 1978), pp. 124, 130.

4. See *Midrash Exodus Rabba*, chap. 2 (section 4).

5. In *Symbols of Transformation*, trans. R. F. C. Hull (London: Routledge and Kegan Paul, 1956), pp. 330–31, 408, 419–20.

6. See André Lacocque and Pierre-Emmanuel Lacocque, *The Jonah Complex* (Atlanta: John Knox Press, 1981), p. 55.

7. Crusoe's first voyage, which ends with the ship foundering off Yarmouth Roads (chap. 1), parallels Jonah's attempted voyage to Tarshish. Like Jonah, he lies in his cabin in a stupor while the storm rages. Crusoe, we remember, had disobeyed his father's command by sailing, and the Master of the ship, when he later hears of this, tells him that "Perhaps this has all befallen us on your account, like Jonah in the ship of Tarshish." His subsequent experiences on the "desert island," I suggest, similarly parallel Jonah's trials in chap. 4 of that prophecy.

8. T. E. Lawrence, *Seven Pillars of Wisdom*, chap. 118 (New York: Doubleday, 1939), p. 638.

9. This and the subsequent quotations from Eliot's poetry are from *Collected Poems 1909–1962* (London: Faber and Faber Ltd, 1963; New York: Harcourt, Brace and World, 1963).

10. "The Vanished Mind: Or *The Waste land* Revisited," in *Scripta Hiero-*

solymitana, vol. XVII, ed. Alice Shalvi and A. A. Mendilow (Jerusalem: Magnes Press, 1966), pp. 228, 231.

11. Florence Jones, "T. S. Eliot Among the Prophets," *American Literature* 38 (1966): 286f.

12. "The Myth and the Powerhouse," in *Myth and Literature*, ed. John B. Vickery (Lincoln: University of Nebraska Press, 1961), p. 115.

13. "The Waste Land: An Analysis," in *T. S. Eliot: A Study of his Writings by Several Hands*, ed. B. Rajan (London: Dennis Robson, 1947), p. 14.

14. From his *Autobiography*, quoted by Paul Fussell in *The Great War and Modern Memory* (London: Oxford University Press, 1975), p. 326.

15. The connection with the Great War is reinforced by the possibility, first mooted by John Peter (*Essays in Criticism*, II, 1952, p. 245), that in "Death By Water" and other parts of the poem, the poet is thinking of a young friend who has died in the war. The probability that this person was in fact Jean Verdenal, who had been killed in the Dardanelles campaign and to whose memory Eliot had earlier dedicated "Prufrock," has been recently discussed by Harry Levin (*The Waste Land from Ur to Echt*, privately printed, 1972, p. 19). A more detailed account of this relationship and its bearing on the poem is offered by James E. Miller, Jr., in *T. S. Eliot's Personal Waste Land: Exorcism of the Demons* (University Park and London: Pennsylvania State University Press, 1977), pp. 11–32 and passim.

16. "A Note on War Poetry" in *London Calling*, ed. Storm Jameson (New York: Harper, 1942), pp. 237–38, and *Collected Poems*, p. 229.

17. See *The Waste Land: A Facsimile and Transcript of the Original Drafts*, ed. Valerie Eliot (New York: Harcourt Brace Jovanovich, 1971), p. 3 and note thereon (p. 125).

18. In *Bluebeard's Castle* (London: Faber, 1971), p. 23.

19. This phrase is actually the title of the poem.

20. From the translation in *The Penguin Book of German Verse*, ed. Leonard Forster (London: Penguin Books, 1978), pp. 435, 437. I am indebted to Professor S. S. Prawer for drawing my attention to this poem.

21. Fussell, *The Great War and Modern Memory*, pp. 3–7.

22. *Travels in Arabia Deserts* (New York: Boni and Liveright, 1923), vol. I, p. 323.

23. Cf. Babylonian Talmud, *Baba Batra*, fol. 74a.

24. From C. N. Bialik, *Selected Poems*, trans. Ruth Nevo (Tel-Aviv: Dvir, 1981), pp. 102–104.

25. Ibid., p. 112.

26. Abba Kovner, *A Canopy in the Desert*, trans. Shirley Kaufman (Pittsburgh: University of Pittsburgh Press, 1973), p. 148.

27. Ibid., pp. 106–107.

28. Ibid., p. 107.

29. Ibid., p. 181.

30. Ibid., p. 140.

31. Ibid., p. 125.

32. Ibid., pp. 184–85.

33. Ibid., pp. 200–202.

34. Ibid., p. 133.

35. Ibid.

36. Abba Kovner, *On the Narrow Bridge* (in Hebrew) (Tel-Aviv: Sifriat Hapoalim, 1981), p. 165.

37. Kovner, *A Canopy in the Desert*, p. 136.

CHAPTER 8: MYTH AND ANTIMYTH

1. Jorge Luis Borges, *The Book of Sand*, trans. Norman Thomas di Giovanni (Harmondsworth: Penguin Books, 1979), p. 10.

2. Ibid.

3. In *Midrash Koheleth Rabba*, chap. 1.

4. Borges, *The Book of Sand*, p. 89. I have benefited by reading Dr. Rosy Pinhas-Delpuech's essay "Le Désert, le livre: De J. L. Borgès à E. Jabès," shortly to appear in a volume of studies in honor of E. Jabès. She distinguishes between Borges's vision of "a circularity which excludes any sense of historical beginning or rupture" and that of Jabès in *Le Soupçon, le désert* and elsewhere.

5. A diagram of the Aleph of the kabbalists, which represents the ultimate Godhead (*eyn sof*) as well as nothingness (*ayin*), is reproduced from Moses Cordovero's *Pardes Rimmonim* (1592) in Gershom Scholem's summary of the kabbalistic doctrines in *Encyclopaedia Judaica*, X, s.v. "Kabbalah" (Jerusalem: Keter 1972), p. 614; see also p. 604.

6. Jorge Luis Borges, *The Aleph and Other Stories: 1933–1969*, trans. Norman Thomas di Giovanni (New York: Dutton, 1977), p. 27.

7. Cf. André Lacocque, "Job or the Impotence of Religion and Philosophy," *Semeia* (Society of Biblical Literature) 19 (1981): 37.

8. See Northrop Frye, *Anatomy of Criticism*, pp. 147–49; *The Great Code: The Bible and Literature* (New York: Harcourt Brace Jovanovich, 1982), pp. 166–67.

9. Cf. Lacocque, "Job or the Impotence of Religion," p. 45, where he speaks of the "ethical emptiness of the universe" of Job and the "laying bare of all structures."

10. *Moby-Dick*, chap. 42, "The Whiteness of the Whale."

11. André Neher, "*Shaddai*: The God of the Broken Arch," in *Confronting the Holocaust: The Impact of Elie Wiesel*, ed. Alvin Rosenfeld and Irving Greenberg (Bloomington: Indiana University Press, 1978), p. 155.

12. *Anatomy of Criticism*, p. 42.

13. *The Great Code*, p. 195.

14. Cf. André Neher, *The Exile of the Word* (Philadelphia: Jewish Publication Society of America, 1981), p. 28.

15. Cf. Frye, *The Great Code*, pp. 50–51.

16. Translated by Michael Roloff in *Selected Poems: Abba Kovner, Nelly Sachs* (Harmondsworth: Penguin Books, 1971), p. 91.

17. Jan Kott, *Shakespeare Our Contemporary* (New York: Doubleday, 1964), p. 104.

18. Elizabeth Freund, "'Give the Word': Reflections on the Economy of Response in *King Lear*," *H.S.L.* (Special issue, 1982): 218.

19. See chap. 4 above, p. 79.

20. U. Z. Greenberg, *The Streets of the River*, p. 216.

21. In *Lifnim Min Hahomah* (Within the wall; in Hebrew) (Tel-Aviv: Schocken, 1976), pp. 51–104.

22. Cf. Babylonian Talmud, *Sotah*, fol. 27b.

23. *Lifnim Min Hahomah*, p. 104, trans. HF.

Index